DK EYEWITNESS ENCYCLOPEDIA OF ANIMALS

THE ULTIMATE GUIDE TO THE WORLD AROUND YOU

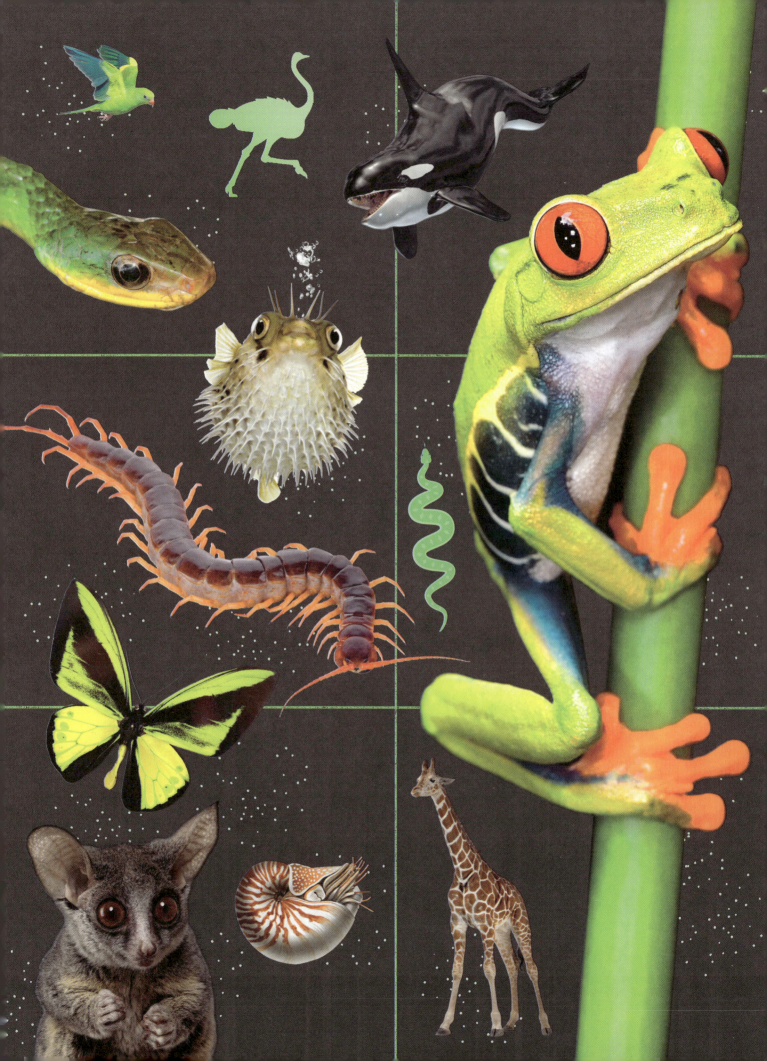

EYEWITNESS
ENCYCLOPEDIA OF
ANIMALS

THE ULTIMATE GUIDE TO THE WORLD AROUND YOU

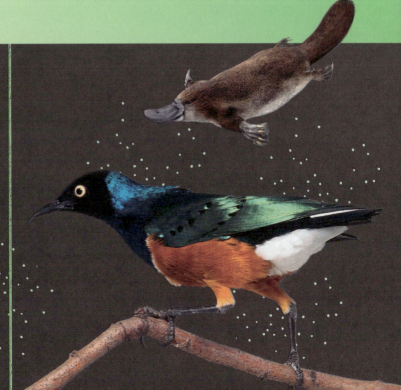

Senior editor Sam Kennedy
Senior art editor Stefan Podhorodecki
Editors Ed Pearce, Binta Jallow, Anna Streiffert Limerick
Senior US editor Megan Douglass
Designers Mik Gates, Beth Johnston
Illustrator Simon Tegg
Picture researcher Geetam Biswas
Deputy picture manager Virien Chopra
Managing editor Francesca Baines
Managing art editor Philip Letsu
Production editor Gillian Reid
Production controller Leanne Burke
Jacket designer Stephanie Tan
Senior jacket designer Rashika Kachroo
Managing art editor (Jackets) Romi Chakraborty
Publisher Andrew Macintyre
Art director Mabel Chan

Authors Dr Kat Day, Cat Hickey, John Woodward

Expert interviewees Professor Colin Beale, Jaime Culebras,
Dr Helen Fox, Dr Michael Murray, Dyan deNapoli, Alex Walters,
Dr Edith Widder, Hamza Yassin

Consultant Derek Harvey

First American Edition, 2025
Published in the United States by DK Publishing,
a division of Penguin Random House LLC
1745 Broadway, 20th Floor, New York, NY 10019

Copyright © 2025 Dorling Kindersley Limited

25 26 27 28 29 10 9 8 7 6 5 4 3 2 1
001–342554–Apr/2025

A catalog record for this book
is available from the Library of Congress.
ISBN: 978-0-5939-6167-4

Printed and bound in China

www.dk.com

This book was made with Forest
Stewardship Council™ certified
paper—one small step in DK's
commitment to a sustainable future.
Learn more at www.dk.com/uk/
information/sustainability

CONTENTS

The story of evolution

FOSSIL **RECORD**

We know about prehistoric species thanks to fossils, such as this one of a T. rex. They tell us what animals looked like and, depending on how deep and in what type of rock layer the fossil is found, when they lived.

Evolution is how life forms change over long periods of time. It happens because offspring differ from their parents. These differences build up over many generations, eventually resulting in new species.

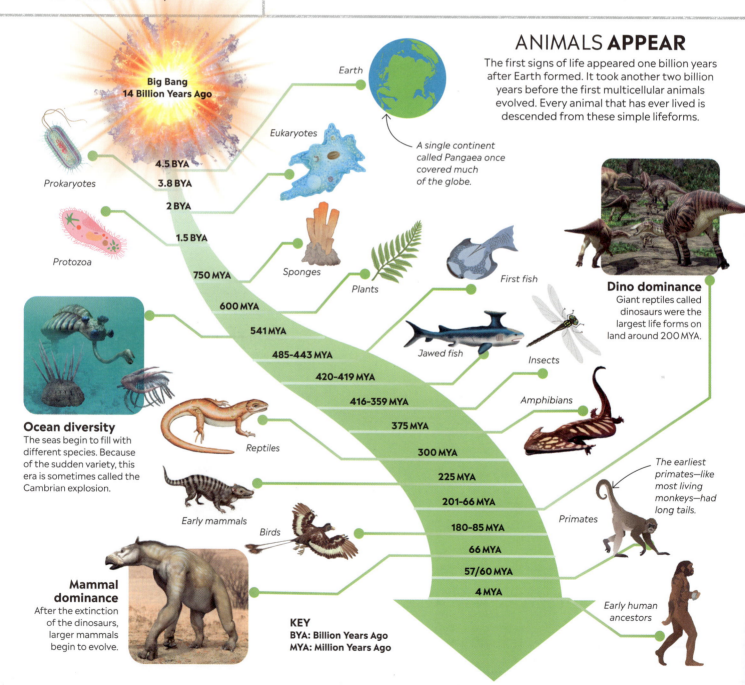

Big Bang
14 Billion Years Ago

Earth

ANIMALS **APPEAR**

The first signs of life appeared one billion years after Earth formed. It took another two billion years before the first multicellular animals evolved. Every animal that has ever lived is descended from these simple lifeforms.

A single continent called Pangaea once covered much of the globe.

Prokaryotes

4.5 BYA

3.8 BYA

2 BYA

Eukaryotes

1.5 BYA

Protozoa

750 MYA

Sponges

Plants

First fish

Dino dominance
Giant reptiles called dinosaurs were the largest life forms on land around 200 MYA.

600 MYA

541 MYA

Jawed fish

Insects

485–443 MYA

420–419 MYA

416–359 MYA

Amphibians

Ocean diversity
The seas begin to fill with different species. Because of the sudden variety, this era is sometimes called the Cambrian explosion.

375 MYA

Reptiles

300 MYA

The earliest primates—like most living monkeys—had long tails.

225 MYA

Early mammals

201–66 MYA

Primates

Birds

180–85 MYA

66 MYA

57/60 MYA

4 MYA

Mammal dominance
After the extinction of the dinosaurs, larger mammals begin to evolve.

Early human ancestors

KEY
BYA: Billion Years Ago
MYA: Million Years Ago

IN 2023 ALONE, 619 NEW SPECIES OF WASP WERE CONFIRMED BY LONDON'S NATURAL HISTORY MUSEUM!

On the main Galápagos islands, giant tortoises have typical domed shells.

On smaller Galápagos islands, mutation has led to unique saddle-shaped shells.

WONDERFUL VARIATION

Parents pass on their genes to their children. Genes mix and sometimes mutate, leading to different colors, sizes, or shapes. On islands, this can produce striking species variations.

NEW SPECIES

Sometimes new species emerge when geographical features form. Around 6 million years ago in North America, the formation of the Grand Canyon divided an area of land, and with it the native squirrel population. Over time, two species evolved, one on each side of the deep gap.

Harris's antelope squirrel lives on the south side of the canyon.

The white-tailed antelope squirrel is found on the canyon's north side.

AMAZING ADAPTATIONS

Animals evolve to "fit" the habitat they live in, and the food available there. This is called adaptation. Penguins are birds that have adapted to dive for prey in cold waters by developing a streamlined body and flipper-like wings.

Wings and feet function as flippers.

SINCE LIFE ON EARTH BEGAN, SEVERAL MASS EXTINCTIONS HAVE CHANGED THE COURSE OF EVOLUTION!

An asteroid colliding with Earth may have caused an extinction event.

NATURAL SELECTION

It's the animals that are best able to survive and breed that can pass on their genes to the next generation. Known as natural selection, this drives evolution and adaptation, as in the case of the Arctic hare.

Color variation
A species of hare living in the Arctic can be born with white or brown fur.

Predator preference
A gyrfalcon easily spots the brown hares on the snowy ground, picking them off.

Camouflage wins
White hares survive and pass on their white-fur genes to the next generation, increasing numbers.

A PINK KATYDID, DISCOVERED IN 2016, IS AN **ANIMAL THAT DISGUISES** ITSELF AS **A PLANT!**

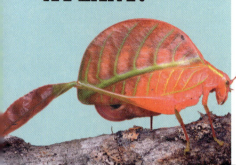

Animal classification

Around 1.2 million different species of animal have been named, and many more are yet to be discovered. Scientists classify and sort animals into different groups, based on their biological characteristics and their earliest ancestors.

Sponges	Cnidarians	Flatworms	Annelids	Mollusks	Nematodes	Arthropods	Echinoderms	Chordates

TYPES OF **ANIMAL**

Every creature in the animal kingdom—from sponges to apes— is sorted into one of several main groups called phyla, the largest of which are shown above. All but one are made up of invertebrates. The final phylum, Chordates, includes the vertebrates.

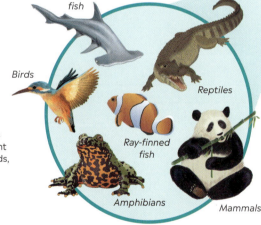

Cartilaginous fish

Birds

Ray-finned fish

Reptiles

Amphibians

Mammals

Vertebrate classes

The Chordates phylum that contains all vertebrates is divided into different classes. These include mammals, birds, reptiles, amphibians, and several classes of fishes.

THERE ARE **MORE THAN 20,000** KNOWN **SPECIES OF BUTTERFLY** IN THE WORLD!

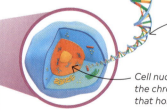

DNA contains genetic information.

Cell nucleus contains the chromosomes that hold DNA.

CELLULAR CREATURES

All animals have bodies made of multiple cells. Specialized cells form tissues and organs that help the animal move, breathe, eat, sense, and reproduce. Each cell's nucleus holds DNA, which determines many things, such as what an individual animal looks like.

Kingdom: Animalia

Phylum: Chordata

Class: Mammalia

Order: Carnivora

Family: Felidae

Genus: Panthera

Species: Panthera tigris

Invertebrates such as this jellyfish make up 97 percent of the entire animal kingdom.

All animals are part of the animal kingdom, including the tiger.

The animal kingdom is divided into different phyla. Chordata is the phylum that contains the tiger.

Each phylum is split into classes. One class of Chordata is Mammalia, which contains all mammals.

Each class is made up of different orders. Carnivorous mammals such as the tiger belong to the order Carnivora.

Each order is made up of different families, such as the Felidae— all big and small cats.

Within a family, animals with very similar biological characteristics form a genus, such as the Panthera.

Each genus contains several individual species, such as Panthera tigris, the tiger.

Genus Panthera consists of the five big cats: leopards, jaguars, tigers, lions, and snow leopards.

ANIMAL
CLASSIFICATION

Scientists have a system to group animal species according to their characteristics. It starts with broad groups, followed by specialized subgroups. This diagram shows all the groups and subgroups that a tiger belongs to.

SPECIES **NAMES**

All species have scientific names. The tiger's is *Panthera tigris*. "*Panthera*" tells us that it belongs to the genus *Panthera* (big cats), while "*tigris*" is its unique species name.

Squirrel (animal kingdom)

Mushroom (fungi kingdom)

Tree (plant kingdom)

KINGDOMS
OF LIFE

All living organisms on Earth belong to one of six main groups, known as kingdoms. Animals, plants, and fungi have their own kingdoms. Single-cell organisms belong to the kingdoms of protozoans, bacteria, or archaea.

Feeding and breathing

Animals eat plants and other animals, and break food down as they digest it. They also extract oxygen from the air or water by breathing, and combine this with digested food to release energy.

DIVERSE DIETS

Animals have evolved many different ways of gathering food. Most are plant-eating herbivores, others—called carnivores—eat other animals. Omnivores combine both plants and meat in their diet, while detritivores eat decaying waste matter.

HERBIVORES
Plants contain sugars, proteins, and vitamins, but plant material can be hard to digest. Dedicated plant-eaters like this caterpillar need to eat a lot to get the nutrients they need.

CARNIVORES
Animals turn digested food into tissues (muscle, bone, skin, and more). These are much richer in nutrients than plant material. A crocodile gets enough food by eating just once a week!

NOT PICKY
Some animals have far more varied diets than a typical hunter or plant-eater. A bear will catch fish or small animals, but also enjoys eating energy-rich fruit, nuts, and honey. And so do many humans!

BUTTERFLIES FIND **SALT** BY DRINKING **ANIMAL URINE** OR SWEAT, AND EVEN **TURTLE TEARS!**

SCRAPS AND LEFTOVERS

Meat may be nutritious, but it takes effort and skill to hunt prey. Some meat-eaters, such as this hyena, also go for easier pickings by scavenging the remains of animals brought down by other predators.

AND **FINALLY ...**

Even the decaying remains of dead organisms, called detritus, are a food source for animals that are prepared to eat them. These detritivores play a vital role in the food chain by recycling dead organic material into nutrients that plants can absorb to begin the cycle all over again.

Earthworms feed on detritus in the soil.

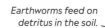

TOOLS FOR THE JOB

Animals have adapted to gather food in many ways. Some tools—such as sharp teeth—have multiple different uses, but others have evolved to deal with specific types of food.

Filter feeder
Many aquatic animals, including this coral, can sift water flowing past for tiny drifting creatures.

Nectar feeder
A butterfly has a long tubular tongue that it uses to sip sweet nectar from flowers.

Nut cracker
The stout beak of a parrot is well adapted for cracking the tough shells of nuts.

SOME SPECIES OF CATFISH HAVE UP TO 175,000 TASTE BUDS!

VITAL OXYGEN

When animals eat, digestion turns the complex organic materials in food into simpler ones, including a sugar called glucose. The oxygen that animals breathe helps turn glucose into vital energy, plus water and carbon dioxide.

Glucose (sugar) + **Oxygen** O_2

Energy
Animals need energy to move, grow, and reproduce.

CO_2
Carbon dioxide

Water

A giant panda eats bamboo shoots and digests them to release sugars.

LUNGS AND GILLS

Land animals breathe air into their lungs. The lungs are lined with thin-walled blood vessels that absorb oxygen from the air and discard waste carbon dioxide and water vapor. Aquatic animals have feathery gills that absorb the oxygen dissolved in water.

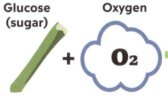

In cold air, the water in animals' breath becomes visible.

Red-crowned cranes

Gills are red due to many tiny blood vessels.

Albino (white) axolotls are rare in the wild. This one has been bred in captivity.

ALTHOUGH IT LIVES IN THE SEA, A WHALE BREATHES AIR THROUGH A BLOWHOLE IN THE TOP OF ITS HEAD!

Sensing and moving

Animals are acutely aware of what goes on around them, thanks to their senses. This means they can react quickly by moving, sometimes very fast! For most animals, the combination of sensing and moving is vital for survival.

A fox's sharp hearing can detect rodents digging underground.

ON THE **ALERT**

The five senses of vision, hearing, scent, taste, and touch are all important to animals, and some creatures have more efficient senses than humans. A fox has super-sensitive ears that can pinpoint the exact location of a mouse hidden in long grass, an acute sense of smell for detecting predators, and touch-responsive whiskers to feel its way in the dark.

SEEING **BY SOUND**

Bats hunt at night using echolocation, emitting a stream of clicks that bounce off objects that can't be seen. This creates an echo, which is picked up by the bat's ears and processed in its brain to form a sonar image.

On target
As a bat closes in on its prey, it produces an extra-fast burst of clicks to create more echoes and improve the quality of the image it creates.

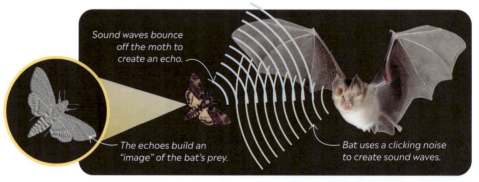

Sound waves bounce off the moth to create an echo.

The echoes build an "image" of the bat's prey.

Bat uses a clicking noise to create sound waves.

SECRET WEAPON

Rattlesnakes and other pit vipers have special sensors that detect heat radiated by prey, especially warm-blooded mammals and birds. Called pit organs, these sensors work like eyes that see in the dark, creating an image in much the same way as an infrared camera.

Pit organ lies between the nostril and eye.

Fatal glow
A hungry rattlesnake can "see" the heat of a mouse hiding in the pitch darkness of its burrow.

BUMBLEBEES CAN SENSE **ELECTRIC FIELDS IN FLOWERS,** HELPING THEM **FIND FOOD!**

Long wings are adapted for soaring.

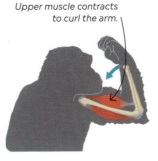

SAILFISH, THE FASTEST FISH IN THE SEA, CAN CHARGE THROUGH WATER AT 68 MPH (110 KPH)!

GLIDING HIGH

Many birds fly vast distances around the world using special techniques. This oceanic albatross can soar on air currents for hours or even days, traveling several hundred miles without beating its wings at all.

SKELETONS AND **MUSCLES**

An animal can move by using its muscles, which are attached to a skeleton. Muscles can only pull, not push, so moving a limb involves a pair of muscles that work in opposition to each other, with one muscle contracting while the other relaxes.

Chimpanzee

Upper muscle contracts to curl the arm.

Lower muscle contracts to uncurl the arm.

Pulling in
To pull the chimpanzee's hand back toward its shoulder, the upper arm muscle contracts while the lower muscle relaxes.

Reaching out
When the chimpanzee extends its arm outward, the upper muscle relaxes and the lower muscle contracts, pulling the arm straight.

RUN FOR IT!

Some land animals, such as snakes, slither along on their bellies, but most have legs to walk and run. A cheetah, the fastest land animal, can run at 75 mph (120 kph).

IN THE **SWIM**

Aquatic animals such as fish, whales, and seals drive themselves through the water with fins or flippers. This penguin uses its short wings in the same way, swimming with the speed and efficiency that it needs to chase and catch its prey.

Grasshopper

Extensor muscle relaxes.

Flexor muscle contracts.

Extensor muscle contracts.

Flexor muscle relaxes.

Folding forward
A grasshopper's leg muscles are attached to its exoskeleton. Here, the flexor muscle has contracted to bring the lower leg forward.

Pushing back
To extend the grasshopper's leg outward, the flexor muscle relaxes while the opposing extensor muscle contracts.

Animal reproduction

Like all living things, animals reproduce to create a new generation. For most, this requires a male and female to mate—a process that can involve elaborate courtship. Many animals then care for their young to give them a good chance of survival.

ONE DEEP-SEA OCTOPUS WAS OBSERVED **GUARDING** ITS **EGGS** FOR MORE THAN **FOUR YEARS!**

SPAWNING AND **MATING**

In sexual reproduction, the female needs a male to fertilize her eggs. Fish can release eggs and sperm into the water to mingle in a process called spawning. But most land animals, including these lime butterflies, come together to mate, so the male passes sperm directly to the female.

A MALE **BLUE-FOOTED BOOBY** DANCES AND **SHOWS OFF HIS FEET TO ATTRACT** A FEMALE!

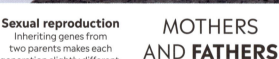

Parthenogenesis
Each generation of young animals is exactly the same as the one before.

Sexual reproduction
Inheriting genes from two parents makes each generation slightly different.

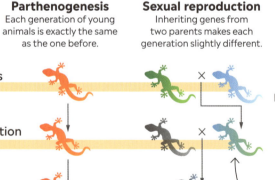

Parents

1st generation

2nd generation

Offspring has characteristics from both parents.

MOTHERS AND **FATHERS**

Some invertebrates and a few vertebrates can breed without a mate. Called parthenogenesis, this creates genetically identical clones of a single parent. But most young animals have a mother and father, and inherit characteristics from both.

PARENTAL CARE

Young animals are easy prey for predators and many do not survive. Some species produce a lot of young to ensure that some will live into adulthood. Others have just a few young, but take great care of them. This waved albatross pair raises just one chick a year and forages together to find food for their offspring.

Chick is fed and protected from danger by its parents.

LAYING **EGGS**

Animals that lay eggs are called oviparous. Birds sit on their eggs to keep them warm and safe. The eggs of most insects, fish, amphibians, and reptiles, however, are left to develop without any help from their parents until eventually they hatch, as with these saltwater crocodile eggs.

HAVING **BABIES**

Viviparous animals give birth to live young instead of laying eggs. The babies grow inside their mother until they are ready to be born, and those of mammals are then nourished by their mother's milk. Crab-eating macaques are pregnant for about five months and nurse their young until they are one year old.

Infant crab-eating macaques are born with sparse black fur, which lightens as they get older.

COURTING
COUPLES

For birds especially, finding a breeding partner may involve a courtship ritual. Many males, including this Raggiana bird-of-paradise, have colorful plumage that they show off in spectacular displays. Females assess the energy, size, singing, and colors of males in order to select a suitable mate.

Male fans its colorful feathers to outdo rivals.

BABY **ELEPHANTS EAT** THEIR **MOTHER'S NUTRIENT-RICH POOP** TO HELP BUILD THEIR **DIGESTIVE SYSTEM!**

Growing up

Animals begin life as small creatures that grow bigger as the cells that form their bodies divide and multiply. For some, growing up can bring about a dramatic change in their form and way of life.

AN OCEAN SUNFISH CAN LAY 300 MILLION EGGS AT A TIME!

DIVIDE AND **GROW**

The very first stage of an animal's existence is an egg: a single cell that holds a nucleus containing DNA. When fertilized, this divides into two cells, then four, then eight, and so on to create the many, many tiny cells that form the animal's body.

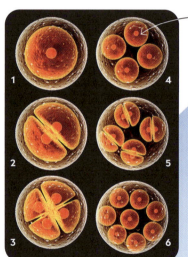

Divided cells are copies of each other.

1 2 3 4 5 6

Reconstruction
In time, the caterpillar makes silk to spin a cocoon. It then turns into a pupa—a stage when its body is rebuilt as an adult moth.

Cocoon made from brown silk contains a pupa inside.

Eating and growing
Each caterpillar feasts on leaves, shedding its skin several times as it grows.

Body can grow up to 5 in (12 cm) long.

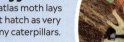

Eggs hatch
A female atlas moth lays eggs that hatch as very small, spiny caterpillars.

FORM **CHANGE**

Some animals completely change their shape as they grow—a process called metamorphosis. For instance, an atlas moth starts life as a soft-bodied caterpillar that spends most of its time eating and growing. It then turns into a winged adult that never eats and does not grow at all.

EGGS TO EMBRYOS

Cell division can be seen in action in frog eggs. As the cells divide, the tiny black spheres grow longer. In time, they become wriggling embryos that later turn into tadpoles.

Embryo has a head and tail.

This round embryo is at an early stage of development.

GETTING **BIGGER**

Like most young animals, a baby orca looks like a small version of its parents. It gets bigger as it grows up, but its growth rate slows down when it becomes an adult.

Wings span up to 10 in (27 cm) across.

Winged beauty

When the adult atlas moth emerges from the cocoon in its new form, it can fly but cannot eat, and lives for just a few days.

Empty, dried out cocoon

Vivid colors are used to attract females.

THE **LARGEST NEWBORN** ANIMAL IS A **BLUE WHALE CALF,** WHICH WEIGHS MORE THAN **A SMALL CAR!**

OLD AGE

All animals eventually grow old, and most die soon after they become unable to breed. But others live longer—some chimps are known to live for up to 60 years. This may be due to their large brains, which are associated with longer lifespans.

SHOWING **OFF**

Animals that don't change form can alter their appearance as they mature. Many, like this male Temminck's tragopan pheasant, develop bright colors or other features to show they are ready to find a mate and fight rivals.

DEEP-SEA **GLASS SPONGES** CAN LIVE FOR **15,000 YEARS** AND CONTINUE **TO GROW SLOWLY** IN OLD AGE!

A glass sponge has a skeleton made of glass-like silica.

INVERTEBRATES

Invertebrates

Animals that do not have a backbone—a spine made up of smaller bones called vertebrae—are called invertebrates. Many are soft-bodied, such as jellyfish and worms, while others, including insects, have hard exoskeletons. Animals that do have backbones are called vertebrates.

WORMS

There are nearly 100,000 species of worms. Best known are the annelids, such as this earthworm, whose bodies are made up of ringlike segments.

CNIDARIANS

These animals live in seas and freshwater and have rings of tentacles carrying stingers. The 11,000-plus species include jellyfishes, anemones, and corals.

MOLLUSKS

Most of these soft-bodied animals, including this nautilus, snails, and clams, have chalky shells. Shell-less mollusks include slugs, octopuses, and squid.

ECHINODERMS

With a name meaning "spiny skin," this group of marine animals includes sea urchins (above), as well as starfish, sea cucumbers, and sea lilies.

Vertebrates: 3%

Invertebrates: 97%

OUT NUMBERED!

The vast majority of all animal species are invertebrates—and most of those are insects. Only a tiny percentage are vertebrates like us.

SHELL SUITS

Snails and other mollusks have hard, unjointed shells into which the creature can retract when threatened by a predator. As the animal grows, so does its shell, allowing the mollusk to use the same shell throughout its life.

Shell grows in a spiral shape so it doesn't get too wide or tall.

Eyes are on long tentacles.

Snail moves by flexing its "foot," and releasing a layer of mucus to help it slide smoothly.

Stinging tentacles snare prey.

STUCK FAST

Most invertebrates move around to find food and mates, or escape predators. However, some aquatic invertebrates are attached to a surface—either with a muscular foot-like disk, like this anemone, or permanently cemented with a kind of "glue," such as barnacles.

SOME **PARASITIC WORMS** SPEND THEIR WHOLE LIVES **INSIDE OTHER** ANIMALS!

1. Egg
Most insects lay eggs. Each egg hatches as an infant form called a larva.

2. Larva
The wingless larva spends most of its time eating and growing bigger.

4. Adult
The fully grown winged insect emerges, in this case a ladybug.

3. Pupa
The larva changes into a dormant stage called a pupa.

METAMORPHOSIS

Many invertebrates change their shape and habits as they grow—caterpillars transform into moths, and ladybug larvae into ladybugs. This process is called metamorphosis and often involves four steps.

DAZZLING DIVERSITY

There are 1.25 million species of invertebrate in about 30 major groups. They vary in size from a few millimeters to the length of a bus and live everywhere—on land, in the air, underground, and in water. The examples shown here just are a tiny sample of the rich diversity of invertebrate life.

CRUSTACEANS
Mostly water-dwelling, all crustaceans have tough, jointed external skeletons (exoskeletons). Examples include lobsters (above), shrimp, crabs, and barnacles.

ARACHNIDS
Spiders, scorpions, mites, and ticks all have eight legs. Many also possess a venomous bite or sting that they use for hunting and defense.

INSECTS
About 75 percent of all animal species are insects. They have six legs, compound eyes, three-part bodies (head, thorax, abdomen), and antennae. Most have wings.

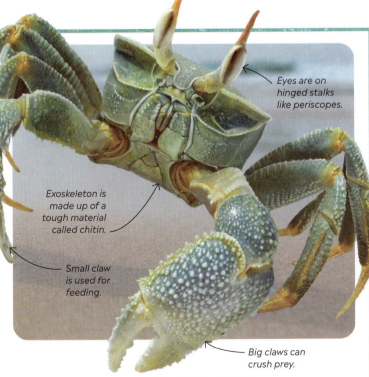

Eyes are on hinged stalks like periscopes.

Exoskeleton is made up of a tough material called chitin.

Small claw is used for feeding.

Big claws can crush prey.

Cicada breaks free of exoskeleton.

NEW SUITS

Exoskeletons do not grow with the animal inside them. Invertebrates with exoskeletons, such as this cicada, have to cast off, or "molt," their outer shell from time to time, then develop a new exoskeleton once they have grown in size.

AWESOME ARTHROPODS

The most numerous invertebrates are arthropods, which make up about 80 percent of all animal species and are found in every habitat on Earth. Arthropods have tough exoskeletons divided into segments connected by mobile joints, like a suit of armor. This group includes insects, spiders, scorpions, and crustaceans such as this fiddler crab.

THE **BIGGEST INVERTEBRATE** IS THE **COLOSSAL SQUID,** AT UP TO **33 FT (10 M)** LONG!

Dragonflies
and damselflies

With glittering wings and eye-catching aerial maneuvers, these dazzling predators dart through the air in search of flies, gnats, and mosquitoes to eat.

AIR **ATTACK**

Fast, agile, and able to hover and fly backward, dragonflies are relentless hunters. They seize flying insects mid-air, wrapping them up in their long, spindly legs.

TAKING **WING**

It can take more than three hours for a nymph to transform into an adult such as the four-spotted dragonfly shown here. The process leaves the insect vulnerable to predators, so it often takes place at night.

1. Pulling out
Having left the water, a nymph attaches itself to a plant stem. Slowly, its case cracks open and the adult body begins to emerge.

The nymph blends in with the plant stalk.

The adult body bursts out of its too-tight nymph casing, or "exoskeleton."

2. Free at last
The emerging dragonfly has to wait for its soft, floppy legs to harden before it can completely pull itself free from its exoskeleton.

The empty skin of the nymph is called its exuvia.

The incredibly thin but strong wings begin to unfurl.

DRAGONFLY NYMPHS CAN **SQUIRT WATER** OUT OF THEIR **BOTTOMS** TO ESCAPE ENEMIES BY **JET-PROPULSION!**

DAMSEL OR **DRAGON?**

The main difference between these insects is that, at rest, damselflies hold their wings together above the abdomen, while dragonflies rest with wings spread horizontally. In both, the thorax is packed with muscles to work the wings and legs. Most of their organs are in the abdomen.

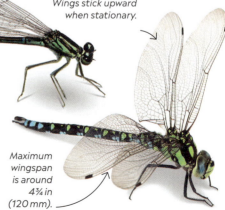

Damselfly has a long, slender body made up of 10 segments.

Streamlined wings can be folded back.

Wings stick upward when stationary.

Maximum wingspan is around 4¾ in (120 mm).

WATER **TO AIR**

Damselflies and dragonflies lay their eggs in water, and these hatch into wingless nymphs. Depending on the species, a nymph can live underwater for months, sometimes years, shedding its skin 5–14 times. When it is ready to become an adult, the nymph crawls out of the water for one final molt.

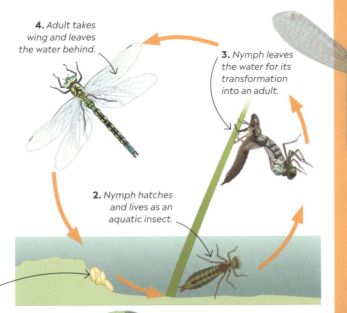

4. Adult takes wing and leaves the water behind.

3. Nymph leaves the water for its transformation into an adult.

2. Nymph hatches and lives as an aquatic insect.

1. Eggs are laid in mud, in rotting logs, or on the leaves and stalks of water plants.

MATING **RITUAL**

When damselflies or dragonflies mate, the male grips the female's head or neck while she curves her body forward to latch onto his. They perch like this for some time, then fly off to the water—often still attached—so the female can lay hundreds of eggs.

3. Fueling up
The dragonfly pumps energizing fluid around its body, especially into the dense network of veins in its wings.

4. Taking wing
Once its wings are hydrated and its body fully extended, the dragonfly is ready to take off!

The folded-back wings begin to take shape.

The colorful body helps the insect regulate how much heat it absorbs and releases.

ALL **EYES**

Dragonfly eyes contain up to 30,000 lenses that help them see in almost every direction, with a small blind spot behind their head. Damselflies also have big eyes, but spaced widely apart.

Dragonfly

Damselfly

STEALTHY **HUNTER**

Nymphs are ferocious predators. Camouflaged by their green or brown coloring, they creep up on prey then shoot out a hinged, retractable jaw that clamps around the victim.

300 MILLION YEARS AGO, INSECTS SIMILAR TO DRAGONFLIES CALLED **GRIFFINFLIES** HAD **WINGSPANS UP TO 30 IN (75 CM)!**

CLOSE **RELATIONS**

Crickets, grasshoppers, and their relatives have biting or chewing mouthparts. Their eggs hatch into miniature versions of their parents, rather than into larvae or caterpillars, before growing into adults.

Mantids
Predatory mantids are known for their elongated bodies and powerful front arms.

Cockroaches
Flat, oval-shaped cockroaches eat dead, decaying matter and live in humid conditions.

Crickets and grasshoppers
Many of these insects use their strong back legs for jumping.

Stick insects
These masters of camouflage include the longest of all insects.

Ear

THE EARS OF A **KATYDID** ARE ON ITS **FRONT LEGS!**

GIANT **WĒTĀ**

Found only in New Zealand, the giant wētā is one of the world's heaviest insects, weighing up to 2½ oz (71g)—about the same as a gerbil. A type of cricket, it spends the day hiding in dark areas and becomes most active at night when it forages for leafy food in forests.

Compound eyes react to the slightest movement.

Sharp mandibles slice through scales.

Limbs have long, interlocking spines to trap prey.

AMBUSH **KILLER**

Armed with powerful spiked forelimbs that can seize a victim within milliseconds, the praying mantis is a fierce predator. By stalking its prey, it can subdue animals much bigger than itself, such as this lizard.

Squirming lizard has no hope of escape.

SOME **GRASSHOPPERS** USE THEIR GIANT HIND LEGS TO **KICK THEIR POOP AWAY!**

File (in orange) is a modified vein with ribbed "teeth."

Hardened inner edge of a wing (in green) is called a scraper, and works like a guitar pick.

SCRAPING **SONG**

Most male grasshoppers, crickets, and katydids attract females with rhythmic "songs" produced by rubbing body parts together. Grasshoppers scrape the inside of a hind leg against a wing. Crickets, however, rub a hardened part of their wing edge along a "file" on the opposite wing.

TOXIC **GRASSHOPPER**

Native to North America, the rainbow grasshopper is named for its bright exoskeleton. It is thought that its coloration is used to warn off potential predators.

LOCUST **SWARM**

The desert locust is notorious for the damage it can do to crops. When food is plentiful, it lives like any other grasshopper, but if their numbers multiply and food runs out, the locusts band together in vast swarms. Living across Africa and Asia, each locust can eat its weight in plants every day.

Long hind legs help locusts hop and leap.

A LOCUST SWARM CAN CONTAIN UP TO 10 BILLION LOCUSTS!

Wings grow longer before swarming.

SOUND **ENGINEER**

A male mole cricket amplifies his courtship song by singing from inside a specially shaped burrow that acts as a megaphone. His sound engineering is so efficient he can be heard up to 1,312 ft (400 m) away from the burrow.

Grasshoppers and **mantids**

Grasshoppers, crickets, mantids, and their relatives, such as the leaf-shaped katydid, are known for their elongated body shape and strong hind legs.

BLOOD **SUCKERS**

Bed bugs are wingless parasites that hide in bedding by day, emerging at night to feast on human blood. Their bites are irritating but not dangerous.

SUGARY **POOP**

Aphids such as this greenfly have to feed on lots of plant sap, because the liquid contains only tiny amounts of the nitrogen they need. But this sap has more sugar than the aphids can use, so they squirt the excess out of their bottoms as a sticky, sweet liquid called honeydew. Ants and other animals feed on honeydew.

A BED BUG CAN SURVIVE FOR UP TO 300 DAYS WITHOUT FEEDING!

The bug is drinking plant sap.

WAX ON **WAX OFF**

The long, waxy tendrils that flower-spike bugs force out of their tail ends help disguise the insect when it's on a plant stem. The waxy coating is also water-repellent.

Body is swollen with liquefied prey.

Middle and hind legs are long and thin. Shorter, thicker front legs can grip prey.

TOXIC **KILLER**

This assassin bug has stabbed a luckless victim with its sharp, hollow beak, through which it injects toxic saliva that paralyzes its prey and dissolves its insides so they can be sucked out.

Shield-shaped back gives bug its alternative name.

SMELLY **SHIELD**

Stink bugs—also called shield bugs—are so-called because of the odor they spray when threatened. Stink bug fluid is not poisonous but it is an irritant and can cause an allergic reaction.

Wings cross over, as with all bugs.

BUG OR **BEETLE?**

A group of bugs called the Heteroptera resemble beetles, but have different wings. A beetle's forewing is completely hard, while only half of a Heteroptera's wing is hard. Also, when these bugs fold their wings, they cross each other, but a beetle's meet in a straight line.

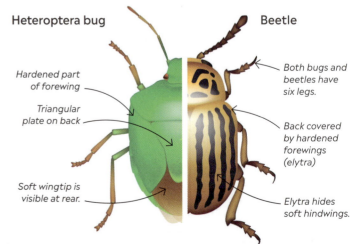

Heteroptera bug

Beetle

Hardened part of forewing

Triangular plate on back

Soft wingtip is visible at rear.

Both bugs and beetles have six legs.

Back covered by hardened forewings (elytra)

Elytra hides soft hindwings.

Beastly bugs

All bugs are insects, but not all insects are bugs. What makes a bug a bug is that it must have mouthparts that let it suck liquid such as sap, water, and even blood.

Sensitive antennae detect prey.

Multi-lens compound eyes notice every movement.

Segmented stabbing beak, called a rostrum, extends from behind head to attack prey.

Pointed lowest segment impales prey.

THE **KISSING BUG** CARRIES **CHAGAS DISEASE,** WHICH INFECTS UP TO **500,000 PEOPLE** A YEAR. IT CAN CAUSE FATAL **HEART DISEASE!**

Thornlike body is very strong.

POND **SKATER**

Tiny, water-repellent hairs on their "feet" help pond skaters stay buoyant, while they use their middle set of legs as paddles to glide across the water. They hold up their front pair of legs, as shown here, to grab hold of prey.

HIDDEN FIGURE

Some bugs are masters of disguise. The thorn bug of the Americas is a sapsucker that clings to a plant stem to feed and lay eggs. Its body is shaped like a sharp thorn, making it almost invisible to hungry birds—and painfully difficult to eat.

AFRICA'S **SHRILL THORN TREE CICADA** IS THE LOUDEST INSECT ON RECORD. AT MORE THAN **106 DECIBELS** IT'S **AS LOUD AS A CHAINSAW!**

CAMOUFLAGE **TACTICS**

Some insects have such perfect camouflage that they are virtually invisible to their predators—especially birds, which hunt by sight.

TROPICAL LEAF INSECTS
These insects look exactly like leaves, and even mimic the scars and markings left by leaf-eating animals.

NIGHT-FLYING MOTHS
Many night-flying moths spend the day flattened against tree bark, concealed by their wing patterns.

SWALLOWTAIL BUTTERFLIES
The young caterpillar of the American eastern tiger swallowtail butterfly looks just like a bird dropping!

MOST **DEADLY**

Some insects feed on blood! They include fleas (right), bloodsucking bugs, and mosquitoes. A few insects carry dangerous diseases such as malaria.

MOST **TOXIC**

The caterpillars of burnet moths eat plants that contain toxins, and use these to make the deadly poison cyanide. When they turn into adult moths, they retain the cyanide in their bodies, making them poisonous to predators.

Warning coloration

FACT PACK!
INSECTS

They may be small, but insects are some of the most amazing creatures on the planet. Many lead extraordinary lives, eating unusual foods and using ingenious tactics to avoid being eaten themselves.

WEIRDEST **DIET**

From dining on wood to eating dung, some insects have diets that don't sound very appetizing to a human.

DUNG BEETLES
These insects gather the poop of large animals, roll it into balls, and feed it to their young.

TERMITES
Many termites are able to eat wood, devouring fences, furniture, and entire wooden houses.

ANTS
Some ants drink the sugary poop of sap-sucking aphids.

MOST **ATHLETIC**

Propelled by spring-loaded muscles, some flea species can jump distances of up to 200 times their body length. This is equivalent to a 5 ft 5 in (1.65 m) human jumping to the height of the Eiffel Tower!

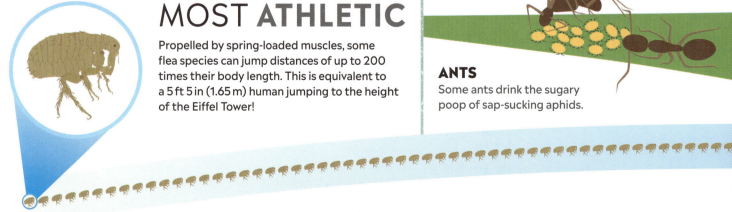

BIGGEST **COLONY**

A single termite colony can contain more than 7 million insects, which work together to build the nest, gather food, and raise young.

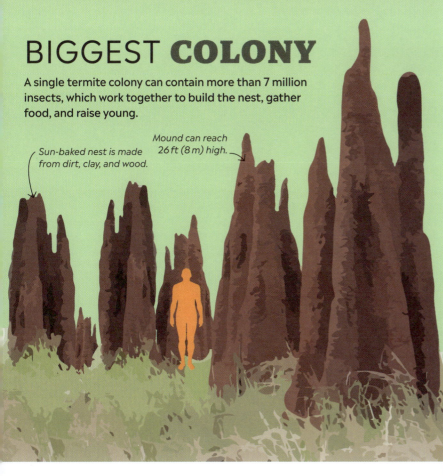

Sun-baked nest is made from dirt, clay, and wood.

Mound can reach 26 ft (8 m) high.

SMALLEST INSECT

A wasp called a fairyfly is the smallest known insect. At 0.01 in (0.25 mm) long, four insects lined up would be the width of a period.

CURIOUS LIVES

Some insects have very short lifespans, while others live in vast colonies where they have just one job to perform.

HONEYPOT ANTS
Living in deserts, these ants store sugary food in the swollen bodies of their nest-mates.

TERMITES
These spend their lives looking after the queen, who produces an egg every three seconds.

PERIODICAL CICADAS
Living underground for 17 years, they emerge to shed their skin and mate. Five weeks later, they die.

MAYFLIES
After living for years underwater, they turn into winged adults that live for as little as a day.

BIGGEST INSECTS

Most insects are small but a few tropical insects are surprisingly large. Here are two six-legged record breakers.

Males have bright green wings.

ADULT FEMALE HAND: 6¾ IN (17 CM) LONG

QUEEN ALEXANDRA'S BIRDWING BUTTERFLY
This tropical forest butterfly is the biggest butterfly in the world. Found in New Guinea, it can have an 11-in (28-cm) wingspan.

Legs are long, slender, and twiglike.

GIANT STICK INSECT
The stick insect *Phryganistria* "chinensis" can reach 24 in (62 cm) long, making it the world's longest insect.

The flea lands on a new host, ready to feed.

Busy **beetles**

A quarter of all known animal species are beetles. There are at least 400,000 different kinds. They live almost everywhere except the ocean, and the smallest is tinier than a pinhead.

THE SOUTH AMERICAN **TITAN BEETLE** CAN GROW TO **6¾ IN (16.7 CM) LONG!**

One of six segmented legs

Battle scar on back from a previous fight

Flight wings are protected by a tough outer wing case.

Beetle can stand on its hind legs as it uses its mandibles to fling an opponent away.

Hook-clawed feet provide grip

BOMBARDIER BEETLES BLAST PREDATORS WITH **HOT, TOXIC CHEMICALS** SPRAYED FROM THEIR **BOTTOMS!**

LIVING **JEWELS**

Many beetles are vividly colorful, and some even glow with a shiny, iridescent rainbow effect. This is created by tiny ridges on the beetle's exoskeleton that reflect different wavelengths of light.

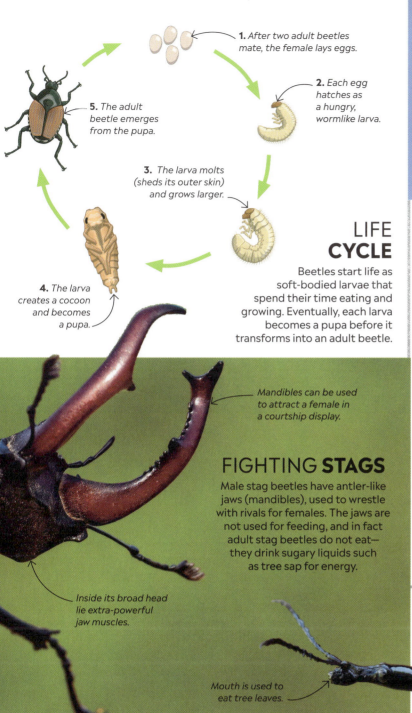

1. After two adult beetles mate, the female lays eggs.

2. Each egg hatches as a hungry, wormlike larva.

3. The larva molts (sheds its outer skin) and grows larger.

4. The larva creates a cocoon and becomes a pupa.

5. The adult beetle emerges from the pupa.

LIFE CYCLE

Beetles start life as soft-bodied larvae that spend their time eating and growing. Eventually, each larva becomes a pupa before it transforms into an adult beetle.

FIRE **FLY!**

Fireflies and glowworms are beetles that glow in the dark to communicate and attract mating partners. Many fireflies flash in coded patterns that identify their species.

UNDERWATER **HUNTER**

Many beetles scuttle around on land, but a few live in ponds, lakes, and rivers. The great diving beetle hunts for fish underwater, using its fringed back legs like oars to move along. It traps an air bubble beneath its forewings so it can breathe and stay submerged for up to 30 minutes.

Mandibles can be used to attract a female in a courtship display.

FIGHTING **STAGS**

Male stag beetles have antler-like jaws (mandibles), used to wrestle with rivals for females. The jaws are not used for feeding, and in fact adult stag beetles do not eat— they drink sugary liquids such as tree sap for energy.

Inside its broad head lie extra-powerful jaw muscles.

Mouth is used to eat tree leaves.

NECK EXTENDER

The Madagascan giraffe-necked weevil has a hugely elongated neck. Males use their long necks to fight each other and perform courtship dances for the females, who have much shorter necks.

BEETLE ANATOMY

Most adult beetles are easily recognized by their tough wing cases called elytra. These are hardened forewings that protect their delicate hindwings. When a beetle takes flight it spreads its elytra wide and unfolds the wings beneath.

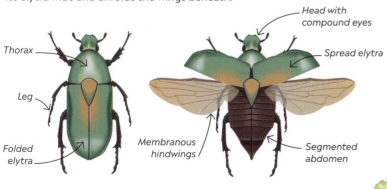

Thorax

Leg

Folded elytra

Head with compound eyes

Spread elytra

Membranous hindwings

Segmented abdomen

Bright red wing case covers its hindwings.

Base of neck is an extension of the body.

Fascinating flies

Some may consider them pests, but flies are astonishing creatures with amazing flying skills, thanks to a special adaptation of their wings. From house flies to mosquitoes, there are more than 110,000 fly species around the world.

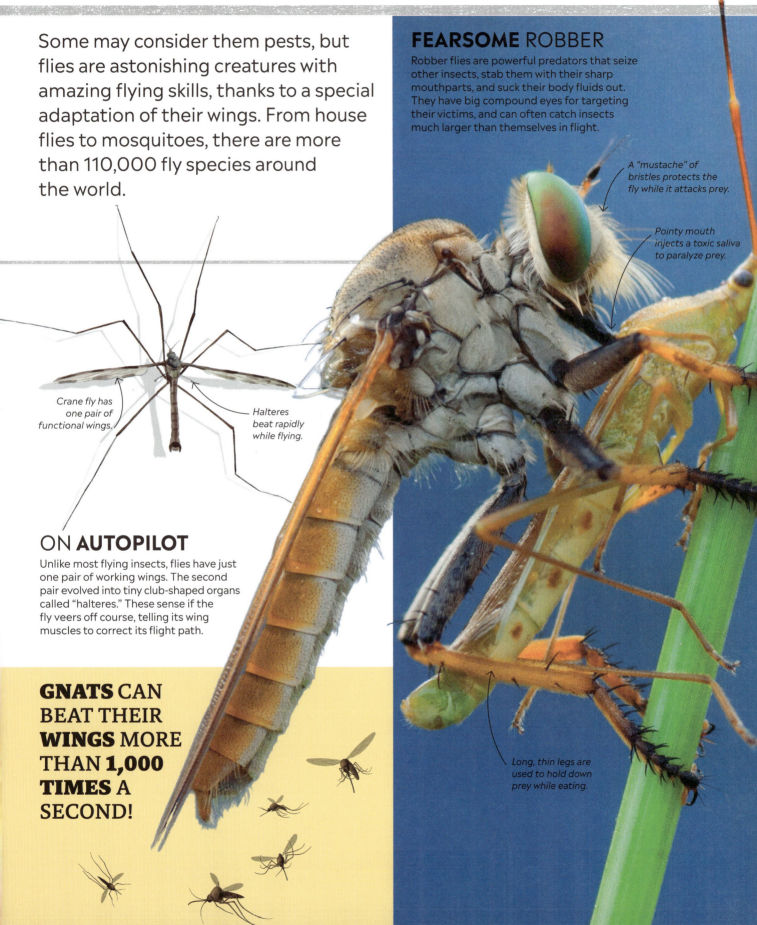

FEARSOME ROBBER

Robber flies are powerful predators that seize other insects, stab them with their sharp mouthparts, and suck their body fluids out. They have big compound eyes for targeting their victims, and can often catch insects much larger than themselves in flight.

A "mustache" of bristles protects the fly while it attacks prey.

Pointy mouth injects a toxic saliva to paralyze prey.

Crane fly has one pair of functional wings.

Halteres beat rapidly while flying.

ON AUTOPILOT

Unlike most flying insects, flies have just one pair of working wings. The second pair evolved into tiny club-shaped organs called "halteres." These sense if the fly veers off course, telling its wing muscles to correct its flight path.

GNATS CAN BEAT THEIR **WINGS** MORE THAN **1,000** **TIMES** A SECOND!

Long, thin legs are used to hold down prey while eating.

SUPER VISION

Most flies have big compound eyes, made up of thousands of lenses that provide a wide field of vision and detect fast movements. Some male flies, such as this hoverfly, have eyes that cover most of their heads to help them locate females.

A hoverfly's compound eyes contain up to 6,000 tiny lenses.

EYES ON **STALKS**

Tropical stalk-eyed flies have eyes mounted on the ends of long, rigid stalks that are up to ⅓ in (1 cm) long, extending from the sides of their heads. Rival males compare their eyespans in territorial contests, sizing each other up head-to-head. The fly with the longer eye-stalks usually wins, and goes on to have more success with females.

LIFE CYCLE

Flies have a four-stage life cycle similar to that of a butterfly: egg, larva, pupa, and adult. The larvae that hatch from their eggs are legless maggots that often feed on decaying matter, such as dead animals or dung. However, some larvae eat other insects, or are parasites that feed on the flesh of big, living animals. Each larva grows into a pupa that will eventually become a winged adult.

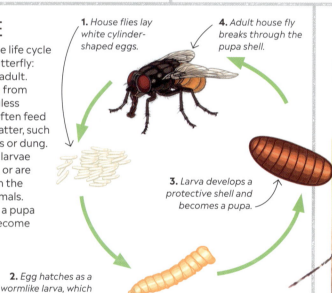

1. House flies lay white cylinder-shaped eggs.

4. Adult house fly breaks through the pupa shell.

3. Larva develops a protective shell and becomes a pupa.

2. Egg hatches as a wormlike larva, which molts and grows bigger.

BLOOD SUCKER

One of the most dangerous flies is the blood-feeding mosquito, which transmits deadly diseases such as malaria. These insects can drink up to three times their body weight in blood.

FOOD PROCESSORS

All adult flies can eat only liquid foods, or foods that they have turned into liquids. Various flies have different types of mouthparts adapted for processing and gathering their food, ranging from soft sponges to sharp needles.

Sponge
The spongelike mouthparts of a house fly drench food with saliva to liquefy it.

Blade
A blood-feeding horse fly slices into its victim's skin with a pair of razor-sharp blades.

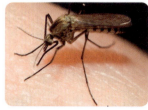

Needle
A mosquito's mouthparts form a sharp, hollow needle ideal for sucking blood.

ONLY **FEMALE MOSQUITOES BITE**—THEY USE THE **PROTEINS** IN BLOOD TO MAKE **THEIR EGGS!**

Yellow and black coloration both acts as camouflage and attracts potential mates.

Butterflies and moths

Delicate and colorful butterflies and their nocturnal cousins, moths, help keep plant and flower habitats healthy through their important role as pollinators.

BUILT **TO SCALE**

As with all butterflies and moths, the wings of this swallowtail are made of hundreds of thousands of tiny overlapping colored scales. The wings are toughened by a substance called chitin.

There are around 600 scales per square millimeter.

UNTRUE **BLUE**

Although it looks blue, the morpho butterfly is actually brown! When they are exposed to light, tree-shaped ridges on its scales reflect the blue light in the spectrum more than all the other colors.

Antennae detect airborne scents.

Hollow wing "veins" give the wing structural support, and contain insect blood, air, and nerves.

LIFE **CYCLE**

Moths and butterflies go through a process called metamorphosis. They start life as caterpillars then go through a pupa stage during which they change into their adult form.

1. *Females lay their eggs on plants.*

6. *The transformation is complete. A butterfly is born!*

4. *Caterpillar wraps itself in a chrysalis (or a cocoon for moths).*

2. *Eggs hatch into caterpillar larvae.*

5. *The caterpillar becomes a butterfly inside the chrysalis, then bursts free of it.*

3. *Caterpillar enters the pupa stage.*

Caterpillar waves whip-like appendages from its two-pronged tail when threatened.

HUNGRY **CATERPILLAR**

Puss moth caterpillars have a range of defenses against birds that try to eat them. Their red face signals danger to potential predators and their green body acts as camouflage. They can also squirt formic acid from their bellies when attacked.

Red coloring warns that this insect may be poisonous.

THE GIANT **ATLAS MOTH** HAS A HUGE **WINGSPAN** UP TO **12 IN (30 CM)**!

Extra-long tongue can reach deep into flowers.

Hummingbird hawk-moth hovers to feed.

VITAL POLLINATORS

Most butterflies and moths feed on flower nectar. As they move from bloom to bloom they spread vital pollen that fertilizes plants. This hummingbird hawk-moth can lick inside long, narrow flowers where others cannot reach—without it, some plants might die out.

AMERICAN MONARCH BUTTERFLIES **MIGRATE** UP TO **2,500 MILES (4,000 KM)** FROM SOUTHERN CANADA TO MEXICO!

BUTTERFLY OR **MOTH?**

Butterflies and moths are in the Lepidoptera ("scaly-winged") order of insects. The main difference is that butterflies are usually active in the daytime, while most moths fly by night.

Moth antennae are feathery; butterfly antennae are club-tipped.

Moth wings tend to be smaller than butterfly wings.

Moth wings are usually dull and dusty-looking for nighttime camouflage.

Butterfly wings are usually multicolored.

A typical butterfly has a slim body.

Butterfly

Moth bodies are often bulky and furry.

Moth

SUPER SENSE!

Night-flying moths have to rely on their sense of smell to find food and mating partners. Some males, such as this emperor moth, have elaborate antennae that can detect the scent of a female more than 1 mile (1.6 km) away.

NAME THAT... MOTH OR BUTTERFLY

How many of these fluttering fliers can you name? Cover up the answers below and find out!

1 Grizzled skipper butterfly
2 Provence burnet moth
3 Queen Alexandra's birdwing butterfly
4 Goliath birdwing
5 Peacock butterfly
6 Zebra swallowtail butterfly
7 Monarch butterfly
8 Clothes moth
9 Blue night butterfly
10 Red glider butterfly
11 Pale clouded yellow butterfly
12 Oleander hawk-moth
13 Broad-bordered grass yellow butterfly
14 Lime swallowtail butterfly
15 Basker moth
16 Helena morpho butterfly
17 Purple hairstreak butterfly
18 Indian leaf butterfly
19 Sulfur butterfly
20 Rajah Brooke's birdwing butterfly
21 Zebra longwing butterfly
22 Dragonfly
23 Tigerwing butterfly
24 American moon moth
25 Green-veined white butterfly
26 Regent skipper butterfly
27 European swallowtail butterfly
28 Luna moth
29 Giant atlas moth
30 Red admiral butterfly
31 Common nawab butterfly

CAN YOU SPOT THE ODD ONE OUT?

The odd one out is number 22, the dragonfly. It has transparent wings, but butterfly and moth wings are colorful and opaque.

PAPER **NEST**

Some wasps that live in colonies build nests made of paper. The worker wasps—which are sterile females—chew up wood pulp and plaster it onto the nest in layers. When completely dried out, it forms a rainproof canopy.

Nest is shaped like an upside-down cone.

Wasps can be aggressive when protecting the nest.

THE TARANTULA HAWK WASP PARALYZES GIANT SPIDERS AND USES THEM AS A FOOD SUPPLY FOR ITS YOUNG!

FUNGI **FARMING**

The leafcutter ants of tropical American forests gather leaf fragments to take back to their nest, forming trails made up of thousands of ants. The leaves nourish a special type of fungus that grows in the nest and which the ants eat.

Sharp jaws can slice leaves into fragments.

Ants, bees, and wasps

Ants, bees, and wasps are members of the same insect group. Ants are essentially wingless wasps, and bees are vegetarian wasps. While all ants live in colonies, different kinds of wasps and bees are colonial or live alone.

SWEET **NECTAR**

Whereas wasps are hunters that kill other insects to feed their young, most bees feed on nectar and pollen. In the process, they transfer pollen from flower to flower, making them important plant pollinators.

Hairy legs help pick up pollen.

Head | Thorax | Abdomen

Venomous stinger

One of six legs attached to the thorax

WASP **ANATOMY**

Like bees and ants, a wasp's body has three sections—the head, thorax, and abdomen. But unlike most ants, wasps also have two pairs of wings that can hook together for more efficient flight.

KILLER **DRILLER**

Ichneumon wasps lay their eggs on insect grubs, and some drill through wood to reach them. When the wasp larva hatches, it eats the grub alive!

Long ovipositor pierces the wood to implant eggs.

Insect grub

Wood bark

THERE ARE AN ESTIMATED **2.5 MILLION ANTS** FOR **EVERY HUMAN** ON EARTH!

Only young leaves are collected.

This ant is one in a line that can reach more than 100 ft (30 m).

Ant follows a scent trail back to the nest.

INSIDE AN **ANT HILL**

Ants are social insects that build underground nests made up of several chambers linked by narrow tunnels. Similar to some species of wasps and bees, ants live in colonies composed of queens and workers.

1. Worker ants find food and look after the queen's brood.

2. Larger queen ant lays eggs in one of the nest's brood chambers.

3. White, legless larvae hatch from ant eggs and later become pupae.

4. Pupae with folded legs and antennae will later change into adult ants.

WASP SPECIES COME IN MANY DIFFERENT COLORS. THE CUCKOO WASP IS A METALLIC BLUE, GREEN, AND RED!

Bees hanging together in a chain is called "festooning."

Honeycomb stores honey, pollen, and larvae.

Brightly colored stripes deter predators.

Honey bees can flap their wings 200 times per second.

Venom sac

Muscles push venom down barbed stinger.

Sting in the tail
A bee uses its stinger for protection. It can survive after stinging insects, but with thicker-skinned animals, its stinger will catch in its victim's flesh and rip from the bee's body, killing it.

AIR CONDITIONING
When a nest gets too hot, worker bees beat their wings to create a breeze. This also evaporates water droplets in the nest, which helps cool the air.

FAMILY UNIT
Bees live in groups known as colonies. The queen bee lays all of a colony's eggs. Thousands of female worker bees carry out the colony's tasks, including gathering food and raising the younger bees. The male drones do nothing except mate with the queen.

HONEY BEES PERFORM WHAT IS CALLED A **WAGGLE DANCE** TO TELL EACH OTHER **WHERE TO FIND NECTAR!**

WHO'S WHO
A colony can have 60,000–80,000 bees. There is one queen and a few hundred male drones. The rest are worker bees, all of whom are the queen's daughters. They are sterile, meaning they cannot reproduce.

Queen
Her long, slender body is specially adapted to carry eggs. She rarely leaves the nest.

Drones
Round and stocky, they have large wings, no stinger, and cannot collect pollen.

Workers
Smaller and more agile than drones, workers have a narrow abdomen.

Hardworking honey bees

"Exiled" queen is protected in the swarm.

Bees play a key role in our planet's biodiversity, spreading the pollen needed to fertilize plants and make seeds. They also make tasty honey and useful beeswax.

CREATING A **COLONY**

If a colony gets too big, the queen and some worker bees fly off to found a rival nest. In the old colony, a new queen emerges from 20 or so young bees raised by "nurse" bees.

CAVE PAINTINGS IN SPAIN SHOW THAT HUMANS KEPT HONEY BEES AT LEAST 9,000 YEARS AGO!

STORAGE **SOLUTIONS**

Every bees' nest is a warren of hexagonal honeycombs made of beeswax (a thick substance secreted from the glands of worker bees). Honey and pollen for food are stored in the cells, and the queen lays her eggs in them too. Drones and potential new queens are raised in larger cells. Worker bees hatch in small, individual "brood" cells.

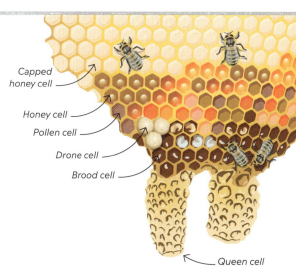

Capped honey cell
Honey cell
Pollen cell
Drone cell
Brood cell
Queen cell

BUSY **MOTHER**

The queen spends most of her life laying up to 1,500 eggs a day! The workers feed and care for her, defending her with their lives if necessary. The queen can live up to five years; workers for just a few weeks or months.

Eggs are deposited inside honeycomb cells.

SWEET **TREAT**

Bees make honey from nectar, a sugary, nutrient-rich liquid produced by plants, by passing it from mouth to mouth and sucking out its water content. Once the nectar is only 18 percent water, it has thickened into honey.

LIFE **ENHANCERS**

Each time a bee feeds, pollen from the flower sticks to its body, and as the bee travels it spreads pollen to different flowers. This fertilizes the flowers, so they can then develop seeds. Many creatures spread pollen—as does the wind—but insects such as bees are by far the most important pollinators.

Bee uses its short tongue to sip nectar.

Basket is used to collect pollen.

Silky spiders

Equipped with eight long legs and a pair of venomous fangs, spiders are efficient predators of insects and other small animals. They all produce and use silk in ingenious ways—to snare prey, build nests, protect their eggs, and even create trapdoors.

SPINNING **SILK**

A spider's body is made up of two parts. The front section, called the cephalothorax, carries its eyes, fangs, and legs. The back section, the abdomen, contains its heart, lungs, and silk glands. At the rear of the abdomen these silk glands are linked to spinnerets, which produce strands of silk that are 1,000 times thinner than human hair. The strands then combine to form strong silken threads.

Strong silk can support the spider's weight.

Spinneret

Liquid silk is stored in the silk glands.

Abdomen

Eight legs

Cephalothorax

Eyes

Fangs

FISHING SPIDER

While some spiders spin webs to trap their prey, others use their agility to hunt. The raft spider lurks in ambush on the edges of pools. They are able to stand on the water's surface and run across the pool to seize insects, tadpoles, and even small fish.

Fish is killed using the spider's venom.

Velvety pads on the spider's legs repel water and stop it from sinking.

WEAVING **EGG COCOONS**

Spider silk has many uses. Many species use it to make silken cocoons in which they hide their eggs from birds and other hungry animals. This yellow garden spider takes great care to give her future family the best possible protection.

Making a start
The spider uses its soft, woolly silk to create a small, dense, cup-shaped web.

Laying eggs
She produces a mass of yellow eggs, placing them beneath the opening of the silken cup.

Covering up
The spider starts covering her eggs in more layers of woolly silk to hide them from view.

Job done
The protective cocoon is complete, and the eggs are sealed safely inside until they hatch.

FLY **SOUP**

The powerful jaws of a wolf spider pinch together to trap prey. Sharp hinged fangs on their ends inject a venom that kills or paralyzes prey, which the spider consumes by regurgitating digestive fluids from its gut into its mouth.

SILKEN **SNARES**

Orb-weavers get their name from the wheel-shaped webs they spin to trap insects. This wasp spider has caught a grasshopper and is quickly wrapping it in fine silk to stop it from escaping. The spider then stabs it with its venomous fangs and starts feeding.

FEMALE SPIDERS ARE OFTEN BIGGER THAN MALES, AND MAY **EAT THEIR PARTNERS AFTER MATING!**

IF **SPIDER SILK** WERE AS **THICK AS STEEL**, IT WOULD BE **STRONGER** THAN **THE METAL!**

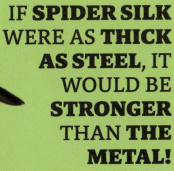

UNDERWATER HUNTER

The diving bell spider is the only spider that spends prolonged periods of time underwater. Needing air to breathe, it spins a dome-shaped web underwater, trapping an air bubble that it sits inside. The spider dashes out from this refuge to catch its prey.

Silk lines act as trip wires for prey.

Trapdoor is light enough for spider to push aside.

TRAPDOOR SPIDERS

Some spiders live in burrows that are hidden by trapdoors made from silk and earth. The spider knows if an insect is nearby because it can sense vibrations along silk lines at the burrow entrance. It can then quickly dart out to grab its unsuspecting prey.

Spider waits, ready to jump out if it senses movement in the silk traplines.

BLOOD SUCKERS

Ticks feed on the blood of animals, including humans. They wait in ambush on plants, grab onto passing victims, and start feeding. When they are full, they drop off to breed.

Tick expands and fills with blood after a meal.

Hungry tick

COURTING COUPLE

Scorpions use their pincers to seize and tear prey apart. As part of a courtship ritual, male scorpions also use their pincers to lead a female in a dancelike walk before mating.

DADDY LONG LEGS

Unlike spiders, which have two main body segments, a harvestman is an arachnid with a one-piece body. Also called a "daddy long legs," its eight legs are often several times longer than its body and can reach 5⅔ in (15 cm) long.

Long tail acts as a sensory organ.

SMELLY DEFENSE

Whip scorpions are named for their long, slender tail that resembles a whip. Like true scorpions, they are hunters, but they do not have stingers. Instead, they spray attackers with an irritating vinegar-like mist to defend themselves.

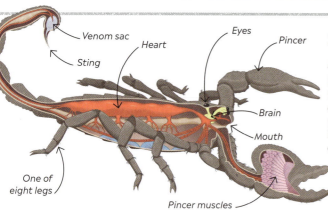

Venom sac

Heart

Eyes

Pincer

Sting

Brain

Mouth

One of eight legs

Pincer muscles

SCORPION ANATOMY

Like other arachnids, scorpions have eight jointed legs and a tough exoskeleton. They also have strong pincers and a powerful stinger, which is mainly used for defense, on the end of a long, segmented tail. Although some species have up to 12 eyes, scorpions have poor eyesight.

Long front legs act as feelers and help find prey.

EVERY HOUSE IS HOME TO MILLIONS OF TINY DUST MITES!

Grasping pincers crush any small animal they can catch.

Awesome arachnids

Arachnids make up a huge group containing around 100,000 different species of spiders, scorpions, mites, and ticks. All have four pairs of legs, no antennae, and fang- or pincerlike mouthparts.

OTHER
ARACHNIDS

Spiders, scorpions, and harvestmen are not the only arachnids. There are around 15 major groups, each containing many species.

Mites and ticks
Blood-sucking ticks are tiny parasites. Mite species eat a variety of foods, from blood to plants and insects.

Pseudoscorpions
Named for their strong resemblance to true scorpions, tailless pseudoscorpions have venomous pincers.

Whip spider
These fierce predators do not have venom and use their long sensory front legs to feel for prey.

Solifuges
At up to 5⅞ in (15 cm) long, solifuges mainly live in deserts, and use their huge jaws to hunt prey up to the size of lizards.

A **HUNGRY** BLOOD-SUCKING **TICK** CAN WAIT **ONE YEAR** FOR A **MEAL!**

TAXI SERVICE

Instead of laying eggs, female scorpions give birth to live young. As soon as they are born, the babies climb onto their mother's back, and she carries them around until they are old enough to find their own prey.

Arched tail is segmented and highly flexible.

Venom gland is covered in sensory hairs.

Baby scorpions are soft-bodied and vulnerable.

EVERY YEAR, ABOUT **3,000 PEOPLE** ARE **KILLED** BY **SCORPION STINGS!**

ZOMBIE WORM

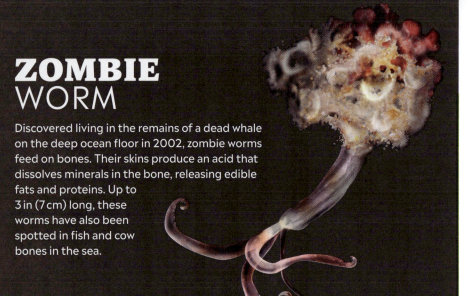

Discovered living in the remains of a dead whale on the deep ocean floor in 2002, zombie worms feed on bones. Their skins produce an acid that dissolves minerals in the bone, releasing edible fats and proteins. Up to 3 in (7 cm) long, these worms have also been spotted in fish and cow bones in the sea.

FACT PACK!
WORMS

Worms are soft-bodied creatures that come in all shapes and sizes. Many are almost microscopic, others are real giants, and some have horror-movie lifestyles.

FEARSOME PARASITES

Many worms live in other animals. This can produce mild effects in their hosts, but some cause serious health problems.

TAPEWORMS
These flat-bodied worms live in their host's intestines, and can cause stomach pain and fever.

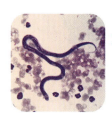

HEARTWORMS
These thin worms live in the lungs and hearts of dogs, causing lung disease and heart failure.

BLOOD FLUKES
These cylinder-shaped worms lay eggs in blood vessels, leading to tummy pain.

Female worm lives within the male.

TYPICAL EARTHWORM: The worms that live in garden soil can grow up to 14 in (35 cm) long.

LONGEST EARTHWORM: The African giant earthworm can grow to 22 ft (6.7 m) long.

LONGEST ROUNDWORM: *Placentonema gigantissima* live in sperm whales, and can reach 25 ft (7.62 m) long.

LONGEST PARASITE: Also found in the intestines of sperm whales, *Tetragonoporus* can be 130 ft (40 m) long.

LONGEST RIBBON WORM: At up to 164 ft (50 m), the ribbon worm *Lineus longissimus* may be the longest animal on Earth.

LONGEST WORMS

Most worms are small, but others can grow to incredible lengths. Here's a selection of record holders.

If threatened, ribbon worms can **shrink** their bodies down to a **tenth** of their extended length!

VIBRANT COLORS

Some worms are brightly colored. Most of these species live on the seabed and retreat into burrows if in danger.

SEA MOUSE
This furry-looking worm has a rainbow-colored shimmer.

CHRISTMAS TREE WORM
Two spiral crowns of tentacles snare prey.

FEATHER DUSTER WORM
This worm has orange, fan-shaped tentacles.

JAPANESE EARTHWORM
Its purple color makes this worm easy to spot.

WORM LIFESPAN

A worm's lifespan can range from just two years to more than two centuries. This graph compares a variety of species.

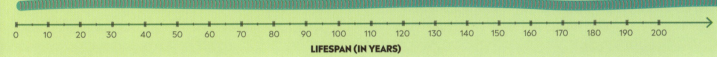

- **ROUNDWORM ASCARIS LUMBRICOIDES:** 2 years
- **COMMON EARTHWORM:** up to 6 years
- **HOOKWORM:** up to 18 years
- **TAPEWORM:** up to 25 years
- **MARINE TUBE WORM ESCARPIA LAMINATA:** 200 years
- **FLATWORM:** May be able to live forever by regenerating and protecting its DNA!

| 0 | 10 | 20 | 30 | 40 | 50 | 60 | 70 | 80 | 90 | 100 | 110 | 120 | 130 | 140 | 150 | 160 | 170 | 180 | 190 | 200 |

LIFESPAN (IN YEARS)

VARIED DIETS

Worms eat all sorts of foods, from soil and dead leaves to half-digested food and even blood!

EARTHWORMS
As they burrow through the ground, earthworms eat soil and digest any decaying plant material it contains.

TAPEWORMS
Like some roundworms, tapeworms live in animals' intestines, soaking up their host's partially digested food.

LEECHES
Some leeches are bloodsuckers but others are predators, feeding on invertebrates such as snails, insect larvae, and earthworms.

NEMERTINES
Most of these ribbon worms are predators found in water. They attack and eat marine snails, sea slugs, and shrimps.

GIANT TUBE WORMS
Living near deep-sea volcanic vents, these worms have no mouth, gut, or anus, and are nourished by food-making bacteria inside them.

SPECIES DIVERSITY

Many types of worms have evolved into thousands of species, each adapted for a slightly different way of life.

EARTHWORMS
There are 6,000 species of earthworm, known for their segmented bodies.

ROUNDWORMS
These consist of about 30,000 species, and are white and threadlike.

FLATWORMS
Most of the 20,000 flatworm species are parasites with flattened bodies.

RIBBON WORMS
Named for their ribbonlike bodies, there are more than 1,300 species.

ENDURING EXTREMES

The Pompeii worm lives close to volcanic hot springs on the ocean floor. Thanks to an insulating blanket of mucus that covers its body and feeds heat-resistant bacteria, it can thrive in hot conditions.

Centipedes
and millipedes

These arthropods were among the first animals to live on land, evolving more than 400 million years ago. While centipedes are fast predators, millipedes are slow vegetarians.

AT 2.6 M (9 FT) LONG, AND LIVING 300 MILLION YEARS AGO, *ARTHROPLEURA* WAS THE **BIGGEST INVERTEBRATE** EVER!

VELVET **WORM**

The ancestors of millipedes and centipedes were most likely similar to the velvet worms that live today in warm, wet forests. They have soft, caterpillar-like bodies and up to 43 pairs of fleshy, stumpy legs.

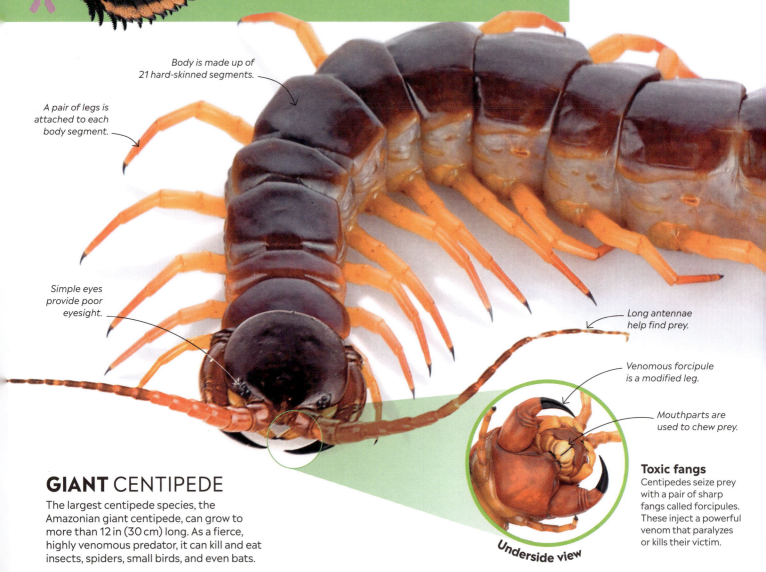

Body is made up of 21 hard-skinned segments.

A pair of legs is attached to each body segment.

Simple eyes provide poor eyesight.

Long antennae help find prey.

Venomous forcipule is a modified leg.

Mouthparts are used to chew prey.

Underside view

GIANT CENTIPEDE

The largest centipede species, the Amazonian giant centipede, can grow to more than 12 in (30 cm) long. As a fierce, highly venomous predator, it can kill and eat insects, spiders, small birds, and even bats.

Toxic fangs

Centipedes seize prey with a pair of sharp fangs called forcipules. These inject a powerful venom that paralyzes or kills their victim.

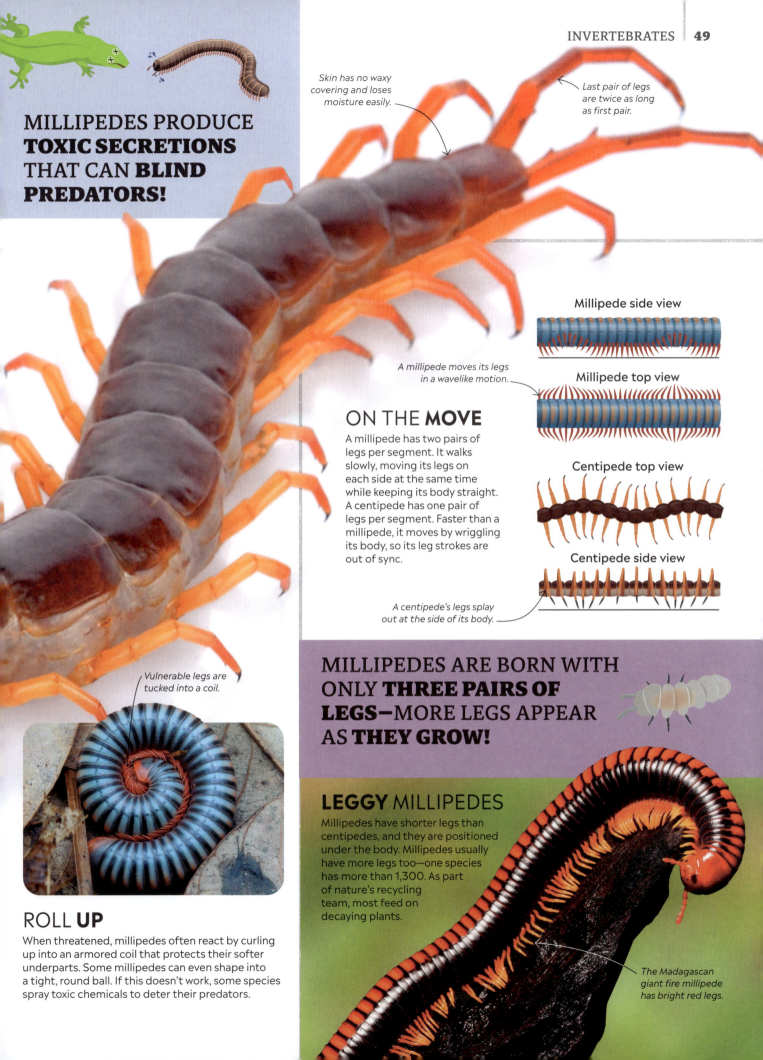

MILLIPEDES PRODUCE **TOXIC SECRETIONS** THAT CAN **BLIND PREDATORS!**

Skin has no waxy covering and loses moisture easily.

Last pair of legs are twice as long as first pair.

Millipede side view

A millipede moves its legs in a wavelike motion.

Millipede top view

ON THE **MOVE**

A millipede has two pairs of legs per segment. It walks slowly, moving its legs on each side at the same time while keeping its body straight. A centipede has one pair of legs per segment. Faster than a millipede, it moves by wriggling its body, so its leg strokes are out of sync.

Centipede top view

Centipede side view

A centipede's legs splay out at the side of its body.

Vulnerable legs are tucked into a coil.

MILLIPEDES ARE BORN WITH ONLY **THREE PAIRS OF LEGS**—MORE LEGS APPEAR AS **THEY GROW!**

ROLL **UP**

When threatened, millipedes often react by curling up into an armored coil that protects their softer underparts. Some millipedes can even shape into a tight, round ball. If this doesn't work, some species spray toxic chemicals to deter their predators.

LEGGY MILLIPEDES

Millipedes have shorter legs than centipedes, and they are positioned under the body. Millipedes usually have more legs too—one species has more than 1,300. As part of nature's recycling team, most feed on decaying plants.

The Madagascan giant fire millipede has bright red legs.

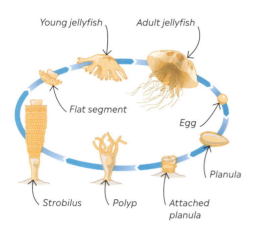

Young jellyfish

Adult jellyfish

Flat segment

Egg

Strobilus

Polyp

Attached planula

Planula

LIFE OF A **JELLYFISH**

Adult jellyfish produce eggs, which grow into larvae called planulae. Each one attaches to a rock and develops into an immobile stalk called a polyp, before changing into a strobilus—a stack of flat segments. Gradually, these break off and become mature jellyfish.

Squishy jellyfishes

Jellyfishes, hydras, anemones, and corals are some of the strangest animals on the planet, often barely recognizable as animals at all. Typically flowerlike in form, they are soft-bodied and use stinging cells to capture prey and protect themselves.

Eight branchlike tentacles line the body.

Blue-green color is caused by microscopic algae called zooxanthellae.

Flattened bell allows the jellyfish to rest easily on the sea floor.

TAKEN FOR A **RIDE**

Sea anemones are polyps crowned with stinging tentacles used to capture prey. Most anemones attach themselves to rocks, but this one is clinging to the shell of a hermit crab. The anemone's stings may help protect the crab from enemies.

REEF CORALS GET THEIR **COLOR** FROM **TINY ALGAE** IN THEIR SKIN!

Ribbed structure helps catch the wind like a sail.

Float is filled with carbon monoxide and air.

Feeding polyps devour prey.

Defensive tentacles can reach 30 ft (10 m) long.

Long, venomous tentacles are used to paralyze and kill fish and crustaceans.

DRIFTING
COLONY

The Portuguese man-of-war looks like a jellyfish, but it is actually made up of four different polyps working together, each specialized for a particular job. One polyp forms a gas-filled float that drifts on the ocean surface. Dangling just below this are feeding polyps, reproductive polyps, and stinging tentacles.

A SEA ANEMONE'S MOUTH IS ALSO ITS BOTTOM!

Barbed stinger shoots out.

Stinger is tucked inside each stinging cell.

Stinging cells
Jellyfish have tiny stinging cells on their tentacles. Each one contains a coiled up harpoon-like stinger. When triggered by touch, the stinger shoots out and injects venom.

UPSIDE-DOWN JELLYFISH
Unlike other jellyfishes, this tropical species lies on the sea bed with its tentacles facing upward. The tentacles carry microscopic algae that use the Sun's energy to make sugar, which feeds the jellyfish. Tropical reef corals get most of their food in the same way.

TYPES OF
CNIDARIA

Jellyfishes, corals, and anemones are all part of a group called cnidaria. While jellyfish are free-swimming, corals and anemones live rooted to one spot.

Jellyfish
Mature jellyfish drift with currents, but can also swim slowly. They are single animals, but they often travel in swarms. Water makes up 95 percent of their bodies.

Sea anemone
These creatures are also single animals. They cling to solid underwater objects such as rocks and wait for food to drift within range of their stinging tentacles.

Coral
Corals are made up of hundreds of thousands of individual polyps. They have separate crowns of tentacles, but their bodies are joined together like tree branches.

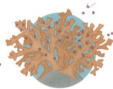

BUDDING BABIES

The freshwater hydra is 1¼ in (3 cm) long, and lives as a polyp attached to a rock or plant. In summer, it reproduces by growing a new polyp from its tiny body, like the bud of a plant. This eventually breaks off to lead an independent life.

Original polyp has tentacles around its mouth.

New polyp grows and breaks off as a clone.

FOSSILS PROVE THAT JELLYFISH HAVE BEEN ON EARTH FOR 500 MILLION YEARS!

CRUSTACEAN **CHARACTERISTICS**

A lobster is a typical crustacean. It has a long body, several pairs of limbs, and a muscular tail with many segments. Although some crustaceans have evolved differently, many have a protective cover called a carapace over the head and front part of the body.

Lobster

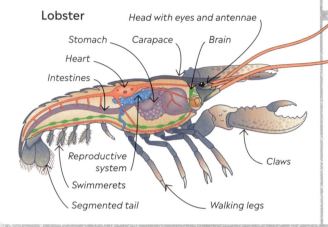

Head with eyes and antennae

Stomach

Carapace

Brain

Heart

Intestines

Reproductive system

Swimmerets

Segmented tail

Claws

Walking legs

Crabs and company

Crabs and their relatives form a group called crustaceans. They are arthropods—invertebrates with tough external skeletons, like insects. But their skeletons are often much stronger than those of insects, and many have ten legs or more.

FLASHY **FIDDLER**

Crabs have eight walking legs and a pair of powerful claws, normally used for feeding. This male fiddler crab has an extra-large claw that accounts for up to half its body weight, adapted to attract females and show off to rivals.

Eyes are on hinged stalks.

Smaller claw is used to gather food.

Leg hinges only bend sideways.

Tough exoskeleton protects soft internal organs.

MARINE COPEPODS LIVE IN SUCH HUGE NUMBERS THAT THEY FORM **THE LARGEST MASS OF ANIMAL LIFE** ON EARTH!

LOBSTERS ON THE **MARCH**

Heavy-bodied crabs and lobsters mostly live on the seabed, hiding among rocks and emerging to hunt or scavenge for food. Most live in the same place for life, but Caribbean spiny lobsters sometimes go on long journeys, marching in single file for 30 miles (50 km) or more to find new feeding grounds.

THE WORLD'S LARGEST CRAB, THE JAPANESE SPIDER CRAB, HAS CLAWS THAT SPAN 13 FT (4 M)!

Oversize claw can regenerate if severed.

CRUSTY **COLLECTION**

Crustaceans come in all shapes and sizes, from tiny drifting copepods to hard-shelled crabs. Their greatest diversity is in oceans and seas, but some also live in freshwater or on land.

Crabs

Lobsters and crayfish

Shrimp and prawns

Copepods

Woodlice

Barnacles

WONDERFUL **WOODLICE**

Only a few crustaceans live on land. The most familiar are woodlice that feed on decaying plant matter. They breathe with gill-like organs that only work well in damp conditions, so most prefer to live under rocks or wood, away from sunlight.

Antennae are sensory organs that help with navigation.

Exoskeleton is divided into seven body segments.

TRAVEL **BUDDIES**

In the rich waters of the Southern Ocean around Antarctica, shrimplike krill multiply to form giant drifting swarms that can be seen from space. These krill swarms are the main prey of the colossal filter-feeding whales that live in these icy seas, and they are also hunted by penguins and seals.

The biggest krill can reach 2½ in (6 cm) long.

NAME THAT... CRUSTACEAN

Are you a canny crabber? Can you tell a louse from a lobster or a crab from a copepod? Try to name these colorful crustaceans without looking at the answers below. Can you crack the odd one out?

1 Yellow cherry shrimp
2 Atlantic ghost crab
3 Blue spiny lobster
4 Sally lightfoot crab
5 Edible crab
6 Slipper lobster
7 Norway lobster
8 Common prawn
9 Ostracod
10 Brine shrimp
11 Banded coral shrimp
12 Camel shrimp
13 Red snow crab
14 Common marble shrimp
15 American lobster
16 Goldenrod crab spider
17 Acorn barnacle
18 Woodlouse
19 Giant tiger prawn
20 Peacock mantis shrimp
21 Blue crab
22 Water louse
23 Sand hopper
24 African rainbow crab
25 Water flea
26 Tadpole shrimp
27 Spider decorator crab
28 Dungeness crab
29 Antarctic krill
30 Goose barnacle
31 Hermit crab
32 Copepod
33 Harlequin shrimp
34 Shore crab

CAN YOU SPOT THE ODD ONE OUT?

The odd one out is the goldenrod crab spider (16). It's a spider, not a crab! Not to be confused with spider crabs, which are crustaceans.

Marvelous mollusks

Snails, clams, squids, and their relatives are all mollusks—soft-bodied animals that sometimes have a hard, protective, chalky shell. Most live in water, but some are land animals.

A SCALLOP HAS UP TO 200 TINY EYES ALONG THE EDGE OF ITS SHELL!

SHELLS AND PEARLS

Mollusk shells are made of chalky minerals, and are lined with a smooth, shiny material called nacre. Some two-shelled mollusks, such as oysters, can coat worms or beads that have got into their shells with layers of nacre to make them less irritating. This process creates pearls.

Pearl

Nacre

Oyster shell

SUPER SLUGS

Some of the most colorful mollusks are sea slugs—gastropods that prey on other marine animals such as sea anemones. Many, including this *Goniobranchus kuniei*, live on coral reefs.

Feather-like gills absorb oxygen from the water.

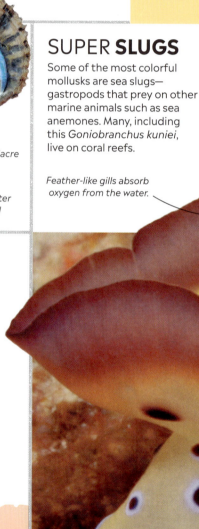

5. *Edible food particles pass through the gut, where they are digested.*

6. *Waste particles are removed in water expelled from the mussel's body.*

Anus

4. *Fingerlike palps around the mouth pass food particles into the gut.*

Gills

Mouth

1. *Water carrying food particles is drawn into the mussel's body.*

2. *Water flows over the gills, where food particles stick to the gill's mucus.*

3. *Microscopic hairs send trapped food particles down toward the mouth.*

FILTER FEEDERS

Clams, mussels, and scallops are called bivalves. They are all aquatic with two shells linked by a hinge, and most spend their lives buried in sand or attached to rocks. A mussel gets food from the sea by filtering water through its body.

INSIDE A **GASTROPOD**

Around 80 percent of mollusks are gastropods—the group that includes snails and slugs, both on land and in water. They are mobile animals that glide along on a slimy "foot." Aquatic snails, like this one, have gills, but some terrestrial ones have a lung. Most have a single, often coiled shell.

Digestive gland

Mantle, a fleshy lining, surrounds the body and protects internal organs.

Strong, spiral coiled shell

Intestine

Gills

Stomach

Foot

LAND **INVADERS**

Most mollusks live underwater and breathe using gills, just like fish. But some have lungs that enable them to breathe air, which allows them to live on land. These land snails and slugs mostly eat plants, although this colorful Cuban painted snail also feasts on fungi and lichens. Its shell keeps getting bigger as the snail grows.

Brightly colored shell is about the size of a grape.

Soft body has no protective shell.

Mantle runs around the edge of the sea slug and forms a flap.

Two long sensory organs called rhinophores help find food and detect predators.

TO GET RID OF PARASITES, SOME SEA SLUGS CAN DETACH THEIR HEADS AND THEN REGROW A NEW BODY!

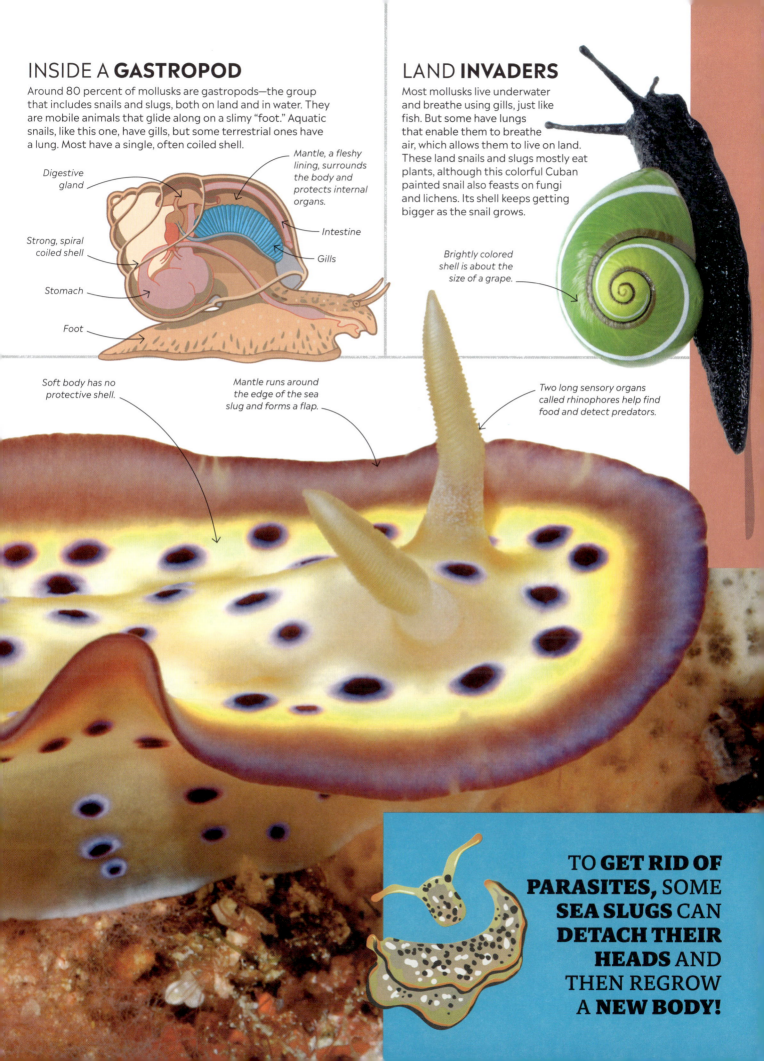

TYPES OF CEPHALOPOD

"Cephalopod" means "head-feet" in Greek, describing how the limbs of these creatures appear to be attached to their heads. There are four main types, which are all soft-bodied except the nautilus.

Octopus
These animals have a large round head and eight arms with clinging suckers.

Squid
Tube-shaped squid have a backbone, eight arms, and two extendable tentacles.

Cuttlefish
A cuttlefish's body has a "cuttlebone," eight arms, and two tentacles.

Nautilus
These are the only living cephalopods to have a hard external shell for protection.

JET PROPELLED

All squid use their fin to swim forward slowly. To move quickly, it can shoot backward by blasting a jet of water from a funnel underneath its body.

Muscular funnel is also used to exhale, lay eggs, and squirt ink.

SOME SQUID **ROCKET** THROUGH **THE AIR** TO A HEIGHT OF UP **TO 10 FT (3 M)!**

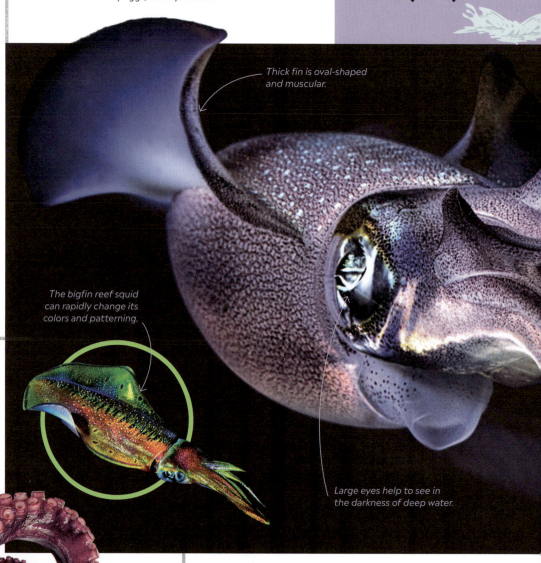

Thick fin is oval-shaped and muscular.

The bigfin reef squid can rapidly change its colors and patterning.

Large eyes help to see in the darkness of deep water.

DEADLY **GRIP**

The arms and tentacles of squids, cuttlefishes, and octopuses are studded with hundreds of powerful cup-shaped suckers that can seize and hold prey, and even pull it apart. Some squid suckers also have hooks to give extra grip on struggling and often slippery prey.

Octopuses can move each sucker individually.

OCTOPUSES HAVE **DOUGHNUT-SHAPED** BRAINS!

LIVING **FOSSILS**

Nautilus are considered "living fossils" because the nine species that live in tropical seas are virtually identical to animals that lived 500 million years ago. They are also similar to fossil ammonites that lived up to the time of the dinosaurs.

Coiled, pearly shell has many internal chambers.

Up to 90 thin tentacles with sticky grooves help catch prey.

Clever cephalopods

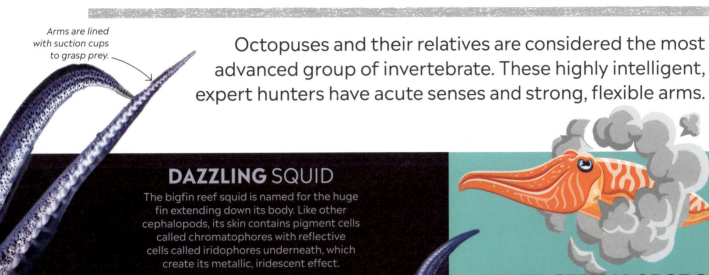

Arms are lined with suction cups to grasp prey.

Octopuses and their relatives are considered the most advanced group of invertebrate. These highly intelligent, expert hunters have acute senses and strong, flexible arms.

DAZZLING SQUID

The bigfin reef squid is named for the huge fin extending down its body. Like other cephalopods, its skin contains pigment cells called chromatophores with reflective cells called iridophores underneath, which create its metallic, iridescent effect.

MANY CEPHALOPODS SQUIRT **CLOUDS OF BLACK INK** INTO THE WATER TO **DISTRACT AND ESCAPE** PREDATORS!

INSIDE A **CUTTLEFISH**

Cuttlefish have eight arms lined with suckers and two tentacles with suckers at their ends. Their internal shell can be flooded with gas to help them float.

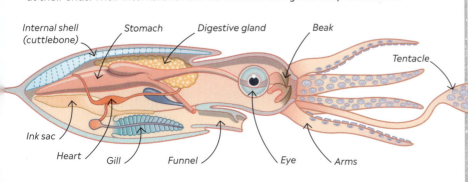

Internal shell (cuttlebone)

Stomach

Digestive gland

Beak

Tentacle

Ink sac

Heart

Gill

Funnel

Eye

Arms

BABY **BIGFIN**

Similarly to other cephalopods, bigfin reef squid lay thousands of eggs. Each egg develops into a tiny embryo, as shown above, and eventually becomes a baby squid. About the size of a grain of rice, the hatchling preys on tiny drifting animals, such as plankton.

Blue-ringed octopuses

Although they are small enough to fit in the palm of your hand, blue-ringed octopuses are a group of extremely toxic cephalopods. Their bite is deadly enough to kill a human.

SWIFT GETAWAY

Normally, a blue-ringed octopus glides slowly with its arms outspread. Like other cephalopods, when in trouble, it escapes by darting head-first through open water with its arms trailing, propelled by a jet of water forced out of its body.

WARNING SIGNAL

When it is alarmed, the tiny blue-ringed octopus performs a dramatic light show, flashing patterns of glowing, iridescent blue. But the dazzling display is a warning to back off, or risk almost certain death.

Well-developed eyes have a blue line running either side of them, like all blue-ringed octopuses.

Glowing blue rings show that the octopus feels threatened.

Head is characteristically large and bulbous.

THE **VENOMOUS BITE** OF THE **BLUE-RINGED OCTOPUS** MAKES IT ONE OF THE **OCEAN'S MOST TOXIC** ANIMALS!

VENOMOUS **BEAK**

The coiling arms of the octopus hide a sharp, parrotlike beak that the creature uses to rip its prey apart and see off threats. As it does so, saliva containing a powerful nerve toxin floods into the wound, paralyzing and often killing the victim.

Sharp-edged beak pierces flesh to deliver venom.

Salivary gland stores venom.

Toothed tongue scrapes against prey.

TIGHT **SQUEEZE**

Since it has no hard skeleton, the octopus can squeeze into tiny spaces. It can slip through narrow gaps in a coral reef or find shelter tucked in an empty clam shell.

THE SOUTHERN **BLUE-RINGED OCTOPUS** ONLY GROWS UP TO **9 IN (22 CM) LONG!**

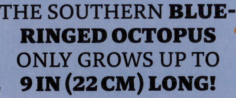

Sucker-covered arms are used to catch prey.

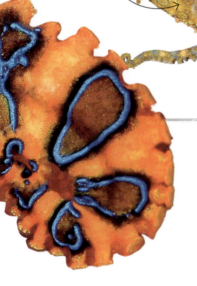

Bumpy skin texture blends in with the surrounding rocks.

SPOT THE **OCTOPUS**

When resting, the octopus uses camouflage to hide from predators lurking nearby. As soon as it settles, the color cells in its skin automatically adjust its color to match its surroundings. The octopus can even change its skin texture to match nearby objects.

Hidden rings

Muscle cell contracts to pull dark pigmented cells over the iridophore and hide its iridescence.

Iridophore

Muscle cell

CHANGING COLOR

The blue-ringed octopus uses iridophores, special kinds of reflective cells in its skin to make its rings flash blue. The iridophores can be exposed or hidden by muscles to switch the flashing on and off.

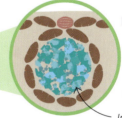

Exposed rings

When the muscle cell relaxes, the dark pigmented cells move out of the way to expose the blue iridophore underneath.

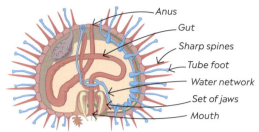

Anus
Gut
Sharp spines
Tube foot
Water network
Set of jaws
Mouth

INSIDE A **SEA URCHIN**

A sea urchin has rows of tube feet (see below) that are connected to a water network. It uses a set of teeth that stick out from its central mouth to nibble on marine algae.

CORAL **SLAYER**

The tropical crown-of-thorns starfish eats coral, pulling its stomach out through its mouth to coat the coral in digestive enzymes. This starfish can destroy entire coral reefs by swarming in vast numbers.

WATER **FILLED**

All echinoderms are equipped with a system of tubes that contain water. The tubes are linked to soft tube feet, which the animals use to move around. The illustration below shows a cross section of a starfish's arm.

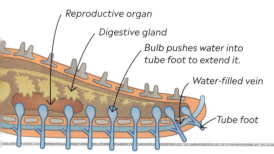

Reproductive organ
Digestive gland
Bulb pushes water into tube foot to extend it.
Water-filled vein
Tube foot

REGROWING **LIMBS**

A starfish has duplicates of its vital organs in each of its arms, so if the creature loses one of its arms, it can grow another to replace it. In some cases, the lost arm can even grow the missing parts of its body to form a new, complete animal.

Brittle stars use their flexible arms to crawl over the seabed.

SWARM OF **SPINES**

Where food is plentiful, parts of the seabed swarm with different types of echinoderms. While sea urchins scrape seaweeds from rocks and brittle stars gather edible debris, typical starfish are predators that feed on clams, corals, and even other echinoderms.

A common sun star, a type of starfish, can grow to 13 in (34 cm) wide.

The common sea urchin is known for its pink shell.

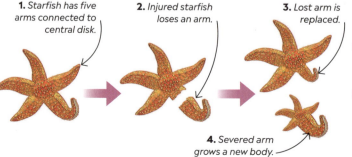

1. *Starfish has five arms connected to central disk.*

2. *Injured starfish loses an arm.*

3. *Lost arm is replaced.*

5. *New arm grows to full size.*

4. *Severed arm grows a new body.*

THE SPINES OF A BLACK SEA URCHIN CAN REACH 12 IN (30 CM) LONG!

Extraordinary
echinoderms

Starfish, sea urchins, and their relatives are known as echinoderms, which means "spiny skinned." They live in seas and oceans, and while some are mobile, others spend most of their lives attached to rocks.

TYPES OF ECHINODERM

All echinoderms have bodies that are starlike or symmetrical. This is clear to see in starfish, but in sea urchins the rays of the star are more like the segments of an orange, forming a ball. Sea cucumbers are similar but with elongated bodies.

Starfish
Most starfish have five arms that are covered in tiny suckers.

Brittle star
These animals coil their sucker-less arms to crawl faster than a starfish.

Feather star
These cling to rocks like sea anemones and have long, feather-like arms.

Sea lily
Sea lilies are similar to feather stars, but have a stalk fixed to the seabed.

Sea urchin
Typical sea urchins are round, and bristle with long, sharp spines.

Sea cucumbers
Using their long, bumpy bodies, sea cucumbers crawl along the seabed.

A SEA CUCUMBER CAN EJECT SOME OF ITS ORGANS TO SCARE OFF PREDATORS!

SEABED SIFTER

Typical sea cucumbers have a long body with a mouth surrounded by feeding tentacles at one end. They live on the seabed—some at great depths—where they sift through the water or soft mud for particles of edible debris. Most sea cucumbers also eat tiny pieces of algae and plankton.

CORAL EXPERT

Dr. Helen Fox is the Conservation Science Director for the Coral Reef Alliance, working to help reefs survive climate change. Based in the US, she has made more than 1,000 dives and once lived underwater for 9 days in the Aquarius Habitat.

Q What first drew you to study coral reefs?

A I was lucky to have parents who enjoyed the natural world, and traveling to explore. I remember snorkeling for the first time when I was 12 on a coral reef in Puerto Rico and being mesmerized. Six years later, I worked on Heron Island, Australia, which is where I learned how to scuba and fell in love with these amazing ecosystems.

Q Why are reefs so important to ocean health?

A Coral reefs are one of Earth's most biodiverse ecosystems. Even though they occupy less than 1% of the ocean floor, they support 25% of all ocean species.

REEF **LABORATORY**

Adorned with vibrant sponges, the Aquarius Habitat is an underwater laboratory in the Florida Keys National Marine Sanctuary. Roughly the size of a school bus, it is permanently anchored to the ocean floor about 63 ft (19 m) below the surface. Housing up to six people, the laboratory is designed to allow scientists to dive and conduct research deeper and longer than they normally could.

Q How have the challenges facing coral reefs changed?

A Challenges for coral reefs have got much bigger over time. Overpopulation and poorly managed coastal development mean more overfishing and pollution. Our increasing use of fossil fuels is causing climate change, which leads to rising ocean temperatures. When the sea is warmer than usual, corals turn so white they appear bleached and are more likely to die.

Q What was it like living in the Aquarius Habitat?

A Being an "aquanaut" and living underwater in the Aquarius Habitat for 9 days was a highlight of my career. I was there to study mantis shrimp in their natural habitat. My dive buddy and I would leave the dry, air-filled habitat to go searching for a type of mantis shrimp living more than 100 ft (30 m) beneath the surface. We couldn't have done this research any other way.

Q What can I do to help coral reefs?

A There are many things! Most are the kinds of things that you would do to help fight climate change and reduce carbon emissions, such as eating less meat and not wasting energy. In addition, if you do travel to a coral reef destination, you could join an organized beach clean-up to help reduce ocean pollution, and avoid buying coral souvenirs, which contribute to habitat destruction.

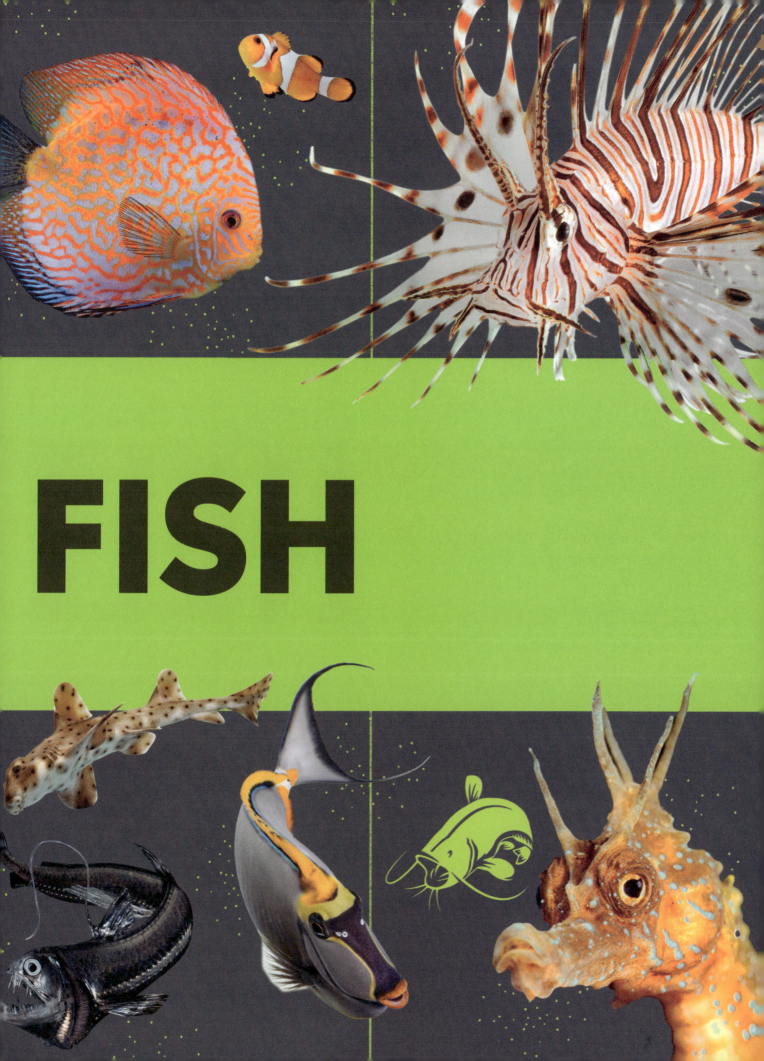

FISH

What is a **fish?**

All fish live in water and most species use gills to extract oxygen. But there are many diverse groups of fish and some are more closely related to land animals than to each other.

PLACODERMS
Placoderms are an extinct group of prehistoric fish. They were among the first creatures to have jaws and teeth.

JAWLESS FISH
The earliest fish had no hinged jaw. Their descendants, hagfish and lampreys, bite and suck food through round mouths.

Placoderms had bony plates for protection.

Fish, like this lamprey, absorb oxygen through their gills. Their ancestors used gills to filter food.

Jawed vertebrates
Hinged jaws evolved to make it possible to bite down on prey.

SALTWATER FISH

Fish that live in the sea are called saltwater fish. They drink lots of seawater and extract excess salt using specialized gills (see p.84). In the vast oceans, some can grow to huge sizes—this manta ray is 26 ft (8 m) across, while whale sharks (see pp.70–71) are the largest of all fish.

Vertebrates
Fish were the first animals with a backbone to anchor their muscles.

500 MYA (million years ago)

Flexible cartilage tail helps shark swim efficiently.

TUSKFISH BASH CLAMS AGAINST ROCKS TO CRACK THEM OPEN FOR FOOD!

FRESHWATER FISH

Rivers, lakes, and wetlands make up only 2 percent of Earth's water, but about half of all fish species spend some or all of their lives in these diverse, low-salt environments. The best known include carp, bass, tetras, and piranhas. Some salmon, eels, and trout move between salty and fresh water at different stages of life.

DEEP-SEA FISH

Deep-sea fish live well below the sunlit surface of the sea and survive low oxygen levels, crushing water pressure, and near-freezing temperatures. In the darkness, a Sloane's viperfish dangles a luminescent lure near its mouth to attract prey.

ANCIENT FISH STORY

Fish are the founders of the vertebrate line. Their adaptations evolved into familiar features for animals in water, on land, or in the air. They include a strong backbone for support, jaws for biting, four limbs to swim and later walk or fly, and gills or air-gulping lungs to breathe.

Bony vertebrates
Early fish had both bone and cartilage. Now most are bony.

Bony fish skeletons have more attachment points for muscles than cartilage.

430 MYA

420 MYA

410 MYA

TETRAPODS
Coastal fish adapted to live on land, and lobes became limbs. All reptiles, amphibians, birds, and mammals are descended from ancient lobe-finned fish.

LOBE-FINNED FISH
These fish use muscular limb buds (lobes) within their fins to push themselves along river or sea beds or even onto land. Some can also breathe air.

CARTILAGINOUS FISH
These fish grow skeletons made of cartilage—the material that gives your ears their shape! It is lighter and more flexible than bone.

Sharks, rays, and skates all have cartilage skeletons.

RAY-FINNED FISH
These make up more than half of all living vertebrate species. Their fins are formed of thin, bony spines connected by a thin layer of skin.

Long snout helps the copperband butterfly fish pull out prey from small gaps.

FISH FEATURES

All fish live in water and have a backbone. Here are six other characteristics that are common to almost all fish species.

1. Lateral line
This narrow strip of sensory cells allows the fish to sense movement, vibrations, and pressure differences.

2. Inside ears
A fish has ears inside its head, one behind each eye.

3. No eyelids
Most fish don't have eyelids because there is no dust underwater.

4. Gills
Most fish have gills to extract oxygen from water.

5. Two-chambered heart
Fish hearts have just two chambers, whereas human hearts have four.

6. Cold-blooded
Most fish do not generate much heat, so their temperature depends on the surrounding water.

REEF FISH

In tropical coral reefs, many fish use bright colors to communicate, for camouflage, or to attract a mate. The clear, still water makes it easy to see these signals, but the reef also has plenty of hiding places.

Sharks and rays

Unlike most other backboned animals, sharks and rays have skeletons made from rubbery cartilage, rather than bone. They are usually covered in tiny, hard scales, so their skin feels like sandpaper.

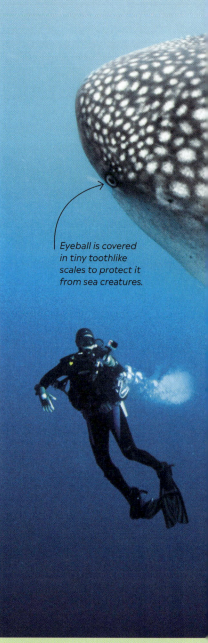

Eyeball is covered in tiny toothlike scales to protect it from sea creatures.

STAYING **AFLOAT**

Cartilage is lighter than bone, so sharks and rays do not need a gas-filled swim bladder to stay buoyant like most bony fishes do. Their flexible cartilage spines also allow them to make sharp turns when chasing prey.

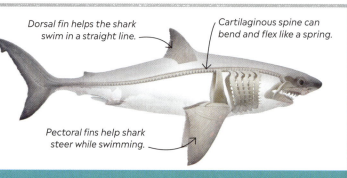

Dorsal fin helps the shark swim in a straight line.

Cartilaginous spine can bend and flex like a spring.

Pectoral fins help shark steer while swimming.

SAWFISH, A TYPE OF RAY, HAVE A **LONG, FLAT NOSE** LINED WITH **SHARP TEETH** THAT LOOKS LIKE **A SAW!**

SUPER PREDATOR

As the world's largest predatory fish, great white sharks have many features that help them hunt. They use sensory organs called ampullae of Lorenzini, located on their heads, to find prey by detecting their electrical fields.

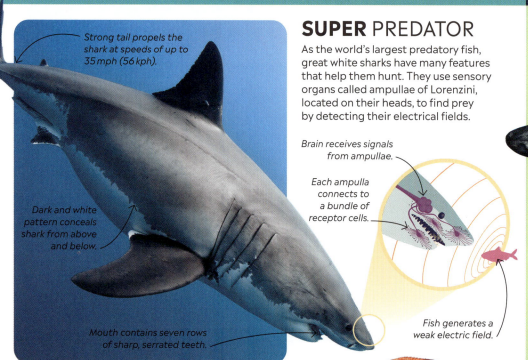

Strong tail propels the shark at speeds of up to 35 mph (56 kph).

Dark and white pattern conceals shark from above and below.

Mouth contains seven rows of sharp, serrated teeth.

Brain receives signals from ampullae.

Each ampulla connects to a bundle of receptor cells.

Fish generates a weak electric field.

GREENLAND SHARKS LIVE FOR ABOUT **400 YEARS!**

Spot pattern is unique to each whale shark, similar to a human fingerprint.

BIG EATER

At 39 ft (12 m) long, whale sharks are the world's largest fish. Found mostly in tropical oceans, these filter-feeders spend eight hours a day swallowing around 10,000 gallons (45,000 liters) of seawater and straining it for small creatures.

One of two dorsal fins on the lower back

Sharks and rays have multiple gill slits on the side of the body.

BABY SHARK

Most female sharks give birth to live young, such as this lemon shark shown here still attached to her newborn by an umbilical cord. Once separated, the lemon shark pup will leave its mother and find cover in mangrove forests.

RADICAL RAYS

Rays have flattened bodies with large winglike pectoral fins. Some have a venomous, barbed stinger on their tails. The blue-spotted ribbon tail ray, a venomous species, is also brightly colored, warning predators to stay away.

WHALE SHARKS ARE 39 FT (12 M) LONG—THE LENGTH OF A SCHOOL BUS!

Hammerhead sharks

The 11 species of hammerhead shark live in tropical oceans around the world. They are known for their wide, flattened heads, which improve their ability to maneuver and heighten their senses for finding prey—even when it is buried in sand.

HAMMERHEAD SHARKS CAN HAVE AS MANY AS 17 ROWS OF TEETH—BOTH ON THEIR **UPPER AND LOWER JAWS!**

SOME HAMMERHEAD SPECIES HAVE DEVELOPED THE ABILITY TO TAN, TURNING THEIR SKIN FROM LIGHT GRAY TO DARK GRAY!

TOOTH FACTORY

Like all sharks, hammerheads have an endless supply of teeth—they are constantly lost and then regenerated. Their small front teeth are sharp and bladelike, while their back teeth are blunter and used for eating shellfish.

Far-apart eyes can quickly scan for prey.

Hammer-shaped head is called a cephalofoil, which means "head wing."

Asymmetrical tail helps propel the shark forward.

New tooth moves up from behind, like a conveyor belt.

Old tooth is about to fall out.

New teeth form in the jaw.

Pectoral fins help the shark balance in the water.

EYES WIDE

Hammerheads have wide-set eyes, which means that, like humans, each eye gets a slightly different view. Their unique eye positioning gives hammerheads a 360-degree view, allowing them to see all around at all times, and enabling them to judge distances.

SCENT DETECTION

Hammerheads' peculiar head shape means they have more sensory organs in their heads (see page 70) than other sharks. Using their acute senses, they sweep their head over the seabed and can even detect prey hiding in the sand.

Brain receives signals from ampullae of Lorenzini.

Tiny pores on its head contain ampullae of Lorenzini—sensory organs that detect electrical fields.

Buried stingray produces an electric field.

THE ONLY PLACE A **HAMMERHEAD CAN'T SEE** IS **ABOVE AND BELOW** ITS HEAD!

Small, hard scales reduce drag, allowing for fast, silent swimming.

Triangular-shaped teeth are arranged in several rows.

Remora fish swims close to the hammerhead to feed on food scraps.

LUNGS AND GILLS

Prehistoric fish probably had both lungs to breathe air and gills to absorb oxygen from the water. Today, some fish, such as lungfish, also have lungs and gills, but most fish just have gills. Most of the air-breathing animals that evolved from fish (see pp.68–69) rely solely on lungs.

Prehistoric bony fish
Fish living more than 400 million years ago may have gulped air into lungs as well as using gills.

Lungfish
Lungfish exist today and still use their lungs to supplement their gills—especially when pools of water dry up.

Ray-finned fish
Most bony, ray-finned fish have a gas-filled swim bladder that evolved from early lungs. It helps keep them buoyant.

Air breathers
Land vertebrates that live today, as well as water-dwelling mammals such as whales, get air through lungs.

Ancient fish

These creatures began evolving differently from other fish hundreds of millions of years ago and have continued to change. Some are more closely related to four-legged land-dwelling creatures than to other fish, breathing through lungs or gulping down air as well as water.

Bony plates (scutes) cover the head and run along the body.

Upper lobe of the tail fin is longer than the lower.

COOL COELACANTHS

These deep-sea drifters have muscular limb buds, like legs, within their fins. They are more closely related to amphibians, birds, and even mammals than to ray-finned fish. It was thought they became extinct 66 million years ago, until living fish were found off the coast of South Africa in 1938.

THE OLDEST KNOWN AUSTRALIAN LUNGFISH IS THOUGHT TO BE MORE THAN 90 YEARS OLD!

GOOD DOGFISH!

Bowfins, commonly called mudfish, choupique, and dogfish, are native to North America and first appeared 250 million years ago. They live at the bottom of seas and lakes, but they can breathe both water and air, allowing them to survive drought conditions that would kill other fish.

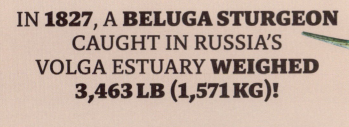

IN 1827, A BELUGA STURGEON CAUGHT IN RUSSIA'S VOLGA ESTUARY WEIGHED 3,463 LB (1,571 KG)!

Sensitive barbels are dragged over the bottom of the lake or river to find food.

Vacuum-like toothless mouth sucks up food.

GULPING **GARS**

With dart-like heavily armored bodies and pointy jaws, gars are deadly predators. Longnose gars (above) have especially long snouts, with which they lunge toward smaller fish, impaling the prey on their sharp teeth. Like bowfins, gars can also gulp down air when needed.

THE LARGEST GAR—THE ALLIGATOR GAR—CAN REACH NEARLY 10 FT (3 M) IN LENGTH!

SPECTACULAR **STURGEON**

Sturgeons have been swimming in lakes and rivers for around 200 million years. They are sometimes considered a "living fossil" because their skeleton is made mostly of cartilage instead of bone. They are bottom feeders, eating fish, crustaceans, and other creatures that live on river and lake beds.

Dorsal fin

Large, muscular pectoral fins allow these fish to "walk."

BIZARRE **BREATHER**

While other fish have gills and gas bladders, lungfish have lungs divided into smaller air sacs—similar to those of land-dwelling animals. When water is scarce they cocoon themselves in mucus and can remain like this for long periods, breathing through their lungs.

WALKING FISH

Mudskippers are fish that have evolved to walk on land, and some even climb trees! They wriggle around in mud to keep their skin moist enough to breathe through, but can also store gigantic gulps of water in their gills—supplying them with extra reserves of oxygen.

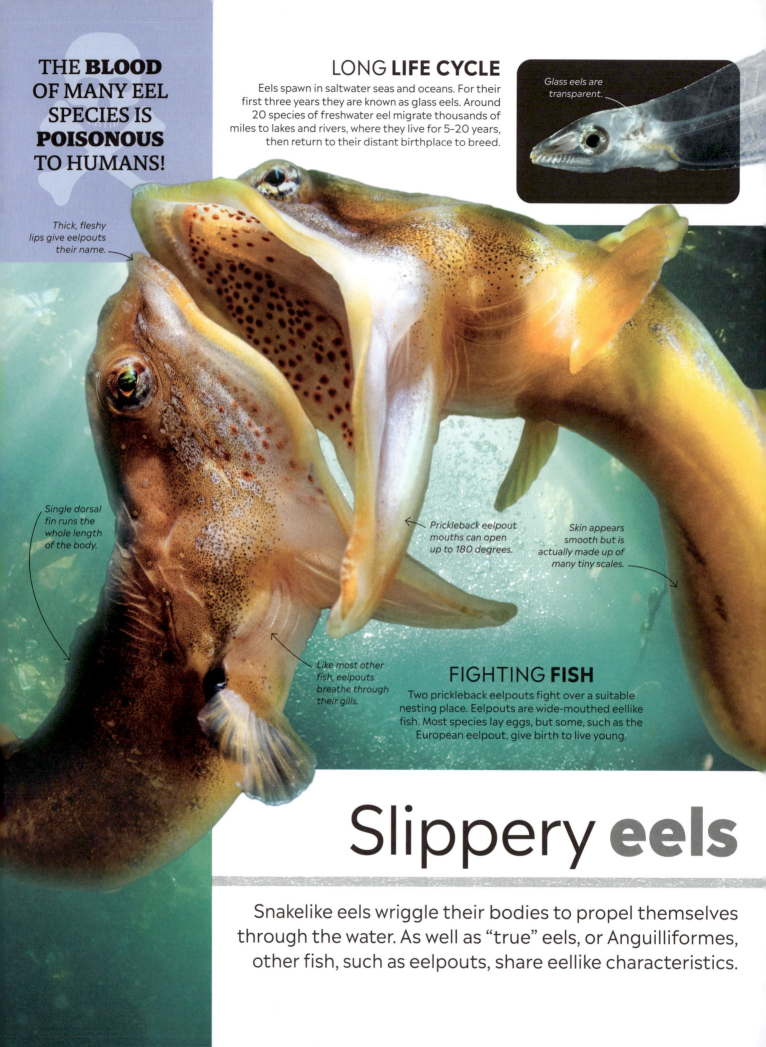

LONG **LIFE CYCLE**

Eels spawn in saltwater seas and oceans. For their first three years they are known as glass eels. Around 20 species of freshwater eel migrate thousands of miles to lakes and rivers, where they live for 5–20 years, then return to their distant birthplace to breed.

Glass eels are transparent.

Thick, fleshy lips give eelpouts their name.

Single dorsal fin runs the whole length of the body.

Prickleback eelpout mouths can open up to 180 degrees.

Skin appears smooth but is actually made up of many tiny scales.

Like most other fish, eelpouts breathe through their gills.

FIGHTING **FISH**

Two prickleback eelpouts fight over a suitable nesting place. Eelpouts are wide-mouthed eellike fish. Most species lay eggs, but some, such as the European eelpout, give birth to live young.

Slippery eels

Snakelike eels wriggle their bodies to propel themselves through the water. As well as "true" eels, or Anguilliformes, other fish, such as eelpouts, share eellike characteristics.

SLICK FISH

Glands under the skin produce the mucus that makes eels and other fish so slimy—and such efficient swimmers. It reduces the surface friction of their skin by more than 60 percent.

Slippery conger eels have no scales.

FRESHWATER EELS HAVE **NEVER** BEEN OBSERVED **MATING** IN THE WILD!

WHO NEEDS WATER?

On land, freshwater eels act like snakes and use their muscular bodies to wriggle in S-shaped waves. They breathe by absorbing oxygen through their skin, which has to stay wet for them to do this.

COLOR SWAP

All ribbon eels are born male and black. As they mature, they turn blue and, after about 20 years, from blue to yellow. At the same time, they change sex from male to female, lay eggs, then die within a month.

ALL CHANGE

In tropical waters, eels have evolved to be colorful, so they can blend in with exotic plants and corals. To guard against predators, garden eels burrow into the sea floor and retract their bodies into the sand when they sense danger.

THERE ARE MORE THAN **1,000 DIFFERENT** SPECIES OF TRUE EEL. THEY RANGE IN SIZE FROM **2 IN (5 CM)** TO **12 FT 10 IN (3.9 M)!**

SHOCKING STUFF

Despite their name and appearance, electric eels are more closely related to catfish than true eels. Their bodies are filled with up to 700,000 cells called electrocytes, each of which generates a tiny electrical charge that, collectively, adds up to around 600 volts.

Eel releases its electrical charge into the water.

Skin conducts electricity outward, so the eel does not shock itself.

Swimming muscles propel eel through the water.

Swim bladder keeps eel buoyant.

Electrocytes are arranged in about 70 rows along the eel's body.

Prey is stunned by electrical waves.

Freshwater fish

Some species of fish spend some or all of their lives in freshwater rivers, lakes, and inland waterways, rather than the salty seas and oceans. Because of the way they absorb water, living in saltwater would cause them to "overdose" on salt and die.

PREHISTORIC PIKE

The pike has existed, largely unchanged, for 60 million years. Found across North America, Western Europe, and Siberia, they are carnivorous, eating other fish, toads, frogs, voles, and small birds. They can grow up to 6 ft (1.83 m) long.

The teeth on the bottom jaw are larger than those on the top and are used to rip and tear at prey.

Gray-green color provides great camouflage in a murky riverbed.

BRIGHT BAND

Colorful tetras are omnivorous and live in rivers across Africa and Central and South America. Only up to 3½ in (9 cm) long—much smaller than their piranha relatives—they are sociable fish that swim in schools. Neon tetras (left), recognizable for their vibrant red and green bands, have even been seen to politely line up when waiting to pass through a narrow space!

RIVERBED LURKER

Living close to the muddy bottoms of rivers and lakes, catfish are identifiable by their barbels—whisker-like sensors above their mouths that inspired their name. These help them detect food in the dark and murky waters in which they swim.

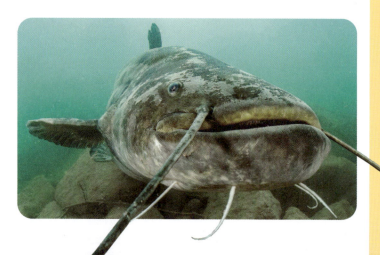

THE MOST COSTLY AQUARIUM FISH, RARE PLATINUM ASIAN AROWANA SELL FOR AROUND $400,000 EACH!

IN 2005, A **MEKONG GIANT CATFISH** WAS DECLARED THE **WORLD'S LARGEST** FRESHWATER FISH. IT WEIGHED **646 LB (293 KG)!**

Reflective layer in the eyes helps the fish see in dark, cloudy water.

Serrated, sharklike teeth interlock when biting.

POINTY-TOOTHED PIRANHAS

Found in the rivers of South America, piranhas usually hunt other fishes. They are rarely more than 24 in (60 cm) long, but the biggest shoaling species may attack larger prey, especially when hungry. Other piranhas live alone and specialize in nipping at the scales of their targets.

PROTECTIVE MUCUS

Tench patrol the bottoms of lakes and rivers, using the short barbels around their mouths to probe for food such as plants and snails. They are covered in a layer of thick, slimy mucus that prevents many of the parasites that live in their weedy habitat from sticking to their scales.

SUPER HEARING

Most freshwater fish species have a series of bones, known as ossicles, that connect a fish's swim bladder (which controls its buoyancy) and its hearing system. Sounds picked up by the swim bladder reach the fish's ears through the ossicles, boosting the animal's ability to hear underwater.

Sound waves from the water travel to the gas-filled swim bladder through the body wall.

Gas in the swim bladder is a better conductor of sound than water.

Ossicles transmit sound from the bladder to the ears.

A WEE PROBLEM!

Known as the vampire fish, the 1-in- (2.5-cm-) long candiru is a skinny Amazonian catfish that burrows into the gills of other fish to feed on their blood. But it is also drawn to human urine—so can accidentally lodge inside the urethra of someone peeing in the water!

the body.

Eyes face up
to see prey
near the lure.

Sea devil anglerfish with l...

Lures only appear
on larger females.

Giant, tooth-filled
mouth can engulf
prey up to twice
the fish's own size!

Stretchy skin
and expandable
stomach to hold
large prey

Fins have little
webbing—anglerfish
barely swim.

FLOAT AND **WAIT**

A predatory fanfin anglerfish is a weak swimmer, so it waits for prey to come to it. Anglerfishes are named for their "fishing-rod" lures that dangle in front of their mouths to attract prey. Many lures have a glowing tip for extra attraction, and all anglerfish have enormous, toothy jaws to munch their targets.

**LONG-SNOUTED
LANCET FISH**
CAN GROW UP TO
6 FT 7 IN (2 M)
LONG—ONE OF
THE **LARGEST**
FISH IN THE
TWILIGHT ZONE!

Deep-sea
fish

Deep-sea fish live far below the sunlit surface of the sea. Here, temperatures drop near freezing, pressures are intense, and there is little food or oxygen. To survive the depths, these fish have some eye-popping adaptations.

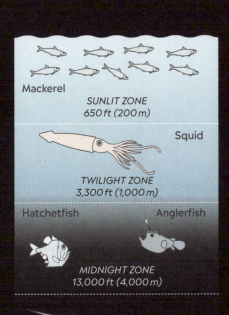

Mackerel

SUNLIT ZONE
650 ft (200 m)

Squid

TWILIGHT ZONE
3,300 ft (1,000 m)

Hatchetfish

Anglerfish

MIDNIGHT ZONE
13,000 ft (4,000 m)

Grenadier

ABYSSAL ZONE
16,000 ft (5,000 m)

Giant amphipod

DEEPEST TRENCHES
16,000–36,000 ft
(5,000–11,000 m)

Huge eyes face upward.

Fangs curve back to lock onto prey.

Skin lacks normal scales.

GOTCHA!

This sabertooth fish has telescopic, upward-pointing eyes that help it spot prey silhouetted against the dim light above. Once snatched, the backward-curving teeth make it impossible for a caught fish to get away.

ORANGE ROUGHIES CAN LIVE FOR 149 YEARS!

INTO THE **ABYSS**

The upper sea is called the photic, or sunlit, zone. Here it is bright enough for photosynthesizing algae but below, in the twilight zone, it is pitch black. With no sunlight, nutrients only reach these depths when decaying plants and animals and poop sink down.

SOME DEEP-SEA FISH EYES ARE **100 TIMES MORE SENSITIVE** TO LIGHT THAN **HUMAN EYES!**

NIFTY NECK

Barbeled dragonfish are only 8 in (20 cm) long, but they have large jaws filled with sharp, fang-like teeth. They can pop open their jaws, thanks to the soft joint that connects their head to their spine. As a result, they can swallow prey that's almost as large as they are!

DEEPEST **DARKNESS**

The deepest-known fish, unofficially named the ethereal snailfish, lives down to 26,000 ft (8,000 m) below sea level. It has a flexible skeleton to withstand the enormous water pressure, along with small eyes and near-colorless skin.

TWINKLE, TWINKLE, **LITTLE FISH**

While some predators of the depths use light to attract prey, smaller fish might use it to communicate to their own kind or confuse enemies. Lantern fishes do it with "spotlight" organs called photophores.

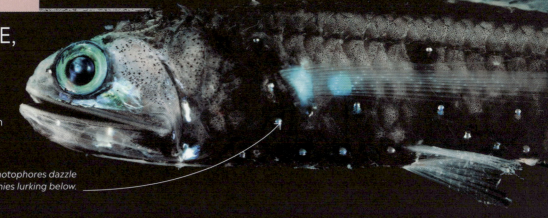

Lower photophores dazzle enemies lurking below.

DEEP-SEA
ILLUMINATIONS

In the darkness of the deep ocean a shrimp expels bioluminescent chemicals to temporarily blind a predatory viperfish, in the same way a bright flash might affect the human eye. As well as a means of defense, some shrimp, squid, and fish use their light-emitting displays to search for prey or as a form of communication.

Ask a ...
DEEP-SEA EXPLORER

Dr. Edith Widder is CEO of the Ocean Research and Conservation Association. A pioneer researcher of bioluminescence (light produced by living things), she has developed a camera called the Eye-in-the-Sea to explore the deep ocean. With the help of an electronic jellyfish (or e-jelly), she attracts glowing sea creatures and captures extraordinary images of them.

Q How did you first become interested in the deep sea?
A I was 11 when I first explored a coral reef. The experience of seeing brilliantly colored fish inspired me to become a marine biologist. Years later, I was researching bioluminescence and deep-sea animals that produce light. I wanted to see what the largest, least explored habitat on Earth, where there is no sunlight but lots of living light, actually looked like.

Q How do you find fish in the dark?
A I use the camera with e-jelly, for attracting squid and fish that think it's prey. Or I use squid as bait to draw creatures into the camera range.

Q What's the most exciting thing you've discovered?

A The first time I used the Eye-in-the-Sea was on an expedition to the Gulf of Mexico in 2004 where we recorded a very unusual squid 6 ft (1.8 m) long that had never been seen before. Then in 2012, we captured the first video images of a giant squid the size of a two story building off the coast of Japan!

Q How does it feel when you're in the submersible?

A I first dived in a diving suit called Wasp because it had a yellow body, a transparent bubble head, and arms with pincers. It was cold and uncomfortable but I didn't mind as I was so excited by all the bioluminescence! It looked like an undersea fireworks display except the flashes and glows were blue. Today, I dive in bubble subs, where I sit inside a transparent sphere. It's like being on the inside of a goldfish bowl with the fish on the outside.

Q What dangers do you face in the deep sea?

A Pressure is the most obvious danger. At 3,000 ft (900 m), which is the deepest I've ever been, the pressure on the outside of the submersible is more than 1,300 psi (9,000 kPa). That's about the same force as an elephant standing on one leg on an area the size of a postage stamp. It sounds terrifying but research submersibles are very safe due to the rigorous checks made before every dive.

Q What do you want to discover next?

A In the deep sea there's no sunlight, so marine snow (clumps of phytoplankton, zooplankton, and droppings) is the primary food source. Much of this is bioluminescent. I want to understand the role bioluminescence plays in how animals find this vital food source.

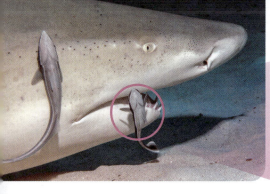

BE MY **GUEST**

Remora fish, also known as suckerfish, have an oval suction disk at the top of their heads, allowing them to press against and lock themselves onto larger marine animals, such as sharks. While attached to a host, they nibble on parasites and even eat their host's poop!

Slat-like structures at the top of the head form rows that create suction.

FISHY **FAMILIES**

There are many different types of saltwater fish: some large, some small, some which migrate between freshwater and saltwater, and even some that glide.

Ocean sunfish
One of the largest bony fish in the world, adult sunfish can weigh nearly 5,000 lb (2,300 kg).

Flying fish
These fish can leap out of the water and use their long, winglike fins to glide above the water for up to 45 seconds.

Salmon
Typically hatching in freshwater, salmon migrate long distances to the ocean, before returning to their freshwater birthplace to reproduce.

Herring
One of the most abundant fish species in the world, herring move together in large schools in coastal waters.

Saltwater fish

More than 18,000 species of fish live in Earth's vast oceans, which cover 70 percent of the planet. Most live in the shallow coastal seas, but others have adapted to swim in great open waters.

SURVIVING IN THE SEA

Seawater is far saltier than a fish's body. This draws water out of the animal while salt seeps in. To counteract these effects, fish constantly drink large amounts of seawater—but excrete the extra salt from their gills and in urine.

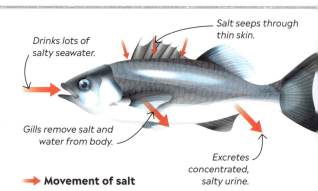

Drinks lots of salty seawater.

Salt seeps through thin skin.

Gills remove salt and water from body.

Excretes concentrated, salty urine.

➡ **Movement of salt**

TERRIFIC **TUNA**

Tuna are huge, powerful fish. The largest species, the bluefin tuna, can reach speeds of up to 43 mph (69 kph). Using its torpedo-shaped body, it dives to depths of up to 3,300 ft (1,000 m).

Bluefin tuna have bright yellow, flexible finlets.

Dorsal fins can retract into slots to reduce drag.

THE LARGEST TUNA EVER RECORDED WAS AN ATLANTIC BLUEFIN THAT WEIGHED 1,496 LB (679 KG)!

SPEEDY **PREDATOR**

Barracudas are large fish with fang-like teeth. They're both predators and scavengers, snapping up smaller sea creatures and following larger ones for leftovers. Known for their speed, barracudas can accelerate from 0 to 36 mph (0 to 58 kph) in seconds.

Bony structures called gill arches support the gills.

Thin gill rakers act like a strainer, keeping food particles in the mouth but letting water escape.

SHOAL **SURVIVORS**

For protection, mackerel often swim together in huge groups called shoals. This makes it harder for predators to pick out and catch an individual fish. A shoal can even split into two smaller groups and reform behind a predator.

FILTER FEEDER

Like most other fish, striped mackerel have gills to extract oxygen from the water. But by opening their mouths incredibly wide while swimming, these fish can also extract zooplankton (tiny sea creatures) from the water, using their gill rakers as a net.

SAILFISH CAN JUMP FULLY OUT OF THE WATER!

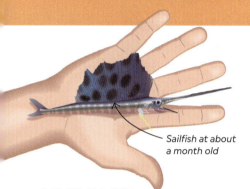

Sailfish at about a month old

LIVE FAST, GROW FAST

A large sailfish can lay millions of eggs, which hatch within two days. The larvae are about 0.1 in (3 mm) long at birth, but grow to 5 ft (1.5 m) long in a single year—that's 5,000 times bigger! In time a sailfish reaches around 10 ft (3 m) long and weighs around 220 lb (100 kg).

HUNTING **SCHOOL**

Sailfish band together to hunt large shoals of fish, herding and harassing them for hours before they close in for the kill. They take turns to attack, signaling their intent by flashing colored stripes and dots on their sides to make sure they don't clash and injure each other.

1. Herd the fish
Predators circle the mass of fish, forcing them together and upward until they are trapped against the surface. Their sails make the sailfish appear larger so the fish do not try to escape.

2. Slash and bash
Using its sail as a stabilizer, the sailfish inserts its bill into the shoal without the fish noticing. It then swipes sideways to strike, knocking individuals off balance and out of the shoal.

MAGICAL **MARLIN**

Marlins are some of the largest and swiftest bony fish in the sea. Their long, muscular bodies are built for explosive power, while long bills, retractable fins, and flashing stripes make them deadly hunters.

Darker topside blends in with ocean depths when seen from above.

Brilliant billfish

Marlin, sailfish, and swordfish live in the open ocean, where they hunt by using their long, bony bills to slash at schooling fish. These billfish have small teeth or none at all, and swallow their catch whole, head-first.

THE LARGEST KNOWN SAILFISH WAS 18 FT (5.6 M) LONG AND WEIGHED **222 LB (100.6 KG)!**

Large dorsal fin stabilizes marlin when hunting.

Concertina structure lets fin fold back for fast swimming.

Sea lions lurk nearby so they can go after the same shoal of fish.

Long, bony bill for tapping and slashing prey.

Large eyes for hunting in dark depths.

Lighter lower fins make fish harder to spot from below, against the light of the Sun.

Stripes flash and change color.

BILLFISH **TYPES**

Billfish are predatory saltwater fish with long pointed bills. There are two billfish families—marlin and sailfish make up the larger one, while swordfish are in a group of their own.

Marlin
Marlin have a large fin but a small sail. Black marlin are the biggest, weighing up to 1,500 lb (680 kg), followed by blue, white, and striped marlin.

Sailfish
Smaller and more agile than most billfish, they only raise their telltale sail for hunting—otherwise it folds back to reduce drag.

Swordfish
Their longer, flatter bill is more like a true sword than the spear-like weapons of marlin and sailfish. They are almost as heavy as black marlin.

BILLFISH HAVE HEAT-GENERATING MUSCLES IN THEIR HEADS TO BOOST BRAIN POWER!

SUPER **SWORDS**

Of all billfish, swordfish have the longest, thickest bills for their size and they use it for defense as well as attack—they are even known to have killed sharks! The sword reaches up to 5 ft (1.5 m) long and can repair itself if damaged, but cannot fully regrow.

Bill makes up one-third of swordfish's length.

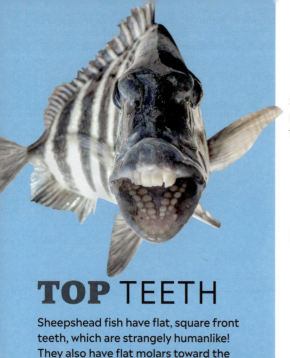

TOP TEETH

Sheepshead fish have flat, square front teeth, which are strangely humanlike! They also have flat molars toward the back of their mouth, used to crush shells.

FACT PACK!
FISH

There are around 37,000 species of fish—as many as all the other vertebrate groups put together. Some have adaptations to catch prey, while others are well camouflaged to hide from predators, and a few can even walk!

BIG WHOPPERS

Some fish species are monstrously huge, and cartilaginous fish such as sharks and rays tend to be the largest. Growing to the size of a school bus, whale sharks are the largest fish in the oceans.

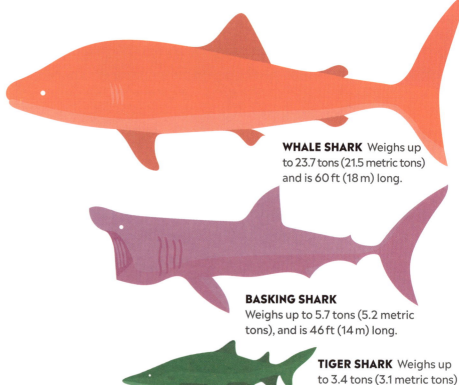

WHALE SHARK Weighs up to 23.7 tons (21.5 metric tons) and is 60 ft (18 m) long.

BASKING SHARK Weighs up to 5.7 tons (5.2 metric tons), and is 46 ft (14 m) long.

TIGER SHARK Weighs up to 3.4 tons (3.1 metric tons) and is 25 ft (7.5 m) long.

BELUGA STURGEON Weighs up to 2.2 tons (2 metric tons) and is 24 ft (7.2 m) long.

GREAT WHITE SHARK Weighs up to 3.6 tons (3.3 metric tons) and is 23 ft (7 m) long.

GIANT OCEANIC MANTA RAY Weighs up to 3.3 tons (3 metric tons) and is 16 ft (5 m) long.

SOUTHERN SUNFISH Weighs up to 3 tons (2.7 metric tons) and is 11 ft (3.3 m) long.

AVERAGE MALE Weighs around 198 lb (90 kg) and is 5 ft 7 in (1.7 m) tall.

TINY TIDDLERS

Just a little wider than the end of a pencil, some fish are almost too small to see. Here are some of the tiniest.

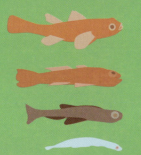

MIDGET DWARF GOBY
0.39 in (10 mm)

DWARF PYGMY GOBY
0.35 in (9 mm)

PAEDOCYPRIS PROGENETICA
0.31 in (7.9 mm)

STOUT INFANTFISH
About 0.27 in (7 mm)

END OF A PENCIL
0.19 in (5 mm)

FIERCEST FISH

Some of the world's most ferocious fish use their sharp teeth, breathtaking speed, or other sneaky adaptations to attack prey.

PIRANHA Well known for their pointy, triangular teeth, piranhas also have strong jaws and a powerful bite.

TIGER FISH This huge, striped freshwater fish has spiked teeth, and is famous for fighting back if caught.

GREAT WHITE SHARK The world's largest predatory fish is also fast, able to reach speeds of 31 mph (50 kph).

MORAY EEL These snakelike fish use two sets of jaws to cram large prey into their narrow bodies.

Pectoral fin

FISH IN FLIGHT

Elongated pectoral fins help the flying fish reach 35 mph (56 kph) while underwater. At top speed, it can break the surface and glide above the waves for up to 655 ft (200 m).

WILD AND WEIRD

With psychedelic stripes, finlike hands, and armor plating, some fish have to be seen to be believed.

PSYCHEDELIC FROGFISH These fish have flat faces and vivid, striped patterns as unique as human fingerprints.

HANDFISH Named for their hand-shaped fins, handfish "walk" along the ocean floor instead of swimming.

ARMORED SEA ROBIN This armor-plated bottom-walker has whiskery "barbels" to sense prey in the dark.

CLEVER CAMOUFLAGE

To avoid being eaten, many fish have developed elaborate camouflage techniques. Here are a few of the hardest to spot.

CROCODILE FISH These creatures use their rough texture to blend in with the sandy seabed.

PAINTED FROGFISH To catch prey, the painted frogfish matches its color to its surroundings.

PEACOCK FLOUNDER This color-changing fish has two eyes on one side of its body so it can lie flat.

SKATE A mottled coloring and flat shape make a skate hard to spot against the seafloor.

TASSELED ANGLERFISH Perfect for hiding in a coral reef, tasseled anglerfish are orange with wavy tentacles.

TRUMPET FISH These fish swim vertically and look like floating sticks or seaweed.

LIPS AND LEGS

Characterized by its pout, the red-lipped batfish uses its modified fins as legs to "walk" along the seafloor. It has a fleshy growth on its head that emits chemicals to attract prey.

WATERY **WALTZ**

Mating seahorse pairs dance together as a bonding activity and to assess when they are both ready to reproduce. During their dance, they entwine their tails and even change color.

Dorsal fin flickers to propel seahorse through the water.

Seahorses wrap themselves around passing debris or even other animals to prevent themselves from getting swept away!

Strong muscles in the tail allow the seahorse to grip onto many items.

Covering of armor-like bony rings limits range of tail movement.

THERE ARE ABOUT **54 KNOWN SPECIES** OF SEAHORSES!

Dancing seahorses

Seahorses get their scientific name "hippocampus" from Greek words meaning "horse" and "sea monster." These armor-bodied fish thrive in shallow, sheltered water, but are not the strongest swimmers.

TINY SATOMI'S PYGMY SEAHORSES **TRAVEL JUST 6–7 IN (15–17 CM) EACH DAY!**

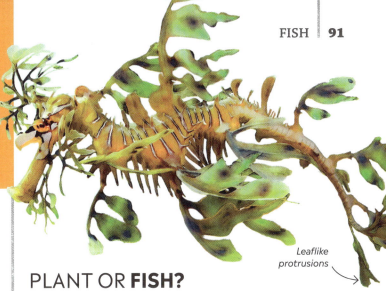

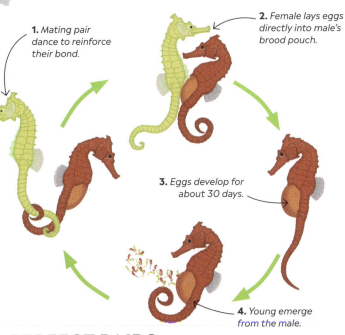

1. Mating pair dance to reinforce their bond.

2. Female lays eggs directly into male's brood pouch.

3. Eggs develop for about 30 days.

4. Young emerge from the male.

PERFECT **PAIRS**

Many species of seahorse form long-lasting pair bonds, sometimes staying together for multiple breeding seasons, with the couple dancing every day. The male carries the eggs, meaning the female is able to quickly produce more.

PLANT OR **FISH?**

Leafy sea dragons have what look like leaves growing out of their body. These don't help with swimming, but they do make great camouflage, allowing them to blend in with nearby seaweed.

Leaflike protrusions

DEDICATED **DADDY**

Seahorses are one of the few animals where males carry the young—in a special brood pouch. The female seahorse deposits up to 1,500 eggs in this pouch, and they develop inside the male before the young seahorses are birthed into the sea.

Each tiny baby emerges fully formed.

A **YOUNG SEAHORSE** CAN EAT UP TO **3,000 TINY SHRIMP** EVERY DAY!

SMALL AND **SNEAKY**

Tiny pygmy seahorses were only discovered by accident in 1969, because they blend in so well with their coral homes. Bargibant's seahorse (above) grows to a maximum of just less than 1 in (2.4 cm) and only lives among corals with its specific pink and red coloring.

EYES ON THE PRIZE

Seahorses have excellent eyesight to spot their prey. Unlike most fish, their eyes aren't fixed and can swivel around in their sockets. Each eye can also move independently of the other, meaning they can look forward and backward at the same time!

The nose of a long-snouted seahorse swiftly swivels round so the tiny mouth can suck in prey.

CLEVER CLEANERS

Big fish of the open ocean, such as manta rays, often visit reefs where different kinds of "cleaner fish" scrub their bodies of dead skin and parasites.

CORAL REEFS EXIST IN **LESS THAN 1%** OF THE OCEAN, BUT ARE HOME TO ALMOST **25% OF ALL** MARINE LIFE!

CHANGING **SEX**

Genicanthus angelfish are one of several fish species that can change sex. In the small groups of up to five in which they live, the biggest and most colorful fish is male. If he dies, the next biggest fish changes from female to male, becoming larger and more colorful.

COOPERATIVE CLOWN FISH

Sea anemones look like plants, but are carnivorous animals. Some species allow clown fish to live and nest among their tentacles, in return for their "lodgers" supplying them with food, keeping them clean, and fertilizing them with feces!

Safety shield

An anemone's stingers protect the clown fish and its eggs from predators, while a mucus layer on the fish's skin stops it from getting stung.

Anemone stingers

Mucus layer

Protect and serve

Clown fish assist anemones by chasing away their predators, such as some species of butterfly fish. They also drop food onto an anemone's tentacles, helping to feed it.

Cleaning service

Clown fish clear away parasites, debris, and dead tentacles from anemones. Nutrient-rich clown fish poop helps the anemone grow.

Of more than 1,000 anemone species around the world, only about 10 play host to clown fishes.

THE OLDEST KNOWN REEF FISH WAS AN 81-YEAR-OLD MIDNIGHT SNAPPER!

MIND YOUR FINGERS

Parrotfish are named for their birdlike "beaks" and striking colors. The beak is actually 1,000 teeth arranged in 15 tightly packed rows.

Teeth are hard enough to crunch through coral.

Tropical reef fish

More than 8,000 types of fish live in and around tropical coral reefs. Many of those who call these rich habitats home sport dazzlingly bright colors so they can recognize each other.

UNDERWATER REFUGE

Clown fish can lay up to 1,000 eggs among the protective tentacles of sea anemones. They live in social groups, controlled by the largest female. Males change sex as they age, replacing the dominant female when she dies.

Each tentacle has thousands of microscopic stinging cells embedded in its surface.

SEABED SECRET

Peacock flounders have the ability to adapt their skin color to their surroundings, disguising themselves among the sand and rocks of the ocean floor. They do this thanks to specialized color-changing skin cells.

Pale sand
Clusters of pigment bunch together to make the skin paler in lighter parts of the sea.

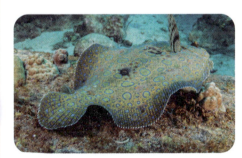

Rocky road
When a change in environment is detected, the pigment disperses, darkening the skin.

PARROTFISH KEEP REEFS HEALTHY BY EATING DEAD CORAL AND OTHER DEBRIS!

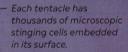

Terribly toxic fish

Some fish have developed poisons and venoms as a way of protecting themselves from deadly predators. Some of these toxic water creatures are even lethal to humans.

Swells into a ball to appear larger.

THE VENOM OF THE STRIPED-FANG BLENNY RELAXES A PREDATOR'S JAW, SO THE FISH CAN ESCAPE!

PECULIAR **PUFFERS**

Puffer fish inflate themselves by sucking in water. This turns them into a big spiky ball that deters predators. They do it as a last resort, because it can harm their bodies. Their liver and sex organs contain a poison called tetrodotoxin that can kill a predator.

POISONOUS **OR VENOMOUS?**

Both poisons and venoms are harmful substances, and are known as toxins. But while a poisonous creature is toxic if eaten, a venomous one may be safe to eat ... if you don't get stung catching it!

Poisonous
Creatures that are poisonous contain toxins that make them harmful if eaten by predators— or humans!

Venomous
Creatures that are venomous have to bite or sting their victims to deliver their toxins.

Venom gland at base of dorsal spine

When pressurized the spine tip shatters and releases venom.

SCARY **STONEFISH**

The venom of this sea creature is perhaps the deadliest of any fish. A stonefish sting should be treated within 15 minutes or it could be fatal.

WHEN A PUFFER FISH EXPANDS IT GROWS UP TO THREE TIMES ITS USUAL SIZE IN JUST 15 SECONDS!

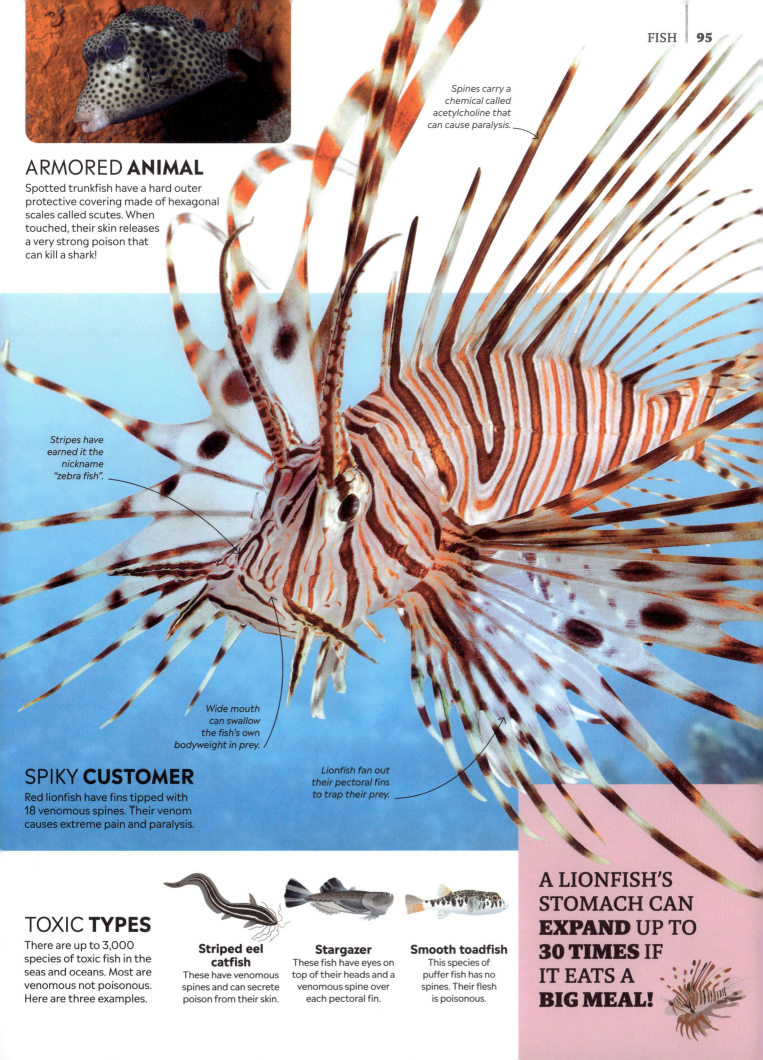

Spines carry a chemical called acetylcholine that can cause paralysis.

ARMORED **ANIMAL**

Spotted trunkfish have a hard outer protective covering made of hexagonal scales called scutes. When touched, their skin releases a very strong poison that can kill a shark!

Stripes have earned it the nickname "zebra fish".

Wide mouth can swallow the fish's own bodyweight in prey.

Lionfish fan out their pectoral fins to trap their prey.

SPIKY **CUSTOMER**

Red lionfish have fins tipped with 18 venomous spines. Their venom causes extreme pain and paralysis.

TOXIC **TYPES**

There are up to 3,000 species of toxic fish in the seas and oceans. Most are venomous not poisonous. Here are three examples.

Striped eel catfish
These have venomous spines and can secrete poison from their skin.

Stargazer
These fish have eyes on top of their heads and a venomous spine over each pectoral fin.

Smooth toadfish
This species of puffer fish has no spines. Their flesh is poisonous.

A LIONFISH'S STOMACH CAN EXPAND UP TO 30 TIMES IF IT EATS A BIG MEAL!

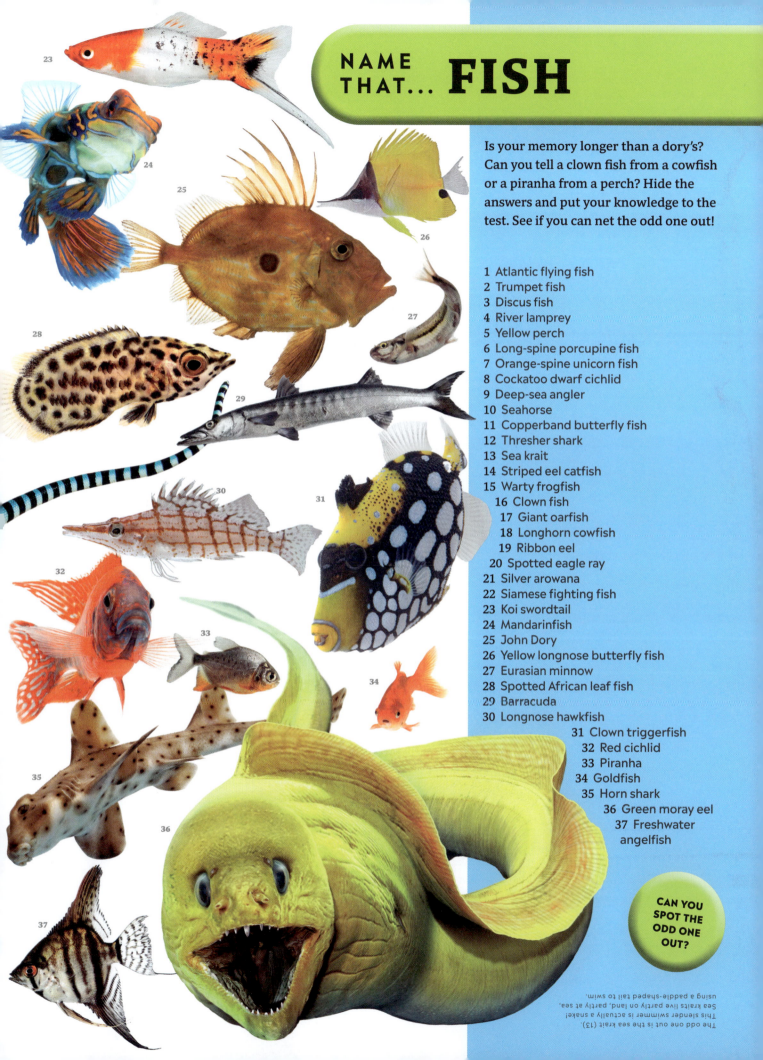

NAME THAT... FISH

Is your memory longer than a dory's? Can you tell a clown fish from a cowfish or a piranha from a perch? Hide the answers and put your knowledge to the test. See if you can net the odd one out!

1 Atlantic flying fish
2 Trumpet fish
3 Discus fish
4 River lamprey
5 Yellow perch
6 Long-spine porcupine fish
7 Orange-spine unicorn fish
8 Cockatoo dwarf cichlid
9 Deep-sea angler
10 Seahorse
11 Copperband butterfly fish
12 Thresher shark
13 Sea krait
14 Striped eel catfish
15 Warty frogfish
16 Clown fish
17 Giant oarfish
18 Longhorn cowfish
19 Ribbon eel
20 Spotted eagle ray
21 Silver arowana
22 Siamese fighting fish
23 Koi swordtail
24 Mandarinfish
25 John Dory
26 Yellow longnose butterfly fish
27 Eurasian minnow
28 Spotted African leaf fish
29 Barracuda
30 Longnose hawkfish
31 Clown triggerfish
32 Red cichlid
33 Piranha
34 Goldfish
35 Horn shark
36 Green moray eel
37 Freshwater angelfish

CAN YOU SPOT THE ODD ONE OUT?

The odd one out is the sea krait (13). This slender swimmer is actually a snake! Sea kraits live partly on land, partly at sea, using a paddle-shaped tail to swim.

AMPHIBIANS
AND REPTILES

Amphibians and reptiles

Amphibians and reptiles are both cold-blooded vertebrates. But while scaly-skinned reptiles lay hard-shelled eggs or give birth to live young, amphibians have smooth, moist skin and most lay soft jellylike eggs.

NEARLY **90 PERCENT** OF AMPHIBIAN SPECIES ARE **FROGS AND TOADS!**

TYPES OF **AMPHIBIAN**

Amphibians fall into three different groups: frogs and toads, salamanders and newts, and caecilians. Scientists believe there are nearly 9,000 living amphibian species.

Long, flat tail helps the newt push through water.

FROGS AND TOADS
Both frogs and toads are carnivorous with short bodies and long legs.

SALAMANDERS AND NEWTS
These animals have lizard-like tails and moist, frog-like skin.

CAECILIANS
Although they resemble a worm, caecilians are limbless amphibians with tiny eyes.

WATERY HABITS

Amphibians are semiaquatic and spend some of their time in water. Newts such as this one live on land for most of the year, but they live in ponds during the spring, when laying eggs.

Webbed feet allow fast, efficient swimming.

MOST FROGS DON'T HAVE **TEETH** ON THEIR LOWER JAW AND **SWALLOW THEIR FOOD WHOLE!**

Born with gills
Like most amphibians, this axolotl began life with gills to breathe water, developing lungs to breathe on land by adulthood.

Metamorphosis
Many have distinct life stages where hatchlings change form as they become adults.

AMPHIBIAN CHARACTERISTICS

Amphibians have roamed Earth for around 400 million years. They have several unique features, which make them different from reptiles.

Thin, moist skin
Amphibians secrete mucus to keep their skin moist, which helps them absorb oxygen.

TEMPERATURE REGULATION

To survive, reptiles and amphibians must regulate their temperature. They are ectothermic, meaning they cannot control their body temperature internally and instead rely on external heat sources such as the Sun.

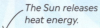

The Sun releases heat energy.

Snake absorbs heat from the hot sand to raise its body temperature.

Shade from the cactus provides a place to cool off when it gets too hot.

Dark coloring at the top absorbs more heat than lighter underside.

ALL HABITATS

Both reptiles and amphibians are found on every continent except Antarctica. However, only reptiles have marine species such as this marine iguana, the only known lizard that spends time in the sea.

TYPES OF REPTILE

There are four different types of reptiles: turtles, crocodilians, lizards and snakes, and tuataras. In total, there are more than 12,000 living reptile species.

CROCODILIANS
These big, predatory reptiles include crocodiles, alligators, and gharials.

LIZARDS AND SNAKES
The main similarity between lizards and snakes is their scaly skin, which sheds regularly.

TURTLES
These creatures are known for their bony shell, which is fused to their ribs and spine.

TUATARAS
With a name meaning "spiny back," lizard-like tuataras are only found in New Zealand.

REPTILE CHARACTERISTICS

Reptiles have a range of adaptations suited for life on dry land. These include lungs to breathe air and tough, scaly skin, which reduces water loss and protects them from predators.

Scaly skin
All reptiles have dry skin covered in scales.

Breathing air
All reptiles have at least one lung from birth.

Lay eggs
Some reptiles give birth to live young, but most lay eggs.

No metamorphosis
Unlike amphibians, infant reptiles look like miniature versions of their parents.

AN **ALLIGATOR'S ROAR** CAN REACH **90 DECIBELS**— AS LOUD AS **A LAWNMOWER!**

Toes help grip tree branches.

FOUR LEGGED

Reptiles are "tetrapods"—which means "four feet." Even some snake species, such as pythons, have tiny leg bones and claws on their undersides.

Spectacular salamanders

These long-bodied amphibians have moist skin and change form as they grow—just like frogs. However, unlike frogs they keep their tails, so they look more like lizards.

Females have darker blue backs.

The smell of algae draws alpine newts to spawning grounds.

Webbed feet are suited to swimming.

Both males and females have orange bellies.

Males have black and white markings down their sides.

NEWT **ROMANTICS**

Alpine newts are salamanders that live in European forests and mountains—they are the only newts found at altitudes of up to 7,900 ft (2,400 m). They live and reproduce in water, where males court females by fanning out their tails.

NEWT OR NOT?

A newt is a type of salamander that spends part of each year living on land and part of it in water. Its body changes to match—the newt on the right is in its aquatic phase, more suited to water than the land-based salamander.

Toes more suited to digging

Long, rounded tail

Coarse, bumpy skin

Glossy skin

Thick tail with fin

Salamander

Newt

SALAMANDER **SELECTION**

There are around 750 species of salamander. Half live in the Americas, the rest in Europe, Asia, and North Africa. Here's a slippery selection.

Marbled newt
Native to Western Europe, adults are around 6 in (15 cm) long.

Tiger salamander
Lives in sandy soils from Canada to Mexico.

Red-backed salamander
Common in North American woodland.

Mudpuppy
Aquatic salamander found in eastern North America.

Japanese giant salamander
Grows up to 5 ft (1.5 m) long in mountain rivers.

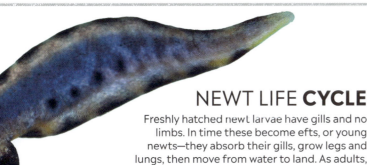

NEWT LIFE **CYCLE**

Freshly hatched newt larvae have gills and no limbs. In time these become efts, or young newts—they absorb their gills, grow legs and lungs, then move from water to land. As adults, newts alternate between living on land and in water—before taking to the water they grow rough skin and a fin on their tail.

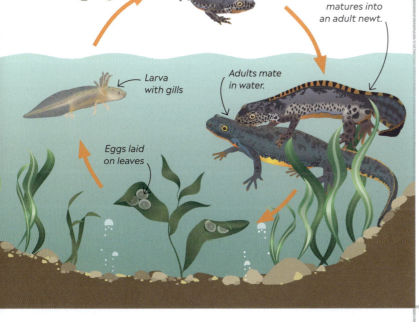

Juvenile eft grows legs and moves onto land.

The eft matures into an adult newt.

Larva with gills

Adults mate in water.

Eggs laid on leaves

RIB-**TICKLER**

When threatened, the Iberian ribbed newt rotates its sharp-pointed ribs so they poke out through its skin—a spiky mouthful for any predator! It even has poison glands for extra protection. Once the ribs retract, the skin soon heals.

Puncture sites are yellow.

NEWT **FOR OLD**

Most vertebrates just cover a big wound with scar tissue, but many salamanders can regrow limbs if they lose one. Their bodies activate special cells called stem cells, which can turn into any type of tissue (muscle, bone, and so on), and direct the cells to grow in the correct shape. The new limb forms in as little as 30 days!

Eastern newt, also known as the red-spotted newt

SUPER **SIRENS**

Lesser sirens have long bodies with just two small limbs near their head. They're vocal—clicking when they meet other sirens and screeching if attacked—and take their name from the mythical sea nymphs that were said to lure sailors to destruction with their song.

FOREVER **YOUNG**

The axolotl is an unusual type of salamander that reaches adulthood without going through metamorphosis. Adults keep their gills and continue to live in water—navigating with their lidless eyes and underdeveloped limbs.

Feathery external gills

Long toes

FROG OR **TOAD?**

Frogs and toads are amphibians: cold-blooded vertebrates, many of which spend part of their lives in water. Toads (see pages 106–107) are really kinds of frog that have shorter legs, smaller heads, and drier, bumpy skin.

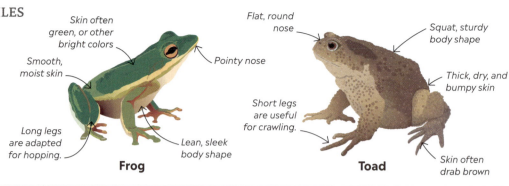

Skin often green, or other bright colors

Smooth, moist skin

Pointy nose

Long legs are adapted for hopping.

Lean, sleek body shape

Frog

Flat, round nose

Squat, sturdy body shape

Thick, dry, and bumpy skin

Short legs are useful for crawling.

Skin often drab brown

Toad

Webbed feet are used for swimming.

LEAP FROG

Due to their powerful leg muscles and specially adapted joints, some frogs can jump more than 20 times their body length. This pool frog can even leap out of water to catch flying insects.

Like other amphibians, frogs have a moist skin to help absorb oxygen from their surroundings.

RED **ALERT!**

Many frogs and toads rely on skin poisons to protect them from predators. Poison frogs from South America, such as this strawberry poison frog, get their toxins from eating toxic mites and ants, and use bright colors as a warning.

Ankle joint helps propel the frog into the air.

Dark spots help the frog blend in while in murky water.

EGG **POUCH**

Gastrotheca frogs are marsupials as well as amphibians. After the female lays eggs, the male pushes them into the brood pouch on her back. There the eggs grow, receiving oxygen and nutrients from the mother.

Eggs will hatch as tadpoles.

LAYING **FROG SPAWN**

When mating, the male frog or toad typically clasps the female to fertilize the eggs as she releases them. In most parts of the world, frog eggs, contained in jellylike frog spawn, are laid in water, but many tropical species lay them in wet places on land.

THE **COMMON FROG** CAN LAY UP TO **2,000 EGGS** AT A TIME, IN **ONE BIG CLUMP!**

GLIDING **HIGH**

Flying frogs cannot fly, but they are able to glide through the air. The Wallace flying frog mostly lives up in trees in tropical rainforests. Using flaps of skin on its arms and webbed fingers and toes, it can descend distances of 50 ft (15 m) or more between branches.

MASTER OF **CAMOUFLAGE**

When asleep, the glass frog has transparent skin and its beating heart and digestive system are visible. But when it is awake, its circulatory system is full of red blood cells that absorb light, making its skin visible.

Eyes about to close in preparation for swallowing.

Soft, sticky tongue begins to extend, ready to shoot out and catch the flying insect.

Vocal sac below mouth amplifies mating calls.

GOLIATH FROGS ARE THE **LARGEST LIVING FROGS** AND CAN GROW TO **15 IN (38 CM)**!

SMALL BUT **DEADLY**

The paperclip-sized golden poison frog is the most toxic of all frog species. Glands in its skin produce a toxin so powerful that each frog contains enough poison to kill 10 people.

Fabulous frogs

Frogs and their relatives, toads, have roamed our planet for more than 200 million years, and were the first land animals with vocal cords. The more than 7,700 species have compact, tailless bodies with long hind legs and feet that many use for jumping long distances.

Terrific toads

Toads include many families of frog-like amphibians with bumpy skin. In many species some of these bumps are wartlike glands that release poisons.

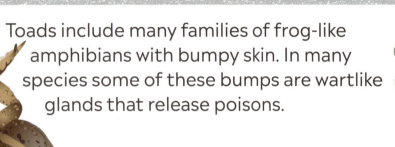

STICKY **SURPRISE**

Toads have long, soft tongues that are coated with thick, sticky saliva. When their tongue hits prey at high speed, the saliva becomes thinner and sinks into creases and pores on the prey's surface, trapping it.

Sticky tongue snares prey.

Catch
Strong muscles in the Common European toad's jaw flick the tongue toward prey at great speed.

... and swallow!
Tongue muscles pull the prey into the toad's mouth where it is swallowed.

Eyes sit atop the head, so they can poke above water when the toad is submerged.

TOADS CAN EAT 50 TO 100 SLUGS, GRUBS, AND OTHER PESTS EVERY SINGLE NIGHT!

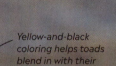

Yellow-and-black coloring helps toads blend in with their wetland environment.

Inflated vocal sac

Toad skin is covered in little bumps.

Clusters of eggs stick to the male's back.

MIDWIFE TOAD

Male midwife toads wrap their eggs around their hind legs, and carry them for around six weeks. After that, they take them back to water to hatch.

TADPOLE TO **TOAD**

Like frogs, toads go through metamorphosis as they age—passing through life stages that look completely different from one another. Most species begin as eggs, hatch into tadpoles, become toadlets and then, finally, turn into adult toads.

1. *The male toad grips onto the female to begin mating.*

2. *As the female releases eggs, the male fertilizes them.*

Eggs are laid in long ribbons.

5. *The toadlet grows into a young adult toad—ready to start the cycle again.*

3. *Tiny, wriggling tadpoles hatch from the eggs.*

Skin grows over toadlet's gills and tail is lost.

4. *Front legs form and the tadpole becomes a toadlet.*

Back legs grow.

CRITTER IN THE LITTER

Leaf litter toads camouflage themselves to look exactly like the fallen leaves in their tropical forest environment. This makes it easy for them to sneakily snap up their favorite meal of passing ants.

Bright underside gives the fire-bellied toad its name.

BACK **OFF!**

The fire-bellied toad can take on a defensive posture to warn off potential predators. By arching their body upward, they expose bright colors—a warning that they could be toxic to eat.

SULTRY **SONG**

American toads mate from March to July. Males travel to shallow ponds then inflate their large vocal sacs and use them to try to lure in local females by creating high-pitched musical trills that can last for up to 30 seconds.

Most toads have horizontal pupils.

THE **OAK TOAD** IS JUST 1⅔ IN (33 MM) LONG—NOT MUCH BIGGER THAN A **FINGERTIP!**

Jaime Culebras is an award-winning wildlife photographer and conservationist. Born in Spain, he currently lives in Ecuador where he works as a reptile and amphibian researcher as well as leading wildlife tours.

FROGTOGRAPHER

Q How did you decide to become a wildlife photographer?

A When I was a child, I often went to the countryside to see animals. Snakes and frogs in particular captured my attention. As I wanted to have memories of my experiences, I thought that photography would be an excellent career, since it would allow me to freeze those moments forever. Later on, when studying conservation in Ecuador, I began to see that the photos I took caught people's attention, and that my photos could help others fall in love with the natural world.

Q What are the challenges of your job?

A The most difficult thing is usually the environmental conditions. When working in tropical forests there are torrential rains, strong winds, and areas with extreme heat or cold.

Q Do you have a favorite photograph that you have taken?

A Many! One of them is a picture of an incredible pink frog from Brazil, called Hoogmoed's harlequin frog. Another I remember fondly shows a female glass frog, where the heart is perfectly visible through the transparent skin and you can even see her eggs inside her body!

Q What is the rarest frog you've seen?

A One of the most elusive is a frog I helped to discover. Called the mutable rainfrog, this frog can change the shape of its skin from spiny to smooth in just one minute. Another super rare frog is one with horns and a big mouth that devours other creatures—earning it the name Pacman frog.

Q How can people learn more about frogs?

A Reading about different species is great, but for me the best way to learn about frogs has been going into the field and observing them. See what local frogs you can spot in watery areas near you!

Q How can I help protect frogs?

A By consuming less, reusing and recycling what we do use, and restoring nature, we can all help the planet, and frogs. Although some frogs are at risk of extinction, there is some inspiring good news too. In 2022 we were able to find a frog that people thought had been extinct for 100 years!

SEE-THROUGH **FROG**

In this photo taken by Jaime, the translucent skin of a female glass frog offers an incredible view of the amphibian's internal organs, including her heart and even the eggs inside her body. Mostly tree-dwelling creatures, glass frogs use their see-through skin to hide among green leaves, fooling would-be predators into thinking they're not there.

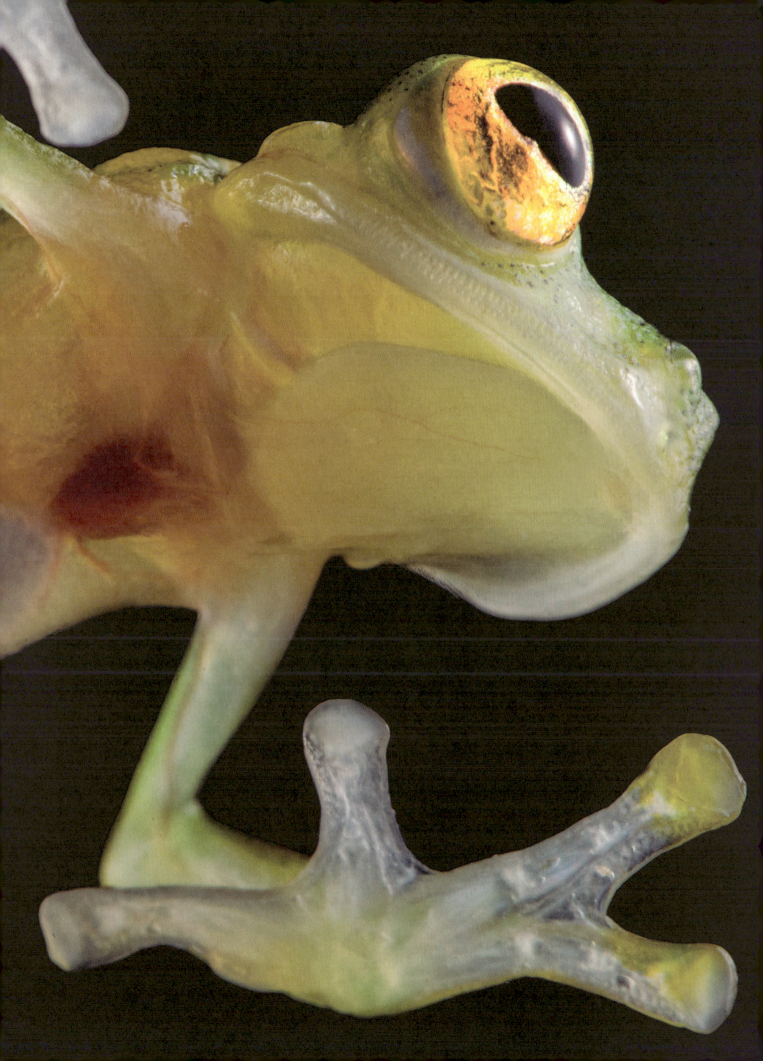

Terrific
turtles

There are 365 known species of turtle, of which around half are mostly aquatic. The other half, called tortoises, live on land. They all have a shell, a hard beak, and scaly skin.

GIANT TORTOISES GROW UP TO **6 FT (1.8 M)** IN SIZE!

Sensitive nose detects food and water.

Strong carapace (upper shell) is made up of an outer layer of interlocking plate

Strong, hard beak to bite through vegetation

Powerful front legs for walking and burrowing

MATING TORTOISES OFTEN MAKE **LOUD QUACKING SOUNDS!**

TURTLE OR TORTOISE?

Tortoises are adapted for life on land with strong limbs to carry their weight. Aquatic turtles are more streamlined to glide through water.

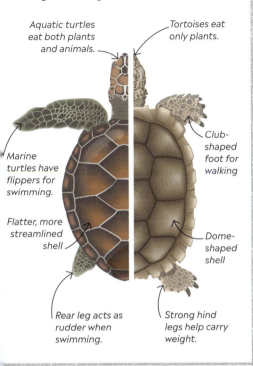

Aquatic turtles eat both plants and animals.

Tortoises eat only plants.

Marine turtles have flippers for swimming.

Club-shaped foot for walking

Flatter, more streamlined shell

Dome-shaped shell

Rear leg acts as rudder when swimming.

Strong hind legs help carry weight.

SUN BATHERS

Turtles are cold-blooded, like all other reptiles. This means that they cannot regulate their body temperature. When they want to warm up, like this terrapin, they lie—or bask—in the sunshine, soaking up the heat. To cool down, they seek out shady places.

HARDBACK REPTILES

A turtle's shell is made of bony plates fused to its ribs and spine. The shell is part of the body, so the turtle cannot survive without it.

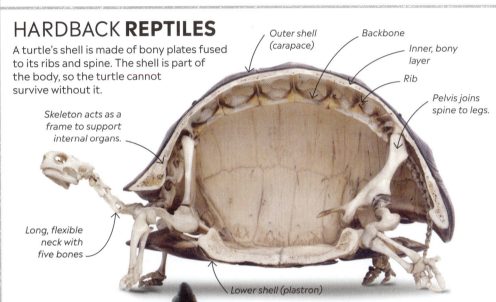

Outer shell (carapace)

Backbone

Inner, bony layer

Rib

Pelvis joins spine to legs.

Skeleton acts as a frame to support internal organs.

Long, flexible neck with five bones

Lower shell (plastron)

SHELL RETREAT

Most turtles can withdraw their head into their shells, usually for protection. The majority retract their head straight back, but around 100 species of turtle bend their head sideways to fit in their shell.

Rear legs tuck in sideways.

Lower shell protects head.

ISLAND GIANTS

The world's largest tortoises live on the remote Galápagos Islands. These tortoises can weigh as much as 550 lb (250 kg) and live for 150 years—just as well considering they move at just 0.16 mph (0.26 kph)!

EPIC MIGRATION

Loggerhead turtles feed and breed on opposite sides of the world. They hatch in Japan then swim 6,800 miles (11,000 km) across the Pacific Ocean to Baja California, Mexico, to feed and mature. They then swim back to mate and breed.

YOU CAN TELL THE AGE OF A TORTOISE BY COUNTING THE NUMBER OF RINGS ON ITS SHELL!

This turtle must be very old.

TOOTHLESS!

Tortoises don't have teeth, but they do have strong beaks that they use to bite and grind food before swallowing. Male tortoises will also sometimes bite females to woo them before mating.

SEA TURTLES NAVIGATE THE OCEANS BY SENSING EARTH'S MAGNETIC FIELDS!

EGGS ON **THE BEACH**

Female turtles dig holes and lay up to 200 eggs in them, often by moonlight. They cover the eggs with sand and return to the ocean. The eggs, and hatchlings, are left on their own!

Strong flippers dig out a nest.

Front flippers rotate and sweep down and back, like oars, to pull the animal through the water.

The shell curves down toward the back to reduce drag.

Rear flippers act like rudders, helping the turtle to maneuver.

The turtles' green color is probably the result of their plant-based diet.

Powerful flippers for swimming and digging

The lower part of the shell is called the plastron.

Green sea turtle

One of the world's largest species of turtle, these reptiles live in the tropical regions of the Atlantic, Pacific, and Indian oceans. Their oar-like flippers and teardrop-shaped shells that cut through the water make them efficient swimmers.

DANGER DASH

Once turtles hatch, usually at night, they face a dangerous journey from their nest to the ocean. As they scuttle along the beach they must avoid predators, including seabirds, crabs, and even dogs!

LIFE CYCLE

Female green sea turtles can reproduce from the age of around 25–35 years. To do this, every 2–5 years they migrate 1,243 miles (2,000 km) or more back to the beach where they themselves hatched to lay their eggs.

Hatchlings are about 2 in (5 cm) long.

The eggs are about the size and shape of ping-pong balls.

Eggs typically **hatch 45–70 days** after they are laid.

Hatchlings dig through to the surface and **make a dash** for the ocean.

Adult turtles typically grow to just under 3 ft (1 m) long.

ONLY ABOUT
1 IN 1,000
GREEN SEA TURTLE **HATCHLINGS** SURVIVE TO **BREEDING AGE!**

AWESOME ATHLETE

Green sea turtles' streamlined shells help them glide smoothly for hours through the water at around 2.2 mph (3.6 kph), and usually much slower. If necessary, they can swim at speeds up to 22 mph (35 kph), but only for a few minutes at most.

Large front flippers provide most of the propulsive force.

Beak has serrated edges, like the teeth on a saw.

SALTY TEARS

As reptiles that live mostly in the ocean, sea turtles drink and absorb lots of salt. Their kidneys expel some but not all of it. Instead, they have evolved special tear ducts in the corners of their eyes from which they "cry" salty tears.

UNDERSEA GRAZERS

Green sea turtles are herbivorous, eating ocean plants such as seagrass or algae that they scrape off rocks with their sawlike beak. Young green sea turtles, however, will eat some meat, foraging for small sea creatures such as shellfish and scavenging fish left by other predators.

GREEN SEA TURTLES CAN **LIVE** FOR MORE THAN 70 YEARS!

CROC **OR NOT?**

There are 28 living species of crocodilians, most of which are crocodiles or alligators. Alligators tend to be darker in color with a rounded snout, while crocodiles are grayish-green with a triangular-shaped snout. Although most alligators and crocodiles live in freshwater habitats, crocodiles can also live in saltwater.

Crocodile

V-shaped snout

All teeth are visible when mouth is closed.

Fourth tooth slots into a notch in the upper jaw.

U-shaped snout

Alligator

Only top teeth are visible when jaw is closed.

American alligator stirs up the water as it swims, disturbing small prey for the egret riding on its back.

FAMILY TIES

Crocodilians are more closely related to birds than to other reptiles, such as lizards and turtles. Both birds and crocodilians are part of a larger group called "archosaurs." Birds and crocodiles look so different today because birds have developed special adaptations such as feathers to help them to fly.

A FEMALE **CAIMAN** CAN LAY UP TO **30 HARD-SHELLED EGGS** PER SEASON!

MIGHTY **BITE**

Crocodiles have a second joint in their jaw, which helps prevent it from twisting or slipping, making their bites very powerful. Nile crocodiles have one of the strongest bites of any animal when clamping their mouths shut and crushing prey.

Pointed teeth are used to catch and hold down prey.

Jaw is more sensitive to touch than human fingertips.

KNOBBLY **NOSE**

Gharials are instantly recognizable by their long, narrow snouts and numerous interlocking teeth. Males also have a bulbous, fleshy knob on the tip of their snout called a "ghara," the Hindi word for a kind of mud pot that has a similar shape. The ghara is used to vocalize and blow bubbles to attract females.

A **CROCODILE BITE** EXERTS MORE THAN **THIRTY TIMES** THE FORCE OF A **HUMAN BITE!**

THE **NILE CROCODILE** CAN **EAT UP TO HALF ITS BODY WEIGHT** IN ONE FEEDING!

STAYING **UNDER**

Crocodiles can hold their breath and stay underwater for up to an hour, partly because they slow their heart rate to just 7–10 beats per minute. They often use this ability to drown their prey, holding captured animals underwater until they suffocate.

Fierce
crocodilians

Crocodiles, alligators, and gharials, collectively called crocodilians, include the biggest living reptiles. These semiaquatic predators have armor-like skin and long, teeth-filled snouts.

GENTLE **PARENTING**

Although known for their powerful bite, crocodiles are able to roll their eggs carefully in their mouths to help them hatch. They also carry their young in their jaws, both to protect them and to transport them to water.

Flexible backbone allows boa to wrap around branch for support.

BRANCH **BOA**

The emerald tree boa lives in South American rainforests and is typically around 6 ft (1.8 m) long. Its bright green color helps it blend in with the leaves in which it lies in wait, its tail coiled around a branch to hold it in place. It targets small mammals or birds, biting into them with long, sharp, but nonvenomous teeth, then squeezing them to death.

Zig-zag "lightning bolt" stripes add extra camouflage.

COLOR **COPY**

By mimicking the warning colors of the venomous Texas coral snake, the nonvenomous Mexican milk snake makes predators think it's more dangerous than it is. Other nonvenomous snakes have also evolved this trick.

Mexican milk snake

Texas coral snake

ALMOST 20% OF THE MORE THAN 4,000 KNOWN SPECIES OF SNAKE ARE VENOMOUS!

VENOM **THIEF!**

Asia's tiger keelback snake has two rows of organs in its neck called nuchal glands in which it stores venom harvested from eating toxic toads. These glands swell up when the snake is attacked, so any predator that bites it gets squirted with a painful jet of poison. Females also lace their eggs with the toxin, to protect their young.

Slithering snakes

Snakes have more vertebrae than most other animals, which makes their bodies extremely flexible. Since they lack limbs, snakes must use their mouths and bendy bodies to manipulate and kill their prey. Their flexibility also means they can crawl, climb, and swim.

EGGS **OR NOT?**

Snakes are either oviparous (egg laying) or viviparous (they give birth to live young). Emerald tree boas are a bit of both: their eggs stay in the mother's body until they are ready to hatch and wriggle out.

Peaks and valleys increase each scale's surface area to reflect less light.

SNAKE **SCIENCE**

The matte black scales on the West African Gaboon viper reflect so little sunlight that scientists have been studying their structure to see if they can use what they learn to make solar panels work more efficiently.

ALL BRAHMINY BLIND SNAKES ARE FEMALE AND THEY REPRODUCE WITHOUT MATING!

SKIN **SHEDDERS**

As snakes grow, from time to time, they have to shed their old skin and grow a new one.

1. Preparing
Snakes do not grow a new skin gradually, as many other animals do. Instead, the new skin grows underneath the old one.

2. Shedding
When the new skin is ready, it separates from the old skin. The snake rubs itself on a rough surface to begin tearing the old skin off.

3. Discarding
Once a tear is made in the old skin, the snake wriggles it off in one piece. Adult snakes shed 2–4 times a year—younger ones perhaps once a month.

RATTLESNAKE VENOM DESTROYS **BLOOD CELLS** AND CAUSES **INTERNAL BLEEDING!**

SUPER **SMELLER**

Snakes have a sensor called the Jacobson's organ in the roof of their mouth that works in addition to their mouths and noses. Using their tongues, snakes flick airborne moisture particles toward this organ, which "tastes" and "smells" the chemical signals they carry.

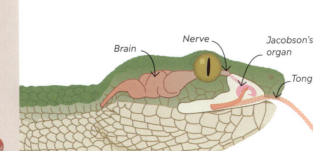

Brain   Nerve   Jacobson's organ   Tongue

SCARY LIZARDS

Some lizards are aggressive and dangerous enough to cause serious injury. Here are a few of the scariest.

Gila monster
After biting, Gila monsters inject venom into the wounds they inflict, causing swelling and a burning pain.

Crocodile monitor
These aggressive lizards have a strong bite and use their long whiplike tails to defend themselves.

Komodo dragon
This large lizard can outrun a human. Their venomous bite releases a toxin that stops a victim's blood from clotting.

DAZZLING DEWLAP

Anolis lizards have a flap of brightly colored skin beneath their jaw called a dewlap. They pulse this flap, usually in a color that contrasts with the lizard's surroundings, as a mating signal.

FACT PACK!
LIZARDS

From dusty deserts to freshwater lakes and rivers, lizards live in a variety of habitats and have adapted different body shapes, sizes, and colors. Most are predators that hunt small invertebrates, and some species have a venomous bite.

LARGEST LIZARDS

Lizards vary enormously in size and weight—the biggest, a komodo dragon, is longer than the average man is tall. Here is a lineup of some of the biggest and heaviest.

AVERAGE MAN
Weighs around 198 lb (90 kg) and is 5 ft 7 in (1.7 m) tall.

Komodo dragons can eat **80 percent** of their body weight in **one meal!**

1 KOMODO DRAGON
Weighs 300 lb (135 kg) and grows 10 ft (3 m) long.

2 ASIAN WATER MONITOR
Weighs up to 55 lb (25 kg) and can grow to 9 ft (2.7 m).

3 CROCODILE MONITOR
Weighs up to 44 lb (20 kg) and reaches over 8 ft (2.4 m) long.

4 PERENTIE
Weighs up to 44 lb (20 kg) and is 8 ft (2.4 m) long.

5 NILE MONITOR
Weighs up to 17.7 lb (8 kg) and can reach 6½ ft (1.9 m).

WHERE'S IT GONE?

Many lizards are camouflage experts that can blend into a range of backgrounds, from tree bark to piles of leaves.

DESERT HORNED LIZARD
These lizards have rough, spiky bodies that blend in with the rocky soil of their desert habitat.

FANTASTIC LEAF-TAILED GECKO
This gecko uses its flat body and blotchy patterning to resemble a decaying leaf.

COMMON FLAT-TAILED GECKO
The speckled skin of a flat-tailed gecko keeps it camouflaged when it clings to a tree.

BLACK-SPOTTED KANGAROO LIZARD
These creatures hide in leaf litter. Their brown coloring makes them difficult to spot.

EYE SPY

To spot predators, chameleons can move each bulging eye independently and process images from both eyes separately. This allows them to look in two different directions at once!

BLOOD DEFENSE

When threatened, the horned lizard has an unusually gory defense. By contracting its eye muscles and cutting off its blood flow to the heart, it can shoot blood from its eyes up to 3 ft (0.9 m) to confuse predators.

THORNY DEVIL

The desert-dwelling thorny devil keeps hydrated using grooves on its skin. These direct rainwater and dew across its body and into its mouth.

LITTLEST LIZARDS

Some lizards are so tiny they could fit on your fingertip. The smallest, the nano chameleon, has a body the size of two sunflower seeds.

2 NOSY HARA LEAF CHAMELEON
1.1 in (28 mm)

3 MINUTE LEAF CHAMELEON
1.1 in (28 mm)

1 NANO CHAMELEON
0.86 in (22 mm)

4 VIRGIN ISLANDS DWARF SPHAERO
1.2 in (33 mm)

5 JARAGUA DWARF GECKO
1.2 in (33 mm)

PRODUCING YOUNG

Here are the different ways in which lizards reproduce, from laying eggs to giving birth to live young, and even reproducing alone!

OVIPAROUS
Most lizards are oviparous, which means they lay eggs that hatch outside their body.

VIVIPAROUS
Some lizards, including the common lizard, are viviparous, meaning they give birth to live young.

OVOVIVIPAROUS
Slow worms (see p.121) are ovoviviparous. They incubate and hatch their eggs inside their bodies.

PARTHENOGENETIC
Some female lizards produce young from unfertilized eggs, with no need for a male at all.

LIZARD LINEUP

There are more than 7,400 species of lizard, and they're found on every continent except Antarctica. The smallest lizards have a body the size of two sunflower seeds at just ½ in (13.5 mm), while the largest can reach just over 10 ft (3 m) long. Here are four kinds of lizard.

Chameleons
These have grasping feet and tails, and some can change color.

Monitors
Monitors have heavy bodies, long necks, and powerful tails and claws.

Skinks
Mostly found in leaf litter or under rocks, skinks have very short legs or even no limbs.

Geckos
Geckos vocalize with chirps or other sounds, and most species lack eyelids.

Scaly lizards

Lizards are reptiles with long bodies covered in horny scales. Most have ear openings, movable eyelids, and four legs to crawl or run.

Bulging eyes can move independently.

Tip of the tongue uses suction to grasp insects.

Sticky tongue shoots forward to catch prey.

THE VENOM OF A GILA MONSTER IS ABOUT AS TOXIC AS THAT OF A DIAMONDBACK RATTLESNAKE!

When tiny crystals in the lizard's skin are compressed together, they reflect short wavelengths of light, such as green.

Relaxed

Male chameleon turns red when showing off to a mate.

Stressed

COLOR CHANGE

Chameleons don't just use their color changing abilities for camouflage—they can also communicate. When relaxed, chameleons tend to be green, but if excited, they're more likely to turn yellow, orange, or red.

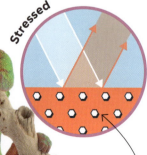

When the tiny crystals are more spaced out, they reflect longer wavelengths of light, such as red.

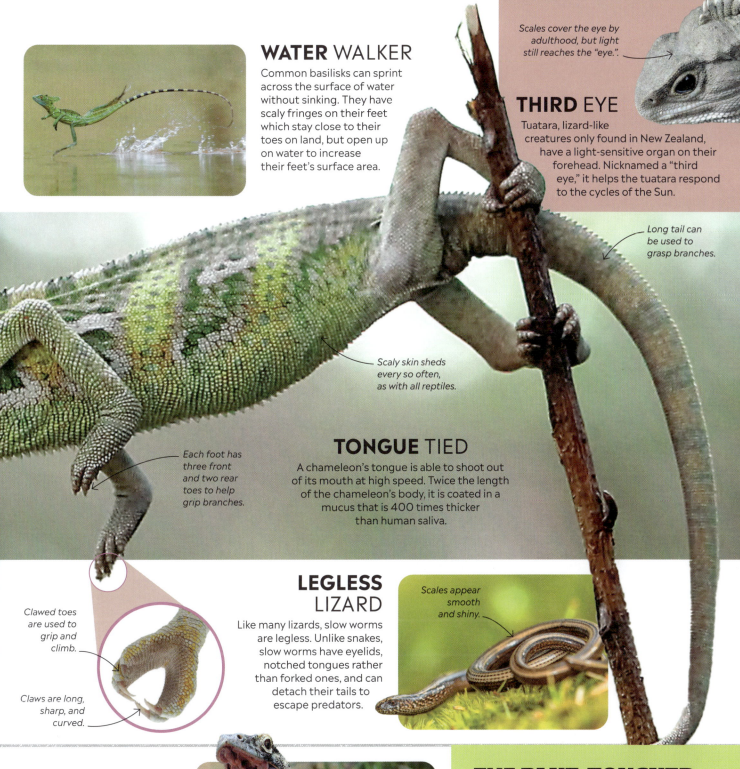

WATER WALKER

Common basilisks can sprint across the surface of water without sinking. They have scaly fringes on their feet which stay close to their toes on land, but open up on water to increase their feet's surface area.

THIRD EYE

Scales cover the eye by adulthood, but light still reaches the "eye.".

Tuatara, lizard-like creatures only found in New Zealand, have a light-sensitive organ on their forehead. Nicknamed a "third eye," it helps the tuatara respond to the cycles of the Sun.

Long tail can be used to grasp branches.

Scaly skin sheds every so often, as with all reptiles.

TONGUE TIED

A chameleon's tongue is able to shoot out of its mouth at high speed. Twice the length of the chameleon's body, it is coated in a mucus that is 400 times thicker than human saliva.

Each foot has three front and two rear toes to help grip branches.

Clawed toes are used to grip and climb.

Claws are long, sharp, and curved.

LEGLESS LIZARD

Like many lizards, slow worms are legless. Unlike snakes, slow worms have eyelids, notched tongues rather than forked ones, and can detach their tails to escape predators.

Scales appear smooth and shiny.

SWIFT GETAWAY

The komodo dragon is the largest lizard in the world, and can weigh up to 366 lb (166 kg)—more than a panda bear. They are able to eat up to 80 percent of their body weight in just one meal, but if they feel threatened, they throw up their food to reduce their weight. This allows them to run away faster!

THE **BLUE-TONGUED SKINK** STICKS OUT ITS **COLORFUL TONGUE** TO SCARE **PREDATORS AWAY!**

Great geckos

The detached tail continues to move after separation!

TAIL **TRICK**

Like many other lizards, most geckos can detach their tail if they meet a predator—distracting the other creature and giving themselves time to get away. Most species can then use special cells called stem cells to grow a new tail in around a month.

Geckos are some of the most acrobatic climbers in the lizard world. Many are able to scamper up vertical surfaces thanks to their grippy toes.

SKIN **SHEDDING**

All reptiles shed their skin as they grow, and geckos are no different. Shedding removes old, damaged skin and protects against infections and mites. Geckos often eat their shed skin to regain lost nutrients and so predators do not catch its scent.

Colorless shed skin comes off in pieces.

SPEEDY **EATER**

Most geckos are insectivores, eating crickets, earthworms, fruit flies, moths, and grasshoppers, but some larger geckos can eat whole infant mice. Despite having lots of teeth, they don't chew their food—they usually swallow it whole!

EGG **HUNT**

Most geckos lay eggs, except for a few species from New Zealand and New Caledonia. Those that do deposit their eggs under rocks, tree bark, and—thanks to their ability to scale vertical walls—even behind window shutters.

A newborn leopard gecko crawls out of its egg.

Dirt sticks to the soft white egg, making it look speckled.

A grasshopper falls victim to a turnip-tailed gecko.

GLOBAL **GECKOS**

Geckos are found everywhere except Antarctica. They've adapted to a wide range of habitats—from chilly mountain slopes to humid rainforests and dry deserts. Here are four from around the world.

Ashy gecko
Brightly colored, and found in Cuba, Hispaniola, and Florida.

Kuhl's gecko
These Southeast Asian geckos have flaps on their bodies so they can glide.

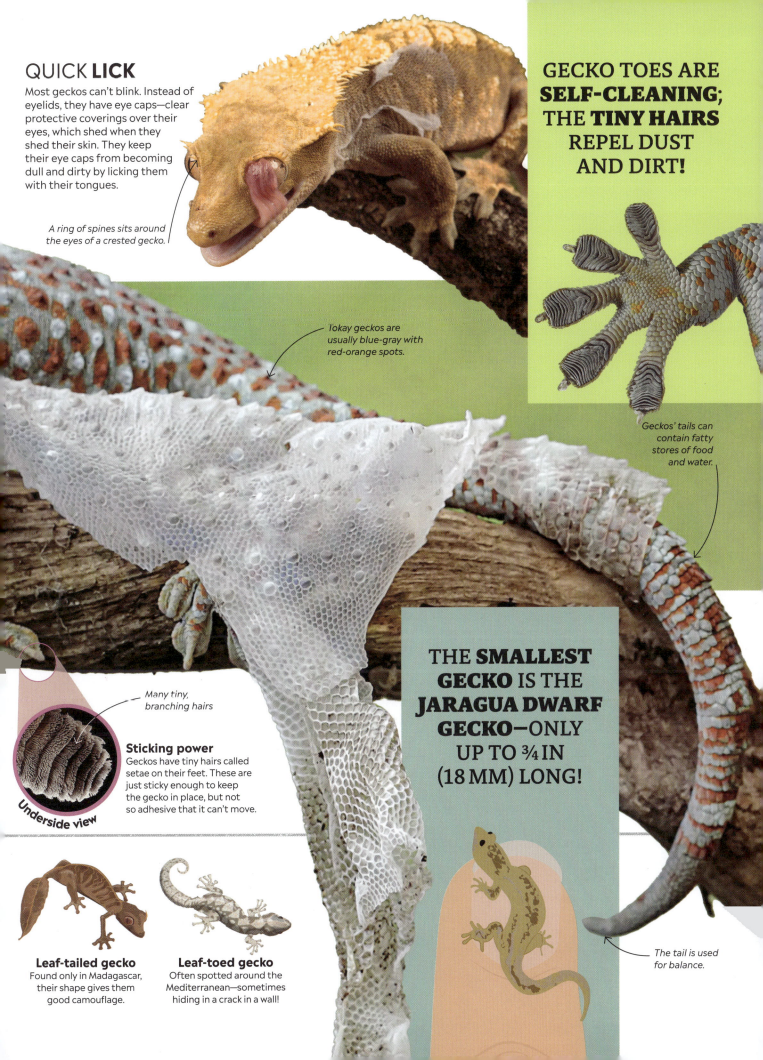

QUICK **LICK**

Most geckos can't blink. Instead of eyelids, they have eye caps—clear protective coverings over their eyes, which shed when they shed their skin. They keep their eye caps from becoming dull and dirty by licking them with their tongues.

A ring of spines sits around the eyes of a crested gecko.

Tokay geckos are usually blue-gray with red-orange spots.

GECKO TOES ARE **SELF-CLEANING**; THE **TINY HAIRS** REPEL DUST AND DIRT!

Geckos' tails can contain fatty stores of food and water.

Many tiny, branching hairs

Sticking power
Geckos have tiny hairs called setae on their feet. These are just sticky enough to keep the gecko in place, but not so adhesive that it can't move.

Underside view

THE **SMALLEST GECKO** IS THE **JARAGUA DWARF GECKO**—ONLY UP TO ¾ IN (18 MM) LONG!

The tail is used for balance.

Leaf-tailed gecko
Found only in Madagascar, their shape gives them good camouflage.

Leaf-toed gecko
Often spotted around the Mediterranean—sometimes hiding in a crack in a wall!

NAME THAT... REPTILE

Are you a wizard at lizards and a devil for detail? Can you tell a snake from a skink or a croc from a dragon? Check out this scaly scattering and name as many as you can.

1 Rattlesnake
2 Smith's green-eyed gecko
3 Eyelash viper
4 Blue-tongued skink
5 Thorny devil
6 Sandfish skink
7 Emerald tree boa
8 Thai water dragon
9 Sinaloan milk snake
10 Slow worm
11 Carolina anole lizard
12 Australian frilled lizard
13 Leopard gecko
14 King cobra
15 Anaconda
16 Gila monster
17 Green tree monitor
18 Bearded dragon
19 Green basilisk lizard
20 Eastern hognose snake
21 Kuhl's flying gecko
22 Armadillo girdled lizard
23 Crested gecko
24 Panther chameleon
25 Caiman
26 Turquoise dwarf gecko
27 Fire skink
28 Northern red-bellied turtle
29 Ornate horned toad
30 Chinese crocodile lizard
31 Short-tailed pygmy chameleon
32 Tokay gecko
33 Alligator snapping turtle
34 Leaf-tailed gecko
35 Green vine snake

The odd one out is the ornate horned toad (29). Frogs and toads are amphibians, with smooth, moist skin. Reptiles have dry, scaly skin.

CAN YOU SPOT THE ODD ONE OUT?

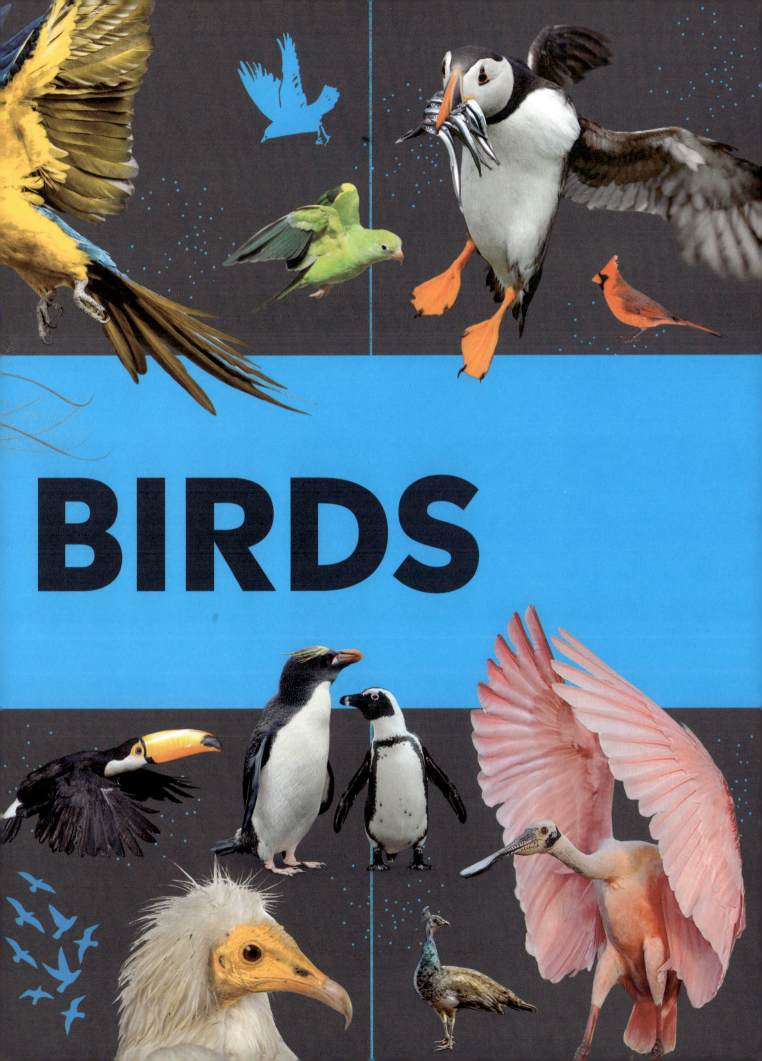

BIRDS

What is a **bird?**

The first feathery fliers evolved from dinosaurs around 160 million years ago. Today, these clever, lightweight animals are the only vertebrate to fly, run, or swim on every continent

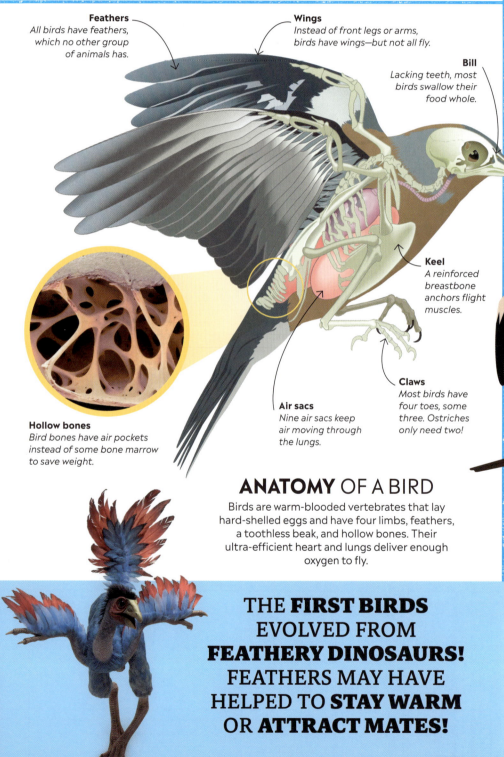

Feathers
All birds have feathers, which no other group of animals has.

Wings
Instead of front legs or arms, birds have wings—but not all fly.

Bill
Lacking teeth, most birds swallow their food whole.

Keel
A reinforced breastbone anchors flight muscles.

Claws
Most birds have four toes, some three. Ostriches only need two!

Air sacs
Nine air sacs keep air moving through the lungs.

Hollow bones
Bird bones have air pockets instead of some bone marrow to save weight.

ANATOMY OF A BIRD

Birds are warm-blooded vertebrates that lay hard-shelled eggs and have four limbs, feathers, a toothless beak, and hollow bones. Their ultra-efficient heart and lungs deliver enough oxygen to fly.

THE **FIRST BIRDS** EVOLVED FROM **FEATHERY DINOSAURS!** FEATHERS MAY HAVE HELPED TO **STAY WARM** OR **ATTRACT MATES!**

FIT THE BILL

Each bird species has a beak adapted to what they eat. Bills are made of a protein called keratin, which also forms feathers, nails, hair, and fur.

SEED-EATER
Crossbills use a sharp, curved bill with overlapping tips to pull seeds out of pine cones.

NECTAR-GATHERER
A long, thin bill, often curved, reaches into flowers to drink nectar. Hummingbird bills are the most specialized.

FILTER-FEEDER
The flamingo's kinked bill dips into the water to sift out algae and tiny shrimp.

MUD-PROBER
Shoreline birds with long, sensitive bills delve into mud for snails and crustaceans.

MEAT-EATER
Birds of prey have sharp, hooked beaks for killing their prey or tearing flesh from larger fish, birds, and mammals.

Bee hummingbird's egg, actual size

THE **SMALLEST** HUMMINGBIRD'S **EGG** IS THE **SIZE** OF A PEA!

Vulture
No vertebrate flies higher than Rüppell's vulture, seen gliding past airplanes at 37,000 ft (11,300 m) above sea level. Try spotting lunch from up there next time you fly!

Air
Large wings and light bones are the classic avian adaptations.

Swift
The common swift spends almost all year in the air—it hunts, eats, drinks, and bathes on the wing, and never touches the ground.

Ostrich
These big birds have become running machines with muscular thighs and small wings. They are tall and fast for life on the open plains.

Land
Flightless runners and heavy wildfowl live mostly on the ground.

ADAPTABLE AVIANS

Birds have adapted to a host of habitats around the world—on land, in the water, and of course high in the air. All early birds flew, but today some prefer to swim, run, or climb. Each species has evolved to find plentiful food, avoid competition, and escape predators.

THE **PITOHUI** MAKES ITSELF **POISONOUS** BY EATING **TOXIC** BEETLES!

Desert sandgrouse
Nests in the desert have few predators, but also little water. Sandgrouse fly 20 miles (30 km) each way to soak special absorbent chest feathers in water so their chicks can drink.

Water
Many birds have learned to "fly" underwater to pursue fish.

Penguin
Too heavy to take off and clumsy on land, penguins are super swimmers, with strong, slim flippers and long, streamlined bodies. Some hunt underwater for 20 minutes at a time.

Tail

Wing

Contour

Down

FEATHER FEATURES
Close to the body lie soft, warm down feathers and contour feathers with a downy lower half and protective upper. Flight feathers on the wings and tail are large and strong to catch the air when gaining height, or to steer when changing direction.

Inner claw

THE CASSOWARY'S **RAZOR SHARP** INNER CLAW GROWS TO **5 IN (12.5 CM) LONG!**

ALL ABOUT **EGGS**

Ratite eggs are far larger than other animals' and come in different colors. Ostriches produce the biggest eggs—about 6 in (15 cm) long—and lay around 60 a year. Kiwis lay one egg at a time, which is 60 percent yolk, giving them the highest yolk-to-egg volume of all birds.

Emu

Ostrich

Cassowary

Rhea

Kiwi

Chicken

COLORFUL **CASSOWARY**

Female cassowaries are about 30 percent heavier than males. Both have jet black body feathers, but the head and neck coloring on the female is far brighter than that of the male. To evade danger, cassowaries can jump almost 6 ft 7 in (2 m) into the air and run at 31 mph (50 kph).

Feathers have a shaggy, hairlike appearance since they do not interlock.

Large crest is called a casque.

THE DEEP, **RUMBLING SOUND** A CASSOWARY MAKES IS ONE OF THE **LOUDEST CALLS** OF ANY BIRD!

Rapid runners

Ratites are flightless birds. Found mainly in the southern hemisphere, they include tall, lanky runner birds that stride across open country—such as ostriches and emus—as well as smaller kiwis who make their homes in thick forest.

A single ostrich stride can be 16 ft (4.88 m) long.

FAST MOVERS

Long legs and strong thigh muscles allow ostriches to reach speeds of 40 mph (64 kph), which is enough to outrun a hyena or a lion. Even kiwis, the smallest ratite, can outpace the average human.

BELLY BUSTER!

New Zealand's kiwis lay the biggest eggs for their size of any bird. Carrying an egg almost as large as the much bigger rhea or emu's, their bellies bulge so much they touch the ground! During egg production female kiwis eat three times their regular intake.

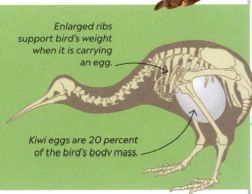

Enlarged ribs support bird's weight when it is carrying an egg.

Kiwi eggs are 20 percent of the bird's body mass.

WELL GROUNDED

Although they have wings, like other ratites this rhea cannot fly. Their bodies are too heavy for the wings to provide adequate lift, and their chest muscles are too weak to flap them. The wings are useful for balance when the bird runs at high speed, however.

Ratites also use their large wings to shade chicks in hot, cold, or too wet weather.

EGGS IN ONE BASKET

Ostriches such as these, rheas and, occasionally, emus live in groups. The first two of these ratites share communal nests, which contain as many as 50 eggs supplied by multiple females each laying 7-10 eggs.

TALL STORY

This lineup of five ratites shows that the biggest bird of all—the ostrich—is taller than a human. The kiwi is the smallest ratite, which suits its preferred means of hunting: digging up buried invertebrates with its long bill.

| Ostrich 9 ft (2.8 m) | Emu 5 ft 11 in (1.8 m) | Southern cassowary 5 ft 3 in (1.6 m) | Rhea 5 ft 3 in (1.6 m) | Kiwi 2 ft (0.6 m) | Human 5 ft 11 in (1.8 m) |

LONG-HAUL **FLIER**

Ospreys breed in the northern hemisphere then fly south for the winter, covering distances up to 3,728 miles (6,000 km). North American ospreys migrate to South America, European ospreys to West Africa, and Central Asian ospreys to South Asia.

EAGLE EYED

Eagles see the world in sharper focus than almost any other animal. Their huge eyeballs fill up to half of their skull space and are packed with one million light receptor cells per square millimeter—that's five times as many as a human eye.

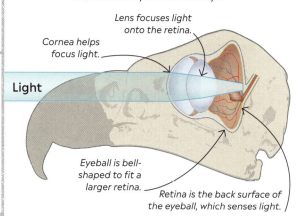

Lens focuses light onto the retina.

Cornea helps focus light.

Light

Eyeball is bell-shaped to fit a larger retina.

Retina is the back surface of the eyeball, which senses light.

Eagles and ospreys

These birds are among the fastest, strongest, and most effective predators in the entire animal kingdom. Majestic eagles can pounce on small and even large mammals, while ospreys expertly snap up fish.

Primary flight feathers help provide lift, keeping the eagle in the air.

Large primary feathers supply most of the wing's power in flight.

Crest feathers pop up when the harpy eagle is startled or worried.

BIG BIRD

Measuring 42¼ in (107 cm) from beak to tail, the harpy eagle of South America is the world's largest and most powerful eagle. Its terrifying talons are up to 5 in (12.7 cm) long and can grab animals as large as sloths, opossums, and monkeys.

A HARPY EAGLE'S **TALONS** CAN BE **BIGGER** THAN AN **ADULT HUMAN'S HAND!**

MASTER **HUNTERS**

When it hunts, the bald eagle can dive down on prey at up to 100 mph (160 kph). Living on a specialized diet of fish, it has large talons with a fierce grip—allowing it to firmly snatch its prize and climb upward again.

Dark pigments help to strengthen wing feathers.

White neck feathers indicate a mature bird of five years or older.

EAGLES CAN SEE UV LIGHT—WHICH MEANS THEY CAN TRACK THE **"GLOWING"** URINE OF THEIR PREY!

Muscular legs are tapered to reduce drag when diving.

Tendon (blue) sits within a ribbed sheath (red).

The sheath and tendon lock together when the toe is clenched.

Spiky soles for gripping

FLEXIBLE **FEET**

Ospreys can carry loads up to 25 percent of their own bodyweight. Most birds lock their clenched toes to grip perches, and ospreys use the same mechanism to hold prey. Their thigh muscles pull on tendons that reach down to the claws and lock inside sheaths with ribbed surfaces.

BRANCHING **OUT**

Eagles and ospreys build their nests in high places. Made of hundreds of branches, these can be 7 ft 11 in (2.4 m) across and 3 ft (1 m) deep. The heaviest ones weigh 1.97 tons (2 metric tons). Mating pairs return to the same nest each year.

American osprey nest—usually lined with soft greenery such as moss, grass, and seaweed

Shaggy mane of feathers makes the bird easy to identify.

UNDER THREAT

With a wingspan of up to 7 ft (2.13 m), the Philippine eagle is one of the largest and rarest of eagles. Fewer than 500 survive today, due to deforestation and hunting. Also known as the monkey-eating eagle, it preys on macaques, snakes, rodents, and even small deer.

HAWK **OR FALCON?**

Hawks belong to the same family as eagles, but falcons are more closely related to parrots! Both groups have evolved similar abilities independently.

Peregrine falcon

Eurasian sparrowhawk

Common buzzard

Falcon
Pointed wings make falcons fast and agile in the air, helping them catch other birds in mid-flight.

True hawk
Broad wings and a long tail help sparrowhawks make quick turns while hunting in forests. They mostly eat small birds.

Buzzard
Soaring high on rounded wings, or perched on high branches, many of these larger hawks scan the ground for small mammals.

Flies high up, looking for prey.

Turns head down and tucks wingtips to "stoop" (dive).

Wings almost fully tucked for speed

DEVASTATING **DIVE**

As a falcon dives, it turns from a bird into a bullet. It tucks its wings back in three phases, each time sacrificing some steering control to reduce drag as it homes in on its prey. At the last moment, it turns feet-first to strike.

AT LEAST **80% OF A PEREGRINE FALCON'S** DIET CONSISTS OF **OTHER BIRDS!**

Wingtips fan out to slow down for landing.

FROZEN **FOOD**

When gyrfalcon chicks are still too small to eat large prey whole, the mother will hide it nearby and bring them small pieces at a time. A gyrfalcon has even been seen chipping pieces off a frozen catch, much like raiding the fridge!

HUNTING **HAWKS**

Red-tailed hawks perch on a tree or circle in the air while searching for prey moving below. Spotting a rabbit or mouse from 100 ft (30 m) up, they swoop down and clamp the unlucky mammal in their claws.

Crural feathers, often called "trousers," stop at the ankle.

PRAIRIE **NEST**

Ferruginous hawks are the largest hawk species. They nest on clifftops, tree stumps, or even at ground level on the open prairie, building huge heaps of sticks lined with cow dung. The nestlings above are white, but adults turn rust-red.

Falcons and hawks

These smaller birds of prey are no less lethal than eagles. Hawks ambush prey at close range, using strong claws to overpower them, while falcons are daredevil divers that can kill a bird on impact with their sheer speed.

FASTEST **FLIER**

No animal on Earth goes faster than a peregrine falcon. It doesn't flap furiously but surrenders to gravity and plummets like a stone, its slim, tapered wings and small head cutting through the air. Special adaptations help it function at breathtaking speed.

Clear additional eyelid blinks often to moisten eye and clear debris.

Narrow wings cut through the air with minimal friction.

Tubercle, a bony cone in the nostril, slows incoming airflow to prevent lung damage.

Pale underside blends in with sky for camouflage.

KILL **BILL**

Unlike most raptors, which crush prey with their feet, a falcon uses its beak to kill. Having stunned a bird in mid-air and brought it to ground, the falcon targets the back of the neck. A sharp "tomial tooth" made of keratin severs the prey's spine with a single, expert bite.

Tomial tooth is on the side and near the tip of the beak.

PEREGRINE FALCONS HIT THEIR PREY **SO FAST** THAT IT CAN **KILL THEM INSTANTLY!**

Large wings compared with body size

Silent owls

With their super-soft feathers and razor-sharp senses, these stealthy predators are perfectly equipped for hunting at night. They can find and catch a mouse in complete darkness.

Large tail provides control when swooping on prey.

Round face disk channels noise to ears on either side of head.

OWL OVER THE WORLD

There are about 260 species of owl, living nearly everywhere except Antarctica. Some are just 6 in (15 cm) long, others span up to 6 ft (1.8 m). Here are a few of the most eye-catching.

Barn owl
This separate family of pale, slender owls live everywhere except deserts and the poles.

Eagle-owl
The largest owls are in this group. They eat rodents, rabbits, birds, and fish.

Snowy owl
This species hunts lemmings in the icy Arctic. Feathered feet keep it warm in winter.

Long-eared owl
Lives in thick northern hemisphere forests. Those tufts are not ears, but feathers!

Elf owl
The smallest raptor of all, from Mexico, is no bigger than a sparrow.

Feathers on front edge are stiff to stop them twisting.

Eyes face forward for better depth perception.

Softly fringed feathers on back edge reduce noise.

BURROWING OWLS SCARE PREY OUT OF THEIR LAIRS BY **IMITATING** THE SOUND OF A **RATTLESNAKE!**

Outer toe pivots backward to help seize prey.

OWL **PELLETS**

Lacking teeth, carnivorous birds swallow smaller prey whole—bones, fur, and all! Every day they cough up a large clump of indigestible parts, called a pellet.

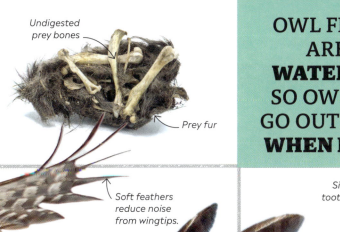

Undigested prey bones

Prey fur

Soft feathers reduce noise from wingtips.

Primary flight feathers are long and strong.

OWL FEATHERS ARE **NOT WATERPROOF**, SO OWLS DON'T GO OUT HUNTING **WHEN IT RAINS!**

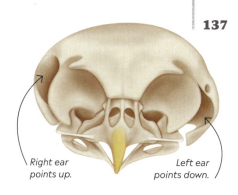

Right ear points up.

Left ear points down.

OWL **EARS**

Owls have a key adaptation to pinpoint their prey—one ear opening is higher than the other! This helps them figure out exactly where a sound is coming from when hunting.

Single egg tooth on end of beak

EGG **TOOTH**

Adult owls are toothless, but like most birds they are born with one tiny tooth on the end of their beak. Chicks use this to break out of their egg, but it falls off a few days later. Reptiles, monotremes, and even spiders have a similar tool.

OWLS CAN **TWIST THEIR HEADS** MORE THAN 180° **TO SEE BEHIND** THEM!

HUNTING **BY EAR**

An owl's ears are so sensitive that it can detect a mouse's heartbeat from 26 ft (8 m) away. This incredible hearing allows it to identify different animals by sound alone, locate and track prey under 2 ft (60 cm) of snow, and make split-second adjustments as it swoops for the catch.

Velvet-soft feather edges glide over each other noiselessly.

NOISES **OFF**

Owls have fantastic adaptations for nighttime hunting. Keen eyes and ears guide them in for the kill, while soft-fringed feathers make flight almost silent, so prey cannot hear them coming. Once the talons lock on, a single peck to the prey's spine finishes the job. This great gray owl is an expert vole-catcher.

Prey moving under the snow

Sound reaches one ear just before the other.

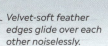

NAME THAT... BIRD OF PREY

Are you eagle-eyed and wise as an owl? Do you have a talent for talons? Swoop in and name these fantastic falcons and ravishing raptors. Can you catch the odd one out?

1 Red-tailed hawk
2 Verreaux's eagle
3 Golden eagle
4 Barn owl
5 Tawny eagle
6 Bald eagle
7 Great gray owl
8 Northern goshawk
9 Turkey vulture
10 Osprey
11 Crested caracara
12 Burrowing owl
13 Northern hawk owl
14 Philippine falconet
15 Snowy owl
16 Secretary bird
17 Tawny owl
18 Egyptian vulture
19 American black vulture
20 Great horned owl
21 White-bellied sea eagle
22 California condor
23 Common kestrel
24 King vulture
25 Peregrine falcon
26 Pel's fishing owl
27 Red kite
28 White-tailed eagle
29 Hen harrier
30 Owl butterfly
31 Eurasian eagle-owl
32 Little owl
33 Rüppell's vulture

CAN YOU SPOT THE ODD ONE OUT?

The odd one out is the owl butterfly (30). It's a butterfly, not an owl! The big, dark circles on its wings look like the eyes of an owl.

Scavenger birds

Scavenger birds are opportunistic feeders. They rarely hunt and kill their own food, but instead seek out carrion—the flesh of animals that are already dead. They pick bones clean after a predator has left, or find animals that died from other causes.

CRITICAL CLEANERS

Scavenger birds are nature's waste disposal units. Their stomach acid can dissolve bones! By gobbling up dead meat they stop it from rotting and perhaps spreading dangerous diseases. But this makes them vulnerable to toxins if the animal has been poisoned.

SAY WHAT?

Griffon vultures use at least 12 different calls to "talk" to each other about food, mating, danger, and other topics. Scientists say they may have an even wider range of calls than parrots.

The white-backed vulture is common in Africa.

ROUGH RASPS ON A VULTURE'S TONGUE HELP IT STRIP MEAT OFF BONES!

Wings are tucked in when eating to keep them clean.

TOOLS OF THE TRADE

Vultures are not built for speed, but to feed. Their beaks have to rip open much larger animals, while their big, heavy bodies must hold a lot of food at once, because it may be many days before the scavenger finds another carcass.

Vultures have weaker claws than hunters, but long toes make walking easier.

A CONDOR CAN **EAT ONE-SIXTH OF ITS BODY WEIGHT** IN ONE MEAL AND **STILL TAKE OFF!**

A marabou stork's bill can grow up to 13¾ in (35 cm) long.

MAKEUP

Egyptian vultures bathe in mud to turn their white feathers orange-brown. This "cosmetic coloration" seems to impress potential mates and may help reinforce bonds between pairs.

NAKED GREED

Like many vultures, the marabou stork has a bare head and neck for easier cleaning after reaching into carcasses. This massive bird stands up to 5 ft (1.5 m) tall, can swallow up to 2 lb (1 kg) of meat in a single gulp, and eats anything, even poop!

TOP **SCAVENGER**

The giant Andean condor of South America always eats first. Even pumas step aside from their kills to let them feed—but not from fear. By ripping open carcasses, stripping off meat, and cracking bones with their sharp, strong beaks, condors help other animals to get their food faster.

Keen eyes spot food from miles away.

Hooked beak for tearing at flesh

Long wings help to soar high in the sky to see farther.

SIGHT AND SCENT

Vultures use sharp senses to home in on food. A griffon vulture (left) can spot a carcass from 4 miles (6.4 km) away, while a turkey vulture has perhaps the best nose of any bird. It can smell a decaying corpse as small as a mouse from 1 mile (1.6 km) away.

HAVING **NO FEATHERS** ON ITS **HEAD AND NECK** HELPS A VULTURE **STAY COOL** IN THE HOT SUN!

HIGH **FLIER**

Condors in the Andes Mountains use rising currents of air called thermals to soar to heights of 21,300 ft (6,500 m). Thermals form when the Sun heats the ground, which in turn warms the air above it. As the air warms, it rises, and condors and other birds ride the swirling current upward, saving them precious energy.

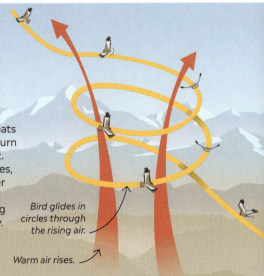

Bird glides in circles through the rising air.

Warm air rises.

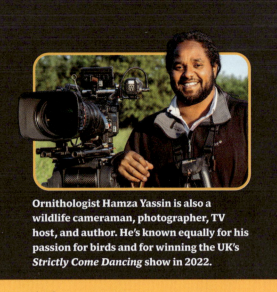

Ornithologist Hamza Yassin is also a wildlife cameraman, photographer, TV host, and author. He's known equally for his passion for birds and for winning the UK's *Strictly Come Dancing* show in 2022.

Ask an ...
ORNITHOLOGIST

Q When did you decide to be a cameraman?
A I used to watch Sir David Attenborough and Steve Irwin shows and thought they had a very cool job. I never dreamed I'd be a presenter but my idea was that if I became a cameraman I could get up close to the animals too.

Q What do you enjoy most about your job?
A I love being outdoors and learning. I am truly just a student still learning about mother nature and that's the beauty of it, there's always something new. I love being one of the only people close to the wildlife, filming it, and it doesn't know I'm there.

Q What's the hardest thing you've done to get close to a bird?
A The longest I've had to wait to capture something on film was probably about a year. The longest I've hidden continuously without moving was three days. I spend a lot of time sitting and waiting!

Q What surprises people about birds of prey?
A Just how big they are. They are so humongous—the talons of a harpy eagle are the same size as a grizzly bear's claws!

Q Can you still see interesting wild birds if you live in a town?
A Yes! There are so many beautiful birds that you can see in an urban environment, from ringneck parakeets, choughs, ravens, and peregrine falcons to starlings, ryenecks, and waxwings. In Berlin, goshawks have been spotted in the middle of the city hunting herons, and nightingales heard singing!

Q What can I do to help birds in my local area?
A Put fresh water and food out, especially in the colder months. Once the feeder is empty, disinfect it before you refill it, to stop disease spreading.

Q How can children take great wildlife photos?
A Patience and practice! It doesn't matter if you use a phone or a camera. Get up before sunrise, go out, drag an adult with you, see what you can find.

Q Which bird would do best in a dance competition?
A Hard to say! Many birds dance to show off and attract a mate. Swans and flamingos do elaborate dances and eider ducks knock their head back, puff out their pink rosy chest feathers, and sound like a surprised person making a strange "awah" noise!

URBAN **NEST**

The world's fastest creature, the peregrine falcon, makes its home in urban environments as well as in the countryside. This female, caught on camera by photographer Luke Massey, is returning to her young chicks nesting in a makeshift shelter on a skyscraper balcony in Chicago.

Soaring seabirds

Feathers not waterproofed for diving

Many seabirds live most of their lives out over the open ocean. Using air currents to stay aloft, some of these majestic gliders return to land only to breed and care for their young.

FLYING **FRIGATE BIRD**

Frigate birds are extremely efficient fliers and foragers. They never swim, dive underwater, or land to take prey, but swoop to seize fish and squid from the water's surface without missing a beat.

Males inflate their red throat pouch to display and call to females.

Gland near nostril excretes excess salt

Long, narrow wings for efficient gliding

Sharp, hooked beak to grab slippery fish and squid

WIND AND **WAVES**

Albatrosses fly in broad loops, using a method called dynamic soaring to harness the energy of the wind. This allows them to travel vast distances with their long, thin wings outstretched, which takes much less energy than flapping flight.

1. Albatross flies into the wind to gain lift from oncoming air.

2. Once high up, in faster air, it turns to glide with the wind.

3. The albatross glides downward and downwind, reaching up to 75 mph (120 kph).

4. At sea level, it turns back into the wind to gain lift for a new loop.

PETREL **POWER**

Giant petrels land on the water to gorge on fish and squid, but taking off on a full stomach is hard work for such a heavy bird. Usually a flapping run-up across the waves does the trick, but sometimes they have to vomit up some food before they can take to the air!

THE **WINGSPAN** OF A **WANDERING ALBATROSS** IS NEARLY **DOUBLE** A HUMAN ARM SPAN!

SHEARWATERS FLY **INTO THE EYE** OF A **STORM** TO AVOID BEING **BLOWN** ONTO LAND!

PIRATES **OF THE AIR**

Frigate birds chase other birds such as boobies, grab their tail feathers, and shake them to make the birds regurgitate their catch. They then dive to gobble up the food before it falls into the sea. Young frigate birds practice by dropping sticks for each other!

Long, forked tail spreads to maneuver or becomes narrow to reduce drag.

TINY **TRAVELER**

The smallest ocean-going bird is the storm petrel. Barely bigger than a swallow, it spends its life at sea, only coming to land to breed on remote islands. It has a unique ability to hover just above the water by flying directly into the wind at low speed, ready to snatch up small prey.

DYNAMIC **DISPLAY**

Albatrosses stage an intricate mating ritual, nodding and circling heads, and rapidly clacking their bills. This forms a lifelong bond, but pairs come together only once every two years to breed.

The male shows off his spectacular wingspan to attract a mate. He also utters a startling shriek, or "moo"!

Diving **birds**

These flying sea birds don't just pluck fish from the water's surface—they plunge into the ocean and swim beneath the waves to pursue their prey.

Wings flatten for maximum streamlining.

Feet tuck in to reduce drag from the water.

GULPING **GANNETS**

Gannets plunge from the sky like a bullet, making themselves as streamlined as possible before hitting the water—one wrong move could mean a broken neck! The speed takes them straight to their prey for a competitive feeding frenzy, as they catch and swallow fish underwater before a rival can rob them.

Sharp, heavy bill helps gannets catch large fish for their size.

Eyes adjust instantly to see underwater.

Webbed feet propel gannet toward fish.

DIVERSE **DIVERS**

Different birds have many ways to hunt at sea. Plunge divers enter the water at high speed from the air, pursuit divers land first then swim down using their feet or wings, and dip-feeders pluck prey from the surface. The deepest divers are penguins, but among flying birds a murre holds the record, at 690 ft (210 m) down!

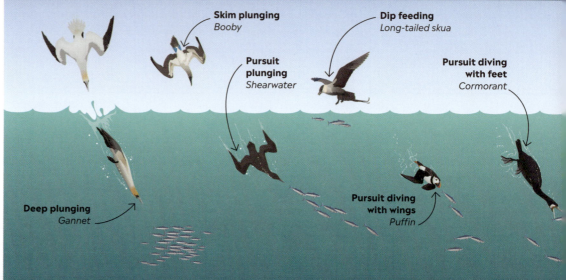

Skim plunging
Booby

Dip feeding
Long-tailed skua

Pursuit plunging
Shearwater

Pursuit diving with feet
Cormorant

Deep plunging
Gannet

Pursuit diving with wings
Puffin

Sand eels are the main prey of British puffins.

Large beak holds 10–60 fish at once.

Spikes pin fish to roof of mouth.

FISH **FACE**

When they have hungry pufflings to feed, puffins try to bring back as many fish as possible. A spiked tongue holds the catch against the roof of their mouth, so the beak can still open to grab more fish.

Claws for defense and digging nest burrows

Webbed feet are used to steer underwater.

Wings both swim and steer underwater.

Water pressure forces air out of surface feathers.

THE **HEALTHIER** THE BLUE-FOOTED **BOOBY,** THE **BLUER ITS FEET!**

CLIFF **NESTING**

Guillemots, like many diving birds, nest on sheer cliffs. This precarious perch keeps their eggs safe from most predators, but makes leaving home a big step—at three weeks old, chicks leap from the ledges, flapping their young wings hard, and splash into the sea!

A **BABY PUFFIN** IS CALLED A **PUFFLING!**

WET AND **DRY**

Cormorants oil their feathers less than other divers, so they don't trap air to stay dry underwater. Instead, water forces air out, making the bird heavier so it can dive more easily. On surfacing, the feather structure drives out water to dry.

Spreading their feathers after a dive squeezes out water.

A **DIVING GANNET** HITS THE WATER AT **50 MPH (80 KPH)!**

FEEDING **YOUNG**

Pelicans don't carry food in their pouch—it's just used as a fishing net—so they swallow their catch on the spot. Like many birds, they regurgitate partially digested meals to feed their young, and the chick has to reach right into their throat to eat.

Scan for fish beneath the waves.

Spot target, start descent.

Turn wingtips back to reduce drag for a faster dive.

Wings tuck back for a streamlined entry into water.

Splashdown! Pelican seizes a fish underwater.

DEADLY **DIVER**

The brown pelican is the only type that dives. It spots prey from the air, tracks its direction, and plunges. Air pockets in its chest cushion the impact as it hits the water, and when it opens its bill underwater to grab a fish, the pouch acts like a parachute to slow it down.

POUCH **POUNCE**

Dalmatian pelicans are the largest in the world at up to 6 ft (1.8 m) long, and eat around 2 lb (1.2 kg) of fish each day. They swim smoothly toward an unsuspecting fish, then dunk their bill suddenly into the water to scoop it up.

Each wing can be 5 ft (1.5 m) long.

Yellow hook at tip of upper bill helps grip slippery fish.

SUPER **SCOOPER**

When a pelican lunges for a fish, water pressure pushes the two sides of its lower jaw apart and expands the elastic pouch between them. The full pouch is up to three times the size of the bird's stomach, so it has to drain the water before swallowing.

1. Plunge and scoop
The pelican lunges with an open bill, collecting a mouthful of fish and water, then closes and raises its bill.

2. Shake and drain
Bringing the bill back toward its body to compress the pouch, the bird tilts or shakes its bill to expel water.

3. Giant gulp!
The pelican tosses its head back, straightens its neck, and swallows the fish head-first.

Powerful
pelicans

These large, social fish-eaters can soar like an eagle and paddle fast on the water. Some hunt in groups, others use stealth or even dive from the sky, but all grab prey in their famous stretchy pouch.

THE **AMERICAN WHITE PELICAN** CAN HOLD **MORE THAN 3 GALLONS** (14 LITERS) OF WATER IN ITS **POUCH!**

Clear additional eyelid protects eye from water.

Nostrils are closed off to keep water out.

A thin bone either side of the pouch holds it in place.

Big webbed feet for landing and swimming on water

FISHING **PARTY**

Some pelican species hunt in teams. Australian, American white, and great white pelicans form a semicircle and swim in line toward the shore, beating the water with their feet and wings to drive fish into the shallows. Once trapped, the fish are easy pickings for the gang.

PELICANS CAN HAVE A **WINGSPAN** OF **MORE THAN 10 FT (3 M)!**

TOP MIGRATIONS

Birds migrate for a range of reasons, from finding food and warmer climates to locating a new nesting spot. Here are a few record holders.

LONGEST NONSTOP MIGRATION
Bar-tailed godwit, 6,835 miles (11,000 km) from Alaska to New Zealand

22,965 FT

HIGHEST MIGRATION
Bar-headed goose, 22,965 ft (7,000 m) altitude over the Himalayas

LONGEST MIGRATION OF ANY ANIMAL
Arctic tern, 55,923 miles (90,000 km) per year

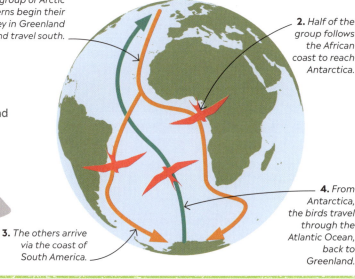

1. A group of Arctic terns begin their journey in Greenland and travel south.

2. Half of the group follows the African coast to reach Antarctica.

3. The others arrive via the coast of South America.

4. From Antarctica, the birds travel through the Atlantic Ocean, back to Greenland.

SMALLEST BIRD

At just 2 in (5.5 cm), bee hummingbirds are the smallest birds in the world. These tiny creatures are found in Cuba and weigh as much as a cashew.

FACT PACK!
TAKING FLIGHT

Flying birds take to the skies to catch prey or escape from predators. Some migrate across the world in long, epic journeys, others soar high above mountain ranges, and a few are super fast.

FASTEST BIRDS

Some birds are known for their impressive speeds. With its long, pointed wings and large chest muscles, the peregrine falcon takes the top spot as the world's fastest animal.

FASTEST DIVING SPEED
Peregrine falcons reach speeds of 199 mph (320 kph) when diving after prey.

FASTEST LEVEL FLIGHT
The gray-headed albatross can fly at 79 mph (127 kph).

FASTEST FLAPPER
A diving ruby-throated hummingbird beats its wings 200 times per second.

FASTEST LONG-HAUL FLIGHT
Great snipes travel 4,200 miles (6,800 km) at a speed of 60 mph (97 kph).

HIGHEST FLIGHT

Different bird species can fly to astounding altitudes. This chart compares the top five highest fliers.

BEARDED VULTURE 23,950 ft (7,300 m)

ALPINE CHOUGH 26,245 ft (8,000 m)

WHOOPER SWAN 32,808 ft (10,000 m)

COMMON CRANE 32,808 ft (10,000 m)

RÜPPELL'S VULTURE 37,000 ft (11,300 m)

BOEING 737 PLANE 41,000 ft (12,496 m)

STAYING ALOFT

The common swift holds the record for the longest time spent in the air by a bird without landing. For 10 months it sleeps, drinks, and mates while in the air as it travels from Europe to sub-Saharan Africa and back.

Wingspan reaches up to 18 in (48 cm).

AMAZING WINGSPANS

Wingspan measures the distance from one wingtip to the other. The biggest ever recorded belongs to a fossil of a *Pelagornis sandersi*, an extinct bird that roamed Earth 25 million years ago.

BIGGEST BIRD WINGSPAN EVER
Pelagornis sandersi: 24 ft (7.4 m)

BIGGEST LIVING BIRD WINGSPAN
Wandering albatross: 11 ft 11 in (3.63 m)

BIGGEST FRESHWATER BIRD WINGSPAN
Great white pelican: 11 ft 10 in (3.6 m)

BIGGEST WINGSPAN OF A LAND BIRD
Andean condor: 10 ft (3.2 m)

HUMAN ARM SPAN
5 ft 8 in (1.73 m)

HEAVY FLIERS

Some flying birds are heavier than they look! The heftiest is the kori bustard, which weighs more than 3 bowling balls.

KORI BUSTARD 42 lb (19 kg)

GREAT BUSTARD 40 lb (18 kg)

MUTE SWAN 33 lb (15 kg)

GREAT WHITE PELICAN 33 lb (15 kg)

ANDEAN CONDOR 33 lb (15 kg)

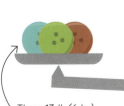
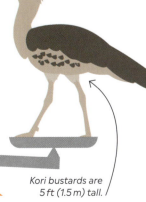

Three 13-lb (6-kg) bowling balls

Kori bustards are 5 ft (1.5 m) tall.

PATTERN IN THE SKY

Geese fly in a V-formation to save energy. The flaps of the leading birds create an updraft of air the birds behind can ride on.

QUICK NAPS

While flying over water for weeks at a time, great frigate birds sleep for about 45 minutes per day in quick 10-second bursts. They do this by shutting down one half of their brain and keeping the other half awake to avoid crashing.

Penguins
on parade

Paddlelike wings and webbed feet leave these birds flightless and slow-moving on land. But in the water they are skilled swimmers, as their dense bones help them to dive deeply and their small, stiff feathers make them streamlined.

EMPEROR PENGUINS ARE THE ONLY BIRDS THAT FEED THEIR YOUNG BY REGURGITATING A MILKY "CURD" FROM THEIR ESOPHAGUS!

TOTALLY **TROPICAL**

Galápagos penguins are the only species that live north of the equator, in the islands off the coast of Ecuador. In 1982, extreme weather killed off fish around the islands and 77 percent of the penguins starved. The population is slowly rebuilding, and today there are almost 2,000 Galápagos penguins.

LINE UP! LINE UP!

There are 18 species of penguin, 11 of them endangered. They are native to the Southern hemisphere, and most live in colder climes, in and around Antarctica. All penguins are flightless and eat fish, krill, and squid. Six species are below.

Pupils become square to limit exposure to light.

49 in (1.25 m)

39½ in (1 m)

29½ in (0.75 m)

19¾ in (0.5 m)

9¾ in (0.25 m)

0

Feet have a pouch for carrying eggs.

WHEN HUNTING, EMPEROR PENGUINS CAN DIVE TO 1,600 FT (500 M) AND HOLD THEIR BREATH FOR 27 MINUTES!

Emperor penguin
Up to 47 in (1.2 m) tall, this is the largest penguin. Bigger than most other birds, they weigh up to 88 lb (40 kg).

King penguin
Growing to 35½ in (90 cm) tall, these birds can eat between 400 and 2,000 fish in one day!

PENGUINS' PREDATORS

Penguins' speed and agility in the water makes them hard for aquatic hunters such as leopard seals and orcas to catch. On land, however, penguin chicks and eggs are vulnerable to birds such as giant petrels or a skua like this, as well as rats, foxes, and snakes.

Gentoo penguin egg

SLIDERS AND DIVERS

Long bodies, short legs, and feet set far back on their bodies force penguins to waddle. So rather than waste energy walking like this, penguins slide over ice on their stomachs. When diving into the water their sleek shape makes it easy for them to quickly reach the depths.

CROWDED COLONIES

Penguins breed in large colonies called rookeries. One colony of chinstrap penguins (like the ones below) in the South Sandwich Islands in the South Atlantic Ocean is home to up to two million birds! Yet, even amid all the noise, chaos, and movement, penguin pairs and their chicks are always able to find each other by their individual calls.

ADÉLIE PENGUINS EAT SO MUCH KRILL (A PALE RED CRUSTACEAN) IT TURNS THEIR POOP PINK!

Longest crest feathers of any penguin

Crest of yellow-orange feathers helps macaroni penguins attract a mate.

Pattern of black spots unique to each animal

Blue feathers are unique to this species.

Macaroni penguin
All adults of this species have red eyes. Males sometimes fight by slapping beaks. Females usually lay two eggs and discard the smaller one.

African penguin
Bare skin above each eye keeps these birds cool in the South African heat. They build nests lined with guano (bird poop).

Northern rockhopper
As their name suggests, these penguins can leap over rocky surfaces with ease.

Little penguin
The world's smallest penguin at just 13 in (33 cm) in height, it is found only in Australia and New Zealand.

Known as The Penguin Lady, Dyan deNapoli helped save 40,000 penguins from an oil spill in South Africa in 2000. Her rapport with the birds is obvious—this curious King penguin approached Dyan to check out her camera!

Ask the …
PENGUIN LADY

Q What made you want to become a penguinologist?

A I call it my accidental career! I'd always dreamed of working with dolphins, but I fell in love with penguins during a college placement at the New England Aquarium. I was later hired as a Penguin Aquarist. Everything I know about penguins, I learned on the job.

Q What did you face when you arrived at the site of the oil spill?

A I was shocked to see so many oil-covered birds. Helping them was the most grueling experience, but also the most rewarding.

Q How do you clean a penguin that is covered in oil?

A We spray them with a degreaser to loosen the oil, then one person holds the bird in hot, soapy water, while someone else scrubs each feather. It can take an hour to remove the oil. Then we hose off the soap, so the penguin can waterproof its feathers again.

Q What happened to the penguins after they were rescued?

A The fully rehabilitated penguins returned to the wild. The rescued penguins lived just as long as un-oiled ones, and bred successfully.

Q What steps are scientists taking to ensure the survival of penguins?

A Lots! From hand-raising abandoned chicks to providing artificial nests. And YOU can help scientists monitor penguin populations by counting them online at penguinwatch.org.

Q Does climate change affect penguins?

A Sadly, yes. Among many other things, it is harder for penguins to find food, because global warming displaces the cold water currents that carry their prey.

Q Do you have a favorite penguin?

A Yes, Sanccob! He was the first chick I raised at the aquarium, and we formed a close bond. He would call out whenever he saw me.

PLUCKY PENGUINS

King penguins live and breed in large colonies on several sub-Antarctic islands, primarily in the Southern Ocean. At the start of the mating season, male King penguins will court females with a ritual display of bowing, stretching, and raising their beaks in the air. Sometimes they may even slap other males with their wings. This plucky behavior is thought to fend off competitors.

STORKS POOP ON THEIR LEGS AND FEET TO KEEP THEM COOL—WHITE REFLECTS HEAT!

Wings raised in courtship display to attract females

Each bird flies behind and above previous bird's wing.

TEAM PURSUIT

Wood storks and other species fly in V-formation to use the "upwash" from other birds' wings. This rising air means those behind use less energy to stay aloft. Birds take turns flying at the front of the V, so they all share the benefits.

SENSITIVE SPOONBILL

Spoonbills are named for the shape of their long bills, which they sweep from side to side in muddy water, mouth slightly open. When special detectors called papillae sense small fish or crustaceans, the bill snaps shut, trapping prey inside.

Flat, spoon-shaped bill has a large surface area.

Sensory pit

Roseate spoonbills go bald on top as they age.

Sensory system
The bill is packed with tiny holes full of nerve endings. These nerves detect subtle changes in pressure when prey brush past.

Feathery "pants" on upper leg for warmth

THE BLACK-WINGED STILT HAS THE LONGEST LEGS FOR ITS BODY SIZE OF ANY BIRD!

Long-legged waterbirds

Many waterbirds stand tall on long, stilt-like legs, which keep their bodies above the water as they fish for prey around lakes, swamps, and mudflats.

GIANT GULP!

Waterbirds cannot break up their prey, so they have to eat their meals whole. By maneuvering fish head-first and straightening its neck, a heron can gulp down a surprisingly large catch, but sometimes the mouthful is just too big!

AMAZING FEET

Waders have long toes to spread their weight and avoid sinking into the mud, but jacanas take this one step further. They are light enough to walk across lily pads in search of prey that lives underneath the leaves.

The American flamingo is one of the largest waterbirds at 5 ft (1.5 m) tall.

ENGAGING EGRET

Male great egrets grow fancy plumes for breeding season. They pick a nest site, scare off rivals, then sway, bow, and stretch their neck to attract a mate. After breeding season, the plumes drop off!

EGG MOUND

Flamingos only produce a single egg at a time. To keep it safe from flash floods and baking heat, they build a waterside nest of mud, straw, pebbles, and feathers. The mound is up to 12 in (30 cm) high and can absorb water from below to keep the egg cool on hot days.

Tiny growths called lamellae catch food.

Tongue

Deep lower bill holds tongue in a V-shaped groove.

Egg kept safe in shallow bowl

THE PINK COLOR OF FLAMINGOS COMES FROM EATING LOTS OF ALGAE AND CRUSTACEANS!

Head down
Flamingos only feed upside down! Their tongue acts like a pump, sucking water in and out across a filter in their mouth to catch algae, crustaceans, and seeds.

MIGRATING **CANADA GEESE** CAN **FLY UP TO 1,500 MILES** (2,400 KM) IN **24 HOURS!**

WEBBED **WONDERS**

Waterfowl are birds that live on or close to water, including geese, swans, and ducks. Most have short legs and long toes with webbed feet for swimming, and broad "duck-bills" for filtering food from the water or grabbing plants. Tightly interlocking contour feathers keep them dry.

— *Mandarin duck*

Males are brightly colored to attract female mates.

Sharp spurs are at least ¾ in (2 cm) long.

Bird spreads wings to appear larger and scare off opponents.

SHOWING OFF

In breeding season, male Golden Pheasants compete for mates, bobbing their heads and puffing out their chests to impress rivals with their size and color. If that fails, they fight, slashing at each other with sharp spurs on the backs of their legs.

Finely striped tail is twice as long as his body.

Fabulous fowl

There are nearly 500 species of fowl, from the ducks, geese, and swans that live on water to land-based cousins such as pheasants and peacocks. Their heavy bodies and muscular legs are adapted to swimming or walking, and males often grow colorful feathers to attract a mate.

EGGS-AUSTING!

Female wood ducks must eat 2.6 oz (75 g) of small invertebrates such as insects and worms to produce one 1.5 oz (43 g) egg. That's about 2,400 prey in total, or one every 12 seconds for eight hours!

1.5 oz

2.6 oz

Wood duck eggs are around 2⅓ in (6 cm) long.

LEAP OF FAITH

Many fowl nest on the ground or in tree hollows, so their chicks are not well hidden. Instead, they are born ready to run, swim, or hide soon after hatching. These day-old wood ducks leap out of their nest to join their parents in the water, even though they cannot yet fly.

Wood ducklings fall up to 65 ft (20 m) and land safely.

SNACKING SWAN

Swans use their long necks to forage up to 3 ft (1 m) deep in river and lake bottoms for vegetation and small fish to eat. Beating their webbed feet in the water helps loosen plants and clingy invertebrates such as snails and shellfish.

Swans don't have teeth—serrated edges on their beaks help them grip their food.

Males poke their beaks into the mound to test the temperature.

Eggs remain at 91.4°F (33°C).

Mounds are around 13 ft (4 m) wide and 3 ft (1 m) deep.

TEMPERATURE CONTROL

Australia's chicken-size malleefowl build mounds for females to lay their eggs in. The male covers the eggs with leaves, which decompose, generating heat to incubate the eggs. He adds or removes leaves to adjust the temperature.

ATTENTION SEEKER

When a peacock wants to attract a peahen, he opens his fan of feathers and shakes them at her. Feathers can be blue, green, gold, or brown, and have an "eye," or ocellus, at the end. They fall off, or molt, after the mating season, then regrow.

A peahen's dull color acts as camouflage when nesting.

The fan, or train, has up to 200 feathers.

THERE ARE MORE THAN 24 BILLION CHICKENS IN THE WORLD!

Hummingbirds and swifts

These surprising relations are fantastic fliers. Swifts swoop and glide tirelessly in the skies for months at a time without landing, while no bird flaps faster than the hovering hummingbird.

Sword-billed hummingbird

RECORD BEATING

Hummingbirds beat their wings incredibly fast. The exact rate varies between species, ranging from 12 to 80 times per second when hovering!

FANTASTIC FEEDER

Hummingbirds are expert feeders—they can hover anywhere and reach deep inside flowers with their long tongue. This nimble flight takes a lot of energy, so they have to visit hundreds of flowers and eat up to three times their body weight in sugary nectar each day.

Eye detects motion twice as fast as a human eye.

Tongue extends and retracts up to 13 times per second.

Forked tip grabs nectar, rather than sucking it up.

Feather structure reflects light as shimmering iridescent colors.

Small, lightweight feet save weight, but are too weak to walk.

BABY SWIFTS DO **PUSH-UPS IN THE NEST** TO PREPARE THEIR **WINGS TO FLY!**

Fewer tail feathers to save weight

Outer feather vibrates in flight—in some species they whistle when diving!

HOVER **CRAFT**

Hummingbirds are perfectly adapted for hovering, with massive muscles for their size, hypermobile shoulder joints, and stiffened wing bones.

Short, stiff wing bones

Hummingbird

Muscles make up 30 percent of body weight.

Typical bird

Muscles make up 15 percent of bodyweight.

Shoulder joint is so flexible that wings can move at any angle.

Larger muscles than in other birds pull wings back up. This resets the wings faster between each beat.

HUMMINGBIRDS ARE **THE ONLY BIRDS** THAT CAN **FLY BACKWARD!**

OUT OF **THIN AIR**

Swifts' legs are too weak to walk or perch—they can only cling to a vertical surface. To build a nest, they catch scraps of plant and feather in mid-air, or break off twigs with their feet while flying, then stick them to a wall using saliva!

WATER **TO GO**

Swifts cannot take off again if they land on the ground or water, so they snatch insects to eat in mid-air, wash when it rains, and skim the surface of lakes to scoop a sip of water. One wrong move and they could be fish food.

Lower jaw extended to catch the water

LONG **HAUL**

With one of the longest migrations of any bird, common swifts commute an incredible 14,000 miles (22,000 km) each year, crossing over 25 countries. They even sleep in mid-air, and only stop to lay eggs and feed their chicks.

Slender, scythe-shaped wings

NO **RELATION**

Swifts can be hard to distinguish from agile swallows and martins, but these two belong to an entirely different branch of feathered fliers. Here's how to tell them apart.

Forked tail with "streamers"

Pale belly extends to upper wing

Dark brown all over

Pale throat patch

White patch on rump

House martin
Smallest of the three, with a white belly and black wings.

Barn swallow
Smaller than a swift, with a pale or rusty belly and dark head.

Common swift
Brown body, short forked tail, and long, boomerang-shaped wings.

TYPES OF NEST

Birds use a variety of materials to make their nests, from feathers to mud pellets. While some birds build their nests from scratch, others reuse old nests and other structures.

ROBINS
Robins build nests in a cup shape from sticks, grass, and leaves.

CLIFF SWALLOWS
Cliff swallows mold mud pellets to form a tubular-shaped nest.

GREBES
Grebes, a water bird, make floating nests from reeds and mud.

BLUEBIRDS
Bluebirds make their nests in tree hollows or in birdhouses.

FACT PACK!
NESTS AND EGGS

Birds do not live in their nests—they use them to raise their young and lay eggs, which vary in color, shape, and size.

BIRDSONG

In hot weather, zebra finches sing an "incubation call" to their eggs. This makes the chicks grow slower and weigh less after hatching to cope better in the heat.

TIME TO HATCH

The time an egg takes to hatch depends on the bird species, and can vary from two weeks to over two months. This chart compares the incubation periods of different birds.

ROBIN EGGS 13 days
CROW EGGS 18 days
CHICKEN EGGS 21 days
BALD EAGLE EGGS 35 days
OSTRICH EGGS 48 days
MALLEEFOWL EGGS 60 days
PENGUIN EGGS 65–70 days
WANDERING ALBATROSS EGGS 77 days

EGG PROTECTION

Birds are fiercely protective of their eggs. They use a range of tactics to hide them and keep enemies at bay, from camouflage to building nests near other predators.

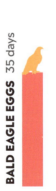

CAMOUFLAGE
Ringed plovers build nests on shingle or sandy beaches, giving their speckled eggs the perfect camouflage.

BROOD POUCH
Male emperor penguins keep their eggs warm enough to survive by standing and covering them with a brood pouch, which is a flap of feathered skin.

RECORD BREAKERS

BIGGEST NEST
The largest recorded bird nest was built in 1963 by two bald eagles in Florida. It was 9 ft (2.9 m) wide and 20 ft (6 m) deep.

SMALLEST NEST
Hummingbirds make the smallest bird nests. They can measure a mere 1 in (2.5 cm) wide and hold eggs the size of coffee beans.

OLDEST NEST
The world's oldest bird of prey nest was found in Greenland on a cliff edge. Up to 2,360 years old, it is still used by gyrfalcons today.

LARGEST COMMUNAL NEST
The sociable weaver in Southern Africa lives in a gigantic bird nest with multiple chambers. Some can house a whopping 500 birds.

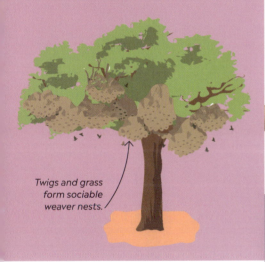

Twigs and grass form sociable weaver nests.

Chicken egg shells are covered in more than **7,000** pores, which let carbon dioxide out and allow oxygen in!

CLUTCH SIZE

A clutch is the number of eggs that a bird lays in one nesting attempt, which often takes place over several days. This chart compares the clutch sizes of different bird species.

GRAY PARTRIDGE: up to 22 eggs

WOOD DUCK: 12 eggs

HOUSE WREN: 8 eggs

AMERICAN ROBIN: 4 eggs

BALD EAGLE: 2 eggs

EMPEROR PENGUIN: 1 egg

LARGEST EGG

The largest eggs ever laid were by the now-extinct elephant bird. The eggs of these flightless birds were big enough to hold the contents of up to seven ostrich eggs.

CHICKEN EGG
Measures 2¼ in (5.6 cm) long.

OSTRICH EGG
Measures 6 in (15 cm) long.

ELEPHANT BIRD EGG
Measured 13 in (33 cm) long.

SNEAKY PARENTS

Brown-headed cowbirds are brood parasites. Instead of raising their own young, they lay eggs in the nests of other birds, which look after the cowbird chicks as their own.

Defenseless young rely on their mother to drive away predators.

MOBBING
Smaller birds often work together to scare away or distract predators, keeping them away from the nest. Mobbing birds can even poop on predators!

PROTECTED BY WASPS
In an unusual approach, yellow-rumped caciques live near wasps' nests for protection. Most predators keep well clear!

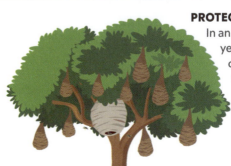

Kaleidoscopic kingfishers

Kingfishers are colorful hunters with compact bodies; big heads; and sharp, heavy beaks. Most live in tropical regions and, despite their name, eat a wide variety of prey.

Minnows, along with sticklebacks, are this species' main prey.

Long, pointed beak is large for its body size, but very streamlined.

Colorful plumage helps attract a mate and scare off rivals.

Compact, stocky body for swift dives and heavy lifting

Special "powder down" feathers keep out water.

FANTASTIC **FISHER**

A river kingfisher powers itself into the air with a fish in its beak. It will stun the minnow on a branch before eating. This expert hunter sits stock-still on a branch, bobs its head to judge the depth of a fish, then plunges. Its long, sharp beak is perfectly shaped for entry.

ONLY HALF OF ALL KINGFISHERS **SPECIALIZE IN** EATING **FISH!**

HUNGRY **MOUTHS**

With six or seven hungry chicks to feed, parents catch up to 120 fish a day for their brood—that's one every 8 minutes per pair! Chicks have such strong stomach acid that it dissolves their food, bones and all. After 25 days in the burrow, the fledglings emerge. Their parents feed them for a few days, then drive them away to find their own territory.

THE PIED KINGFISHER IS THE **LARGEST** BIRD THAT CAN **HOVER!**

Long flight feathers spread for maximum lift.

DINNER **DATE**

In breeding season, male kingfishers court females with food offerings such as this tasty frog. If the gift is refused, the male will eat it himself and continue the search for a mate.

Black-capped kingfisher

FOREST **FISHER**

Tree kingfishers don't catch fish, but hunt small invertebrates, amphibians, and reptiles. Rather than burrowing, some nest in termite mounds, which keep a constant temperature perfect for incubating eggs.

FEARLESS **FEEDER!**

Kookaburras are the largest kingfishers. Famous for a cackling laugh and dangerous diet, they can kill a snake up to 3 ft 3 in (1m) long by grabbing it behind the head and smacking it on the ground.

Bee-eaters
This bird can grab a bee, bash it on a branch, cut off the stinger, and swallow the rest! Watch for the long central tail feather, which rollers do not have.

Rollers
Named for their spectacular tumbling courtship display of mid-air loops and dives, rollers gather in groups to feast on locusts.

Hoopoes
Hoopoes often walk along the floor to browse for insects with their downward-curved beaks. Their crest rises when they are excited.

COLORFUL **COUSINS**

Kingfishers' relatives share their vivid colors and the long, pointed beaks that make them fearsome predators. They also nest in tree-holes, burrows dug into sloping soil, or termite mounds.

Woodpeckers and toucans

These brilliant-beaked birds both live in forests and nest in tree holes, but their bills have evolved in different ways. Woodpeckers delve into trees for live prey, while toucans mostly pick fruit.

Short wings for brief flights

TOP **BILLING**

Toucans use their giant bills to pluck seeds and berries that other birds cannot reach. Four times the size of a toucan's head, the beak displays dazzling colors to attract a mate, and even doubles as a dueling weapon.

Beak coated in tough keratin

Hollow center

Light but strong network of bony fibers

V shape helps channel food to mouth.

Serrated edge helps crack nuts and peel fruit.

Food picked with bill tip, then tossed down throat

Two front claws and two at the back help toucan grip and climb.

HOLLOW **BEAK**

A hollow center and many smaller holes make the toucan's beak much lighter—if it were solid, the bird would fall over! The huge surface area helps toucans stay cool in hot weather—they increase blood flow to their beaks to shed heat.

SHOCK **ABSORBER**

Woodpeckers' heads undergo G-forces of up to 1,200 g when pecking trees. That's 12 times enough to concuss a human! Scientists are still researching how the birds hammer so hard and so often without brain injuries.

Red-breasted toucan

Abandoned hole of woodpecker or other animal

NEST **HOLE**

Toucans and woodpeckers nest in tree cavities to keep their eggs safely hidden. Toucans cannot dig their own, so use other animals' old holes. Their chicks are born with a small bill and stay in the nest for at least six weeks until ready to feed themselves.

TOUCANS ARE **NOT GREAT FLIERS.** THEY ONLY FLAP FROM **ONE TREE TO THE NEXT!**

TOUCANS HAVE **FENCING MATCHES** WITH THEIR **BEAKS** TO SET THE **PECKING ORDER** IN GROUPS!

Large tail for balance when climbing

Tongue stored in tubes all the way around skull

ACORN **STASH**

Every fall, acorn woodpeckers store thousands of acorns in individually pecked holes. Each takes 20 minutes to drill, and a small group works together to build and defend its "granary" year after year.

Muscles contract to push tongue around and out.

Long, bristled tongue to extract grubs from trees

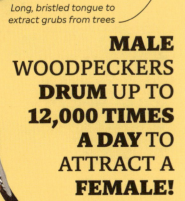

MALE WOODPECKERS **DRUM** UP TO **12,000 TIMES A DAY** TO ATTRACT A **FEMALE!**

TONGUE **TIED**

Toucans and woodpeckers have incredibly long tongues, which they poke into trees for food. When not in use, the woodpecker's tongue curls all the way round its skull to the base of its beak, and may help cushion the shock of hammering!

Acorn stashed for when food is scarce

Preening parrots

These flamboyant fliers are colorful, noisy, and very clever. Sharing a strong, curved beak, paired claws, and vivid plumage, most parrots live in tropical and subtropical regions. Some sociable species are uncanny mimics and copy the sounds of other animals, including humans!

Broad wings for fast take-offs

MATES **FOR LIFE**

Many parrots are loyal lovers who stay together for life—about 30 years for scarlet macaws like these two! They reinforce their bond by preening each other's feathers and picking off parasites.

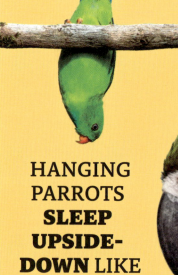

HANGING PARROTS **SLEEP UPSIDE-DOWN** LIKE BATS!

Blue-and-yellow macaw, one of the larger species.

Strong, curved beak ideal for cracking nuts

THE **PARROT FAMILY**

There are around 430 species of parrot. They probably evolved in or near Australasia, where New Zealand parrots and cockatoos still live. True parrots include parakeets, lories, and lorikeets.

Kakapo

New Zealand parrots
Kakapo and kea exist only in New Zealand.

Sulfur-crested cockatoo

Cockatoo
Noisy parrots with a movable crest

Green-winged macaw

True parrot
Clever, hook-billed birds such as macaws

Plum-headed parakeet

Parakeet
Small true parrots, mostly green

Rainbow lorikeet

Lory & lorikeet
Rainbow-colored nectar lickers

Tiny papillae stand up when tongue extends

NECTAR POINTS

Unlike other true parrots, lories (left) and lorikeets have brush tongues. The tip is covered in tiny hairlike papillae that collect nectar from flowers. These delicate brushes fold away when not in use.

THE **BUFF-FACED PYGMY PARROT** IS ABOUT THE **LENGTH** OF AN ADULT **HUMAN'S FINGER.**

ONE OF A **KIND**

The kakapo is a large, nocturnal, flightless parrot native to New Zealand. With a pale, owllike face, strong legs, and booming mating call, it is unlike any other parrot. Despite being flightless, it remains an agile climber and can use its wings as a parachute.

SUPER **SPEAKERS**

Parrots possess a special "song system"—an area in the brain for learning and producing new sounds. While many birds can imitate individual sounds, only a few parrot species can mimic human words and voices. One African Grey learned 1,700 words!

Bright colors help parrots recognize their own kind.

MACAW **WOW!**

Parrots are strong fliers and nimble climbers, able to use their beak like a hand to grab branches. Their beak cracks nuts, a dry scaly tongue can tap into fruit, and they hold food in one claw while they eat.

Large tail helps the parrot maneuver.

THE OLDEST KNOWN BIRD, A PINK COCKATOO CALLED "COOKIE," LIVED TO THE AGE OF 83!

Parrots have two facing pairs of claws to climb and pick up food. Most birds have three claws at the front, one at the back.

ZEBRA FINCHES SING SLOWLY AND REPEAT PHRASES TO HELP THEIR YOUNG LEARN TUNES!

Sitting pretty

Sixty percent of all birds are passerines, often called "perching birds." Many of these are also songbirds, which learn to sing complex tunes. A few can imitate almost anything they hear!

When breeding, males grow brilliant blue plumage to attract females.

PERCHING PATTERN

Passerines have four toes—three facing forward, one backward. An automatic locking system, common to most birds, clamps their feet shut when perched so they need less effort to hold on and can grip even when asleep. These red-legged honeycreepers don't have to worry about falling off.

Automatic perching

Muscle bends leg.

Tendon pulled tight around heel

Tightening tendon pulls claws shut.

Claws locked in place until leg straightens

SHAKE A **TAIL FEATHER**

Tail can be up to 22 in (55 cm) long.

Male perching birds compete for mates by singing, dancing, giving gifts, or even fighting. The superb lyrebird grows 16 long tail feathers to show off in extravagant courtship displays. He struts his stuff and sings while vibrating and fanning his tail to attract a female.

SYRINX SONG

Mammals and reptiles speak using the larynx, but birds have a unique structure lower down the windpipe—the syrinx. Several vibrating surfaces and movable "lips" produce an amazing range of sounds. In songbirds, the syrinx sits where two airways join the main windpipe, so they can sing with two different voices at once, one from each lung.

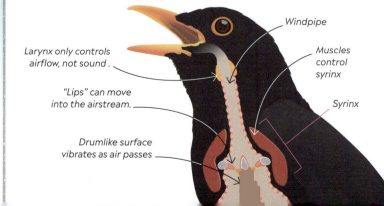

Windpipe

Larynx only controls airflow, not sound.

Muscles control syrinx

"Lips" can move into the airstream.

Syrinx

Drumlike surface vibrates as air passes

DYNAMIC **DUET**

Songbird couples sing for many reasons: to build bonds, defend territory, care for chicks, and more. In some species only the male sings, in others there is call and response, and a few combine their songs so closely that they sound like a single bird!

Female listens to some songs and joins others in a call-and-response pattern.

Male red-backed shrike sings to female. In breeding season, he also performs a courtship dance.

After breeding, males molt to replace blue feathers with green ones for camouflage.

HUNGRY MOUTHS

Born bald and blind, songbird chicks need a lot of feeding to grow up fast, so parents bring them protein-packed insects rather than fruit or seeds. Continuing to develop outside the egg lets these robin chicks grow larger brains for their body size than birds that hatch ready to move.

NEARLY HALF THE **WORLD'S** BIRDS ARE **SONGBIRDS!**

THERE ARE MORE THAN **1.5 BILLION RED-BILLED QUELEA** LIVING IN THE WILD!

SECOND **HOME**

Keeping eggs and chicks safe is hard work, so Cape penduline tits build an ingenious nest with two chambers to puzzle predators. The family stays in the larger space with a hidden entrance, while the other hole acts as a decoy.

Snake searches empty nest but finds no prey.

Concealed entrance to main nest

Open entrance to decoy nest

Bird and eggs stay safe in main chamber.

Crafty crows

The agile, clever, and surprisingly colorful corvid family includes not just crows, rooks, and ravens, but also jays, choughs, and nutcrackers.

MAGPIES CAN RECOGNIZE THEMSELVES IN THE MIRROR!

A JAY MAY HOARD 5,000 NUTS READY FOR THE WINTER!

CORVID **COMPANY**

Eurasian jays usually live alone, but when they come together their brief gatherings are noisy and energetic. They enjoy speedy play-chases and play-fighting, but there are also serious tussles where feathers fly.

Powerful beak to crack open acorns

Eye-catching blue wing panel with black stripes

Long tail for balance

TOOL **MAKER**

Wild New Caledonian crows make tools to reach food. To test them, scientists placed treats in a closed box with a narrow slit along one side. The crows had to join two short sticks together to reach the treats.

1. Tool short
Crow finds the sticks are too short to reach the treat and plugs one into the connector to join two together.

2. Tooled up
The double-length stick is long enough to push the treat out of the box. Success!

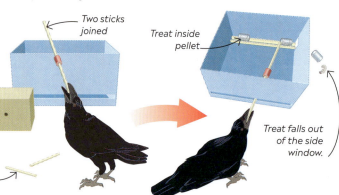

"Tool kit" of sticks with connectors

Loose sticks

Two sticks joined

Treat inside pellet

Treat falls out of the side window.

MOB **MENTALITY**

When crows spot a dangerous bird of prey nearby, they team up to drive it away by "mobbing" the intruder. They swoop, call loudly, and even peck at it until the harassed raptor moves on.

Broad wings help to maneuver between trees.

Streaky crest feathers are raised when communicating.

Legs extended to grapple for dominance

White "rump" is more visible when bird is in flight.

Tail feathers fan out to help with mid-air maneuvers.

THE ALPINE CHOUGH NESTS HIGH IN THE HIMALAYAS— 16,400 FT (5,000 M) UP!

Crow
Crows have a straight, dark beak and tidy, jet-black feathers. They make a hoarse triple "caw."

Rook
Rooks have a domed head and a thin gray beak with pale skin at the base. They make a noisy "caw-caw" call.

Common raven
Ravens have shaggy throat feathers and a long, thick beak. Their call is deep and gravelly.

ROOK, **CROW**, RAVEN

These hefty, black-feathered birds look less alike than you might think. Common ravens are the biggest, spanning up to 5 ft (1.5 m); crows have a smooth, glossy sheen; and rooks have loose, oily-looking feathers.

ROWDY **ROOKERY**

Rooks nest in noisy, sociable groups—an extended family of children, siblings, and cousins. Parents mostly take care of their own young, but some crows "adopt" neighbors' chicks, and all adults defend the rookery from predators.

SURPRISING **SOAP**

Crows and jays take "ant baths" by sitting on the ground to let the insects crawl all over them! It is thought that acid from the ants cleans and protects the birds' feathers. Some even pick up an ant in their beak to rub on their wings.

NAME THAT... SONGBIRD

Can you tell a finch from a flycatcher? A blackbird from a bunting? A magpie from a myna? Spot as many sensational songbirds as you can, but beware fowl play—there's an odd one out!

1 Eurasian jay
2 European goldfinch
3 Eastern bluebird
4 Blue-and-white flycatcher
5 Eurasian magpie
6 Southern masked weaver
7 Scarlet tanager
8 Crimson sunbird
9 Barn swallow
10 Gouldian finch
11 Splendid glossy starling
12 European starling
13 Northern cardinal
14 Domestic cockerel
15 Common hill myna
16 Eurasian tree sparrow
17 Chestnut weaver
18 Superb starling
19 Carrion crow
20 Blue tit
  21 Chaffinch
    22 Red-billed blue magpie
  23 Rook
    24 Eurasian blackbird
25 Willow warbler
26 Painted bunting
27 Brambling
28 House sparrow
29 Blue jay
30 Emerald starling
31 Orange-headed thrush
32 House finch
33 Orange weaver finch
34 Bearded tit
35 Red-winged laughing thrush

The odd one out is the domestic cockerel (14)—not every loudmouth is a songbird! Chickens and cockerels are fowl, like turkeys and ducks.

CAN YOU SPOT THE ODD ONE OUT?

MAMMALS

What is a **mammal?**

Mammals range from tiny rodents and flying bats to mighty elephants and whopping whales—not to mention humans. More than 6,600 mammal species can be found around the world, living in many types of habitat.

MAMMALS LIKE THE BOWHEAD WHALE HAVE A LAYER OF FAT UNDER THEIR SKIN CALLED BLUBBER TO KEEP WARM IN COLD WATER!

COMMON FEATURES

All mammals are warm-blooded vertebrates and most have fur or hair to help regulate their temperature. Almost all mammal mothers give birth to live young and feed the newborns their milk. The only exceptions are the monotremes—they lay eggs!

WARM-BLOODED
Mammals use energy from food to keep a constant body temperature whatever the weather. Snow leopards stay warm even in icy winters.

VERTEBRATE
Mammals have an internal bony skeleton, including a spine, as shown on this X-ray. The skeleton helps this cat hold up its body and move.

MAMMAL TYPES

Mammals can be grouped by how they give birth. Most are placental, meaning babies are nourished in the womb and born looking like miniature adults.

Placental-land
These give birth to young that have grown inside the mother's body.

Marsupials
Tiny, premature newborns climb into the mother's pouch and develop there.

Monotremes
These lay soft-shelled eggs. After hatching, babies nurse on their mother's milk.

Walking
Large, heavy, grazing mammals such as rhinos walk across the land to feed on grass and find water.

Running
Cheetahs and other predators have to run fast to catch food—but prey are often good runners too!

Hopping
Kangaroos use their strong back legs as giant springs to hop across their flat, open habitats at speed.

Climbing
Tree-living species such as koalas nest on branches and climb around to find tasty leaves to munch on.

ON THE **MOVE**

Each mammal species has adapted to move in the optimal way to survive in their habitat. This helps them avoid predators and find food, whether they live on land, in the air, or in water.

A blue whale swims easily in water, but is too heavy to move on land.

60% OF MAMMAL SPECIES ARE RODENTS OR BATS!

HUMAN **NURTURE**

Humans are placental mammals. We spend about nine months developing in the womb, fed by our mother through the placenta and umbilical cord, and are born with all our vital organs in place. Like other mammals, newborn humans can't manage by themselves, so they need an adult to feed and take care of them until they are older.

FUR OR HAIR
Most mammals have fur or hair on their bodies. This red panda's thick coat traps air, which helps retain body heat and protects the skin from scrapes and bruises.

LIVE BIRTH
Most mammals give birth to live young. Some newborns are ready to walk right away, such as this zebra, but other babies take a bit longer to get moving.

PRODUCE MILK
All mammal mothers produce nutritious milk to sustain their young until they are ready to digest solid food. Elephant calves drink 3 gallons (12 liters) a day!

SOME SHREWS AND OTHER SMALL MAMMALS LIVE FOR LESS THAN ONE YEAR!

Some places are only accessible to mammals that fly.

Dense jungle is easier to navigate for mammals that climb and swing.

Flying
Bats are the only mammals with wings. Some fly to feed in fruit trees, others grab insects in mid-air.

Gliding
Flying squirrels leap from a branch and spread furry skin flaps to glide to a new tree without touching the ground.

Burrowing
Black-tailed prairie dogs and other burrowing animals use their long front limbs and sharp claws to dig through soil.

Swimming
Whales and dolphins, such as orcas, live and hunt in water. Many land-based mammals are good swimmers too.

DOMESTICATED **MAMMALS**

More than 10,000 years ago, humans began domesticating wild animals. As animals were bred for transportation, milk, meat, farm work, or companionship, their traits changed so that tame species now look very different from their wild ancestors.

Domestic pig breeds have little hair.

Wild boars have thick fur.

Long tusks grow from the jaws of wild pig species.

Tail is half the length of the tiger's body.

Ears rotate like radar dishes—a tiger's hearing is five times better than a human's.

Every tiger has a unique pattern of stripes on its head and body.

POWERFUL POUNCE

Tigers are fast, muscular, and can leap up to 33 ft (10 m). They have the widest range of all big cats, from the Asian tropics to the colder climes of eastern Russia. They usually hunt at night, launching a surprise attack from the side or behind.

Sharp claws are retracted until needed to keep the tips razor sharp.

Ligament holds the claw in protective skin sheath when not in use.

Big cats

From the lions of Africa to the tigers of Asia, the leopards of both regions, and the jaguars of the Americas, these supersize felines are among the most fearsome predators on the planet.

FEWER THAN ONE IN THREE LION HUNTS IS SUCCESSFUL!

TOP CATS

There are 46 species of cat, large and small. Most of the larger cats belong to the genus *Panthera*, and of those only these four have the ability to roar.

Tiger
The biggest cat: Siberian, or Amur, tigers can be 13 ft (4 m) long and weigh 661 lb (300 kg).

Lion
Generally smaller than tigers, lions live in packs called prides and hunt in open grassland.

Jaguar
The largest cat in the Americas, jaguars have large heads, short legs, and live and hunt around water.

Leopard
This cat hunts at night. The smallest big cat, it loves to climb and is often found up a tree.

ROAR SOME

Special folds in a lion's vocal cords mean that its roar is louder than any other big cat—and most other animals. It can be heard from 5 miles (8 km) away.

LEAVING A MARK

Aside from roaring, big cats communicate in other ways. Urine sprays and anal gland secretions on trees mark their territory, as do scratch marks on bark and strategically placed piles of feces.

TIGER PEE SMELLS LIKE BUTTERED POPCORN!

TREE LARDER

Leopards hide the animals they catch in trees so jackals and other scavengers cannot steal them. They also use trees to lie in wait for prey and as places to rest.

TOP OF THE FOOD CHAIN

All big cats are apex (top) predators, which means no creature in their ecosystem is capable of hunting or eating them. In addition, apex predators such as the jaguar prey not just on herbivores but also on other predators including coatis and caimans.

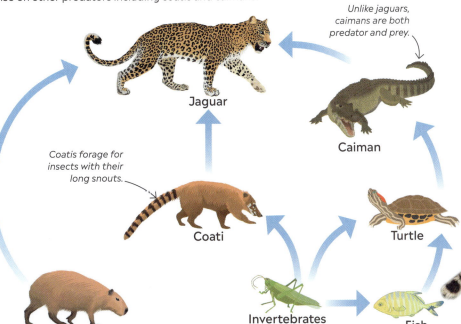

Unlike jaguars, caimans are both predator and prey.

Jaguar

Caiman

Coatis forage for insects with their long snouts.

Coati

Turtle

Invertebrates

Fish

Capybara

Herbivores such as the capybara solely eat plants.

Plants are the basis of the food chain.

Plants

JAGUARS HAVE THE STRONGEST BIG CAT BITE. IT'S TWICE AS POWERFUL AS A TIGER'S!

CAT TONGUES HAVE **TINY SPIKES** THAT **STRIP MEAT** FROM PREY!

AGILE **MARGAY**

A tree-climbing specialist, the margay lives in forests in Mexico and Central and South America. Its adapted claws and feet allow it to travel up and down tree trunks with ease. It mostly hunts tree-living animals, such as birds, frogs, and small rodents.

Margays can climb down headfirst because their back feet can rotate to grip the trunk.

Large eyes for good night vision

Claws grip the bark.

LONG-LEGGED **SERVALS** OFTEN HAVE BOTH **SPOTS AND STRIPES** ON THEIR **FUR!**

CAT COUSINS

Although they aren't cats, these creatures, like their feline relatives, are all mainly carnivores that hunt or scavenge prey. They tend to have clawed toes and many can climb trees.

Civets
African and Asian civets are nocturnal, live in trees, and have long tails.

Mongooses
Mongooses live mainly on the ground and are active by day.

Fossa
The largest predator on Madagascar, the fossa hunts in trees and on the ground.

Hyenas
The biggest and most distant cat-cousins live in open habitats.

Small cats

Most of the nearly 40 species of small cat are solitary and live in forests. Like big cats, they are carnivores that usually ambush their prey.

Caracals can jump high enough to catch birds in the air.

FLEXIBLE FELINES

Most small-cat species have bodies made for climbing and jumping. Once in the air, they can twist their bodies so they always land on all fours.

SNOW PAWS

The Canadian lynx lives in forests that are cold and snow-covered for large parts of the year. Its huge paws make padding across deep snow an easy feat, because they distribute its weight to stop it from sinking.

Wide paws work like snowshoes.

EXCELLENT EARS

The caracal is easily recognizable because of its big ears, crowned by long, black ear tufts. Twitching and swiveling, they are believed to play a part in how caracals communicate with each other.

Strong legs for leaping up to a vantage point.

GONE FISHING

Unlike domestic cats, many wild species are happy in the water. The fishing cat hunts for fish and crustaceans in rivers and wetlands throughout southern Asia. Its front toes are webbed, which helps it swim and capture prey in water.

DESPITE THEIR NAME, **MEERKATS** ARE MORE **RELATED** TO **MONGOOSES!**

KEEPING **CUBS**

A female cheetah lives a solitary life, so when she has cubs there is no family group to rely on. At first, she hides them while going hunting, but from six months, she teaches them how to stalk prey. They are ready to leave their mom after 15–18 months.

Chasing
cheetah

Like a mammalian racing car zooming across the African savanna, a cheetah can quickly reach incredible speeds to catch its prey. But it can't keep the pace up for long, so not every hunt is successful.

Muscular tail acts as a counterbalance during high-speed leaps.

Elongated, flexible spine enables mid-air twists.

Long, slender legs stretch out for sprint speed.

Cheetah claws are always exposed, providing traction—like running spikes.

CHEETAH SPEAK INCLUDES **PURRS, BLEATS, BARKS, GROWLS, HISSES,** AND **CHIRPS!**

PURR POWER

Cheetahs can't roar like other big cats. But like small cats, they are great at purring, a skill that big cats lack. This is because a cheetah's larynx (voice box) and a bone called the hyoid are structured differently from those of big cats. Purring can be a sign of contentment, especially when a mother and her cubs are bonding.

Air inhaled and exhaled passes through the larynx.

Trachea (windpipe)

Small, densely padded vocal cords in the larynx produce purring.

Rigid hyoid bone, connected to the back of the jaw, vibrates to amplify the purring sound.

SPOT THE DIFFERENCE

Cheetahs and leopards are both spotty predators stalking the savanna. While leopards sometimes use trees to ambush and store prey, cheetahs take to the long grass to hunt. Both species need to blend in with their surroundings, but a closer look at their spots reveals who's who.

Cheetah
The cheetah's pale fur is covered with oval or round black spots of different sizes.

Leopard
The leopard has distinctive black and brown spots on its fur. Resembling the shape of a rose, they are called rosettes.

HAIR APPARENT

Adult cheetahs don't have a mane, but cubs do. From birth, long, fluffy, pale hair extends over their head, neck, and back. Perfect for disguising them in the long grass while their mom is on a hunt, this baby mane disappears as the cubs grow.

THE FASTEST LAND ANIMAL ON EARTH, CHEETAHS CAN REACH 75 MPH (120 KPH)!

AGILE ASSASSIN

Equipped with large lungs and a body made for sprinting, a cheetah can increase its speed by 6 mph (10 kph) in a single stride, and is built for taking down prey. Its top targets are gazelles and antelopes. These are also fast runners that can swiftly change direction, so a cheetah needs to be in great shape to succeed.

The slender throat of this springbok is where the cheetah bites—if it can catch it.

Thin lines of black fur form anti-glare stripes

CHEETAHS CLIMB UP ON TERMITE HILLS TO SEARCH THE SAVANNA FOR PREY!

FACIAL FEATURES

All cheetahs have two distinct black stripes running from their eyes down to their mouth. These absorb light to reduce the glare of the Sun. This helps cheetahs hunt in the daytime (as opposed to lions, who prefer dusk and nighttime).

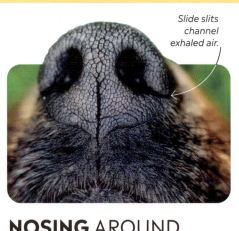

FOXES HAVE **VERTICAL PUPILS,** LIKE CATS—ALL OTHER CANINES HAVE **ROUND** ONES!

Clever **canines**

Dogs, wolves, foxes, and their relatives are hunters that tend to chase down rather than ambush their prey. Most have bushy tails and long muzzles, and many are sociable and live in family groups.

Slide slits channel exhaled air.

NOSING AROUND

Canines use their noses to assess each other's health, find food, and detect danger. Two large nostrils continuously inhale air and scents, while air is exhaled through slide slits. This ensures exhaled air doesn't interfere with incoming smells.

Tail moves for balance in mid-air.

SNOW **HUNT**

A red fox can pinpoint the movements of prey deep under the snow using their super-sensitive hearing. When they have judged their distance from the target, they leap up to pounce nose-first through the snow, right on top of the mouse or lemming hiding below.

Ears are pricked up to take in sounds coming from under the snow.

THE **MANED WOLF'S** FAVORITE **SNACK** IS A FRUIT CALLED **WOLF APPLE!**

Wolf apples are up to 8 in (20 cm) in diameter.

PUP **REARING**

Depending on their species, pups grow up with their mom, with both parents, or in a pack. Ethiopian wolf pups (above) are the offspring of the pack's dominant female, but rearing them is a communal pack job! The pups even suckle milk from other females, and the pack will guard and provide food for them.

Paws and jaws ready to grab the prey

The fox pierces through the snow, surprising the prey deep below the surface.

Gray wolf
Length: 5 ft 3 in (160 cm)

Fennec fox
Length: 9½ in (24 cm)

THE **LARGEST CANINE** SPECIES IS **6 TIMES BIGGER** THAN THE **SMALLEST!**

PACK LIVING

Gray wolves live together in packs, with larger groups headed by a dominant male and female. The rest of the pack is made up of their pups, relatives, and, at times, new arrivals. Each wolf knows its role. Together, they hunt and defend their territory from other packs, but there's time for rest and play too.

BODY **LANGUAGE**

Communication is key for canines, especially in large packs. In addition to yelps and growls, canines signal via the dip of a head, changing shoulder shapes, and ear and tail movements.

Bowing with wagging tail means "I want to play!"

Hunched, with ears back and tail between legs: "you are my leader"

Head and tail high, confident stare: "I'm the boss"

Belly shown, ears flat, and tail between legs: "I'm not fighting, don't hurt me!"

NAME THAT... DOG BREED

Are you terrific at terriers? Do you know a dalmatian from a dachshund, or a pointer from a pug? Identify these dashing domestic dog breeds and sniff out the impostor.

1 Vizsla
2 Afghan Hound
3 Golden Retriever
4 Bernese Mountain dog
5 Husky
6 Beagle
7 Great Dane
8 Doberman
9 Corgi
10 English Bull Terrier
11 Yorkshire Terrier
12 Pug
13 Labrador
14 Pointer
15 Miniature Schnauzer
16 Staffordshire Bull Terrier
17 Dachshund
18 British Bulldog

19 Australian Shepherd
20 Cocker Spaniel
21 Chihuahua
22 Basset Hound
23 Bichon Frise
24 Border Terrier
25 Fennec Fox
26 Dalmatian
27 Corded Standard Poodle
28 Whippet
29 Toy Poodle
30 West Highland Terrier
31 German Shepherd
32 Irish Terrier

CAN YOU SPOT THE ODD ONE OUT?

The odd one out is number 25, the fennec fox. It belongs to the dog family, but is a wild animal, not a pet! These tiny foxes, up to 16 in (40 cm) long, live in the North African desert.

Ears (and nostrils) close when the otter goes underwater.

Thick, two-layered fur stops water from reaching the skin underneath.

Webbed feet with sharp claws for swimming and holding on to slippery fish

URBAN **SCAVENGER!**

Raccoons are intelligent problem-solvers that use their dexterous paws to grab food. In urban areas, they home in on bird feeders, fish ponds, and pet food. As unfussy scavengers and omnivores, they regularly raid garbage cans too.

Otters
and relatives

Otters, weasels, raccoons, and relatives are slinky assassins and include the smallest true carnivores of the mammal world. Their sharp teeth are ideal for hunting prey and slicing meat, but some also eat fruit and scavenge.

FISH FEAST

This giant river otter has just got its webbed paws on a tasty catch and eats it head-first. Fish make up most of a giant otter's diet, but they can kill caimans and anacondas too. Giant otters hunt and play in South American rivers and waterways, and make their dens on riverbanks.

Sensitive whiskers (vibrissae) help detect fish movements in murky river water.

WILD WOLVERINES

Roaming the wilderness in northern parts of Eurasia and North America, wolverines can gallop quickly and catch prey, such as reindeer, with their wide, sharp-clawed paws. But they are equally happy to eat carrion left by other predators. What they can't eat right away, they hide for a later meal.

SKUNKS CAN USE MUSCLES TO AIM THEIR SPRAY AT ANYTHING THAT SCARES THEM!

WHICH WEASEL?

Members of the weasel family look similar, but range in size. Fast and clever, they have long, slender bodies with short legs, and can pursue prey, such as rats, into narrow burrows. Here are 3 of the 20 or so weasel species.

Least weasel
The smallest of the mammalian carnivores is only 5 in (13 cm) long. In cold, snowy habitats, it changes its brown coat to thick white in winter.

Stoat
Larger than weasels, stoats have longer tails that end in a "paint brush" tip. They are feisty fighters that take on prey three times their size.

Ferret
Domesticated from wild polecats, ferrets were bred to hunt rabbits. They are extremely inquisitive and have a sharp bite.

FORAGING BADGERS

The European badger sniffs out earthworms, grubs, snails, and slugs. Its paws are perfect for both digging for food and expanding its family sett (burrow). The sett is kept tidy, with new leaves regularly added for comfy bedding.

Sharp curved claws for scratching through soil

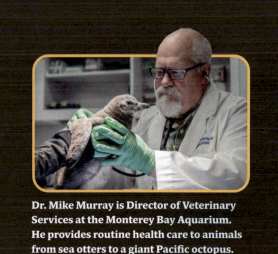

Dr. Mike Murray is Director of Veterinary Services at the Monterey Bay Aquarium. He provides routine health care to animals from sea otters to a giant Pacific octopus.

CHIEF VET

Q What drew you to marine medicine?
A I was always attracted to water and my parents encouraged this. One Christmas when I was about 10 years old, I came downstairs and found they had assembled a whole aquarium with live fish in it. To this day I don't know how they did it, but I loved it.

Q What is your typical day?
A We start with rounds at 7:30 a.m. There are tens of thousands of animals in the aquarium—it's the size of a medium city—so a day is rarely typical.

Q Do the animals eat each other in the tanks?
A We like to say we have "low predation" not "no predation," because sometimes it happens. Generally the animals are fed well enough that they don't need to expend the energy to hunt.

Q How difficult is it to diagnose what's wrong?
A We don't have any over-worriers! Unlike humans, wild animals tend to hide it if they are unwell. If they look weak a predator might try and eat them. So it can be difficult if they're trying to hide something. It gets trickier if they need to stay in the water. Then we have to put them in what I call a reverse scuba tank, where we pump water with a little bit of anesthetic in it over their mouths and gills while we treat them.

Q What does it feel like to release an animal back into the wild?
A It's rewarding. The team puts a lot of blood, sweat, and tears into getting to this point. Your brain wants to say to the animal "Could you at least wave while you're swimming away?," but you know it won't. I don't feel mournful. I know it's the right thing to do.

Q What about animals that live in the aquarium—is it right to keep them in captivity?
A Living exhibits can help change public attitudes in ways that benefit wild ocean animals and ecosystems by inspiring people to care about and act on behalf of the ocean. There are cases when keeping animals isn't in their best interests, but the creatures at the Monterey Bay Aquarium have won the lottery. They don't have to worry about finding food. They have a bunch of naked apes (us) running around inventing toys for them. And they're curious about us. We did some major renovation in the kelp forest tank a couple of years ago, and when the divers left, the fish would line up to look at the work that they had done. It was like a bunch of 12-year-olds checking out a construction site.

OTTER RESCUE
Surrogate sea otter mother Kit holds and grooms a 10-week-old pup as part of the Monterey Bay Aquarium's Sea Otter Rescue Program. Dr. Mike helped devise this program, which partners rescued sea otters with otters living in the aquarium. The youngsters learn valuable skills from the moms to prepare them for their return to the wild.

Sensitive nose parts

STELLAR NOSE

The star-nosed mole possesses 22 pink, fleshy parts that fan out from around its nostrils. Covered with thousands of touch sensors, they help catch the tiny creatures that wriggle around in the waterlogged soil where this mole hunts .

Moles, shrews, & hedgehogs

Hedgehogs, moles, and shrews don't see very well. Instead, they use their noses to sense and hunt bugs and worms. They all prefer the solitary life, while the shrewlike solenodons are more social creatures.

Silky soft fur offers no resistance when the mole moves backward and forward in tunnels as it can easily lie both ways.

Hairless nose surrounded by whiskers

Pointy teeth to bite through juicy earthworms

HEDGEHOGS ROLL UP INTO A **PRICKLY BALL** TO PROTECT THEMSELVES FROM **PREDATORS!**

RARE SIGHT

Moles are usually busy digging with their spade-like feet. They rarely emerge from under the ground, but may pop out while making shallow feeding tunnels. Their eyes are hidden by fur, but they can detect light. To find prey in the tunnels, moles rely on their highly sensitive noses.

STIFF HAIRS ON THEIR FEET HELP **WATER SHREWS** SCAMPER **ACROSS WATER!**

TOXIC **SOLENODON**

There aren't many venomous mammals, but the Caribbean solenodon, like some of its distant shrew relatives, produces venomous saliva. It injects this into its prey through special grooves in its incisor teeth.

Teeth funnel toxic saliva.

BRISTLY **HEDGEHOGS**

Hedgehogs have a coat of 5,000 to 7,000 stiff, sharp, hollow spines, each measuring around 1 in (2.5 cm). Newborns quickly grow a set of white baby spikes, replaced by adult spines over the first few weeks. Some hedgehog species hibernate in winter, but in warmer months they come out to forage for worms and beetles after sundown.

JITTERY **SHREW**

Like most shrew species, this Eurasian shrew is very small. It needs to be on high alert to stay alive, and it is quick to move, either to escape predators or catch prey. If a shrew doesn't eat every few hours, it starves to death.

Long whiskers help orientation.

BURROW ENGINEERS

Living most of their lives underground, moles construct extensive burrows with several specialized areas. They make permanent tunnels deep in the soil, which run between sleeping chambers and larders. Feeding tunnels close to the surface are used to catch worms and other prey.

Powerful front paws, always turned outward for digging and shoveling soil

Mole hill formed from earth shoveled up from below

Mole digging a feeding tunnel

Permanent tunnel

Nesting chamber

Larder for storing worms

Burrow of a colony of European moles

Riveting
rodents

The largest group of mammals, rodents are found around the world. Making up more than 2,660 species, they vary in size, shape, and habits. But they have one thing in common—their teeth never stop growing.

Thick fur keeps the beaver warm, both in and out of water.

RIVER RODENT

Up to 4 ft 2 in (1.3 m) long, capybaras are the world's largest rodents. They live in wetlands and near rivers in South America. Fantastic swimmers with webbed feet, they spend a lot of time in water, where they wallow, feed on aquatic plants, or hide.

BEAVERING AWAY

Beavers put their teeth to good use. They gnaw through tree branches to get materials to build dams and lodges in rivers. When hungry, they chew on leaves, sprigs, and bark. Often, they bite off more than they can eat right away, to build up a supply to keep inside their lodge for winter.

Molars for grinding down leaves

Orange incisors are strengthened with iron.

Strong jaws support gnawing action.

Fortified teeth
Like other rodents, a beaver has four long, curved incisors, with hard enamel on their outer surfaces. Gnawing keeps them sharp and stops them from over-growing.

RATS GRIND THEIR TEETH TO PRODUCE AN ULTRASONIC CLICKING WARNING SIGNAL!

RODENT **HOMES**

Many rodents are clever engineers, creating safe spaces for storing food and sleeping, and they even build nurseries for their young. From river banks to forests, rodents make their homes in a wide range of places.

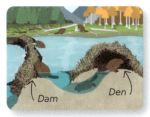

Beaver lodge
Beavers build dens from sticks and branches, with a hidden underwater entrance. The dam creates a protective moat.

Dam
Den

Built-in food supply

Naked mole rat colony
A queen reigns over a complex underground burrow for hundreds of mole rats. Roots and tubers provide food.

Squirrel tree nest
Squirrels fill holes they find in trees with bedding made of feathers, moss, leaves, or shredded bark

SUPER **SMELLERS!**

Rats have an incredible sense of smell, which they use to find food and navigate the world. They are intelligent and light on their feet, so some rat species have even been tasked with sniffing out land mines hidden in the ground.

African pouched rat sniffing for the TNT used in land mines

MANY RODENTS **EAT** THEIR **OWN POOP** TO GET **BACTERIA** THAT HELP THEM **DIGEST FOOD!**

Mouse droppings

TAIL TALENT

A harvest mouse can use its tail almost like an extra hand for climbing tall grass and reed stalks. This helps it reach berries and seeds, and build nests woven around stems at a safe distance from the ground.

Prehensile tail grasps stem.

QUILL OR BE KILLED

Porcupines run backward to lodge their detachable quills (spines) in an attacker's skin. With sharp tips, the quills are the perfect defense, and predators and other animals tend to give porcupines a wide berth.

Quills raised in defense

Black and white pattern is a visual warning of the danger.

Guard hairs protect the quills when they lie flat.

Hollow quills rattle when shaken together as warning to predators.

NAME THAT... RODENT

Prove you know a jerboa from a gerbil by naming these gnaw-some rodents with ever-growing incisors. Is your knowledge as incisive as they are? Don't forget to spot the odd one out!

1 Southern flying squirrel
2 Crested porcupine
3 Harvest mouse
4 Hazel dormouse
5 European hamster
6 Prairie dog
7 Malagasy giant rat
8 Agouti
9 Arabian spiny mouse
10 Eastern gray squirrel
11 Eurasian red squirrel
12 Mongolian gerbil
13 Guinea pig
14 Brown rat
15 Degu
16 Bobak marmot
17 South African springhare
18 Coypu
19 Striped grass mouse
20 Naked mole rat
21 Wallaby
22 Fat dormouse
23 Bank vole
24 Norway lemming
25 Long-eared jerboa
26 Chinchilla
27 European wood mouse
28 North American beaver
29 Patagonian mara
30 Capybara
31 Eastern chipmunk

CAN YOU SPOT THE ODD ONE OUT?

The odd one out is the wallaby (21). It's a marsupial, not a rodent!

Trees provide roosts for fruit bats.

Gray-headed fruit bats

HANGING AROUND

Bats gather together, or roost, in trees, caves, and sometimes inside buildings. They sleep upside down, wrapped in their wings, for most of the day.

BRACKEN CAVE IN TEXAS IS HOME TO MORE THAN 20 MILLION BATS!

Brilliant bats

Bats come in all shapes and sizes. There are more than 1,400 species, making them the second largest group of mammals after rodents. Their extra senses come into play at night, when they hunt and feed.

FLIGHT READY

This bat, an Indian flying fox, is about to take off. Hanging by its feet, it spreads its wings before letting go to swoop off into the night.

Large ears to catch echolocation signals

SUPER SENSES

All bats have good eyesight. But those that hunt insects at night, such as this horseshoe bat, need to find prey in the dark. To do this, they use echolocation. They send out a pulse of sound through their mouth or nose and pick up the echo (signal bouncing back), which tells them where prey, and obstacles, are.

Nose leaf, used to direct echolocation signals from the nose

JUST 1 IN (3 CM) LONG, THE KITTI'S HOG-NOSED BAT IS THE WORLD'S SMALLEST BAT!

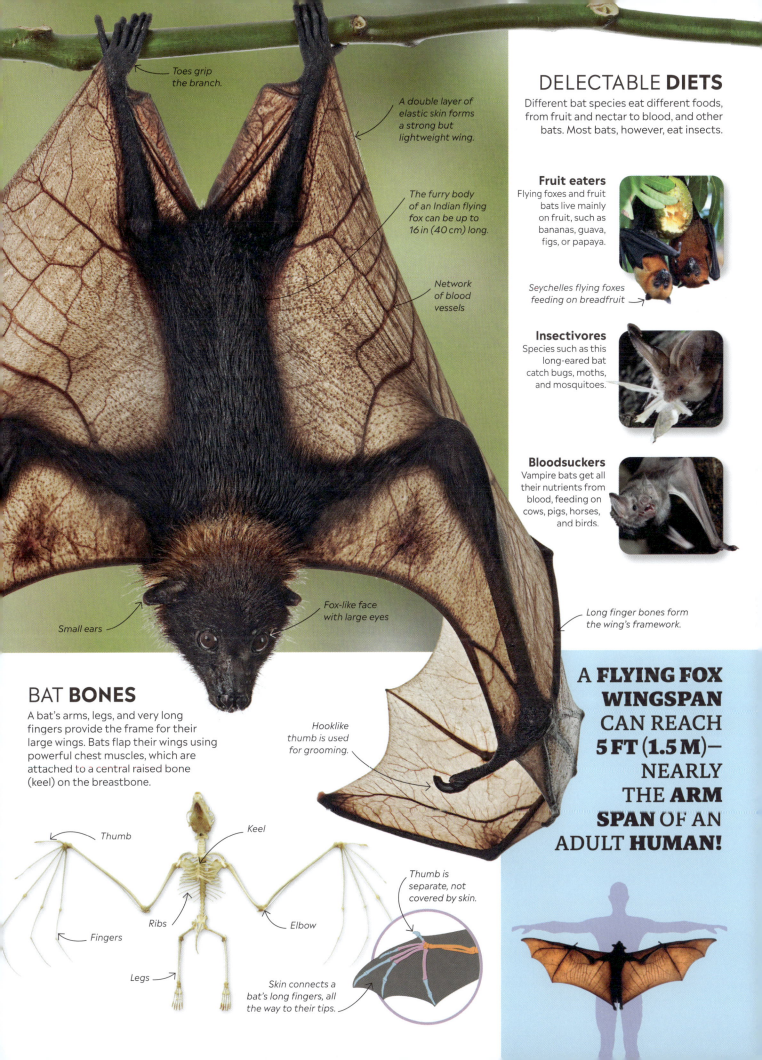

Toes grip the branch.

A double layer of elastic skin forms a strong but lightweight wing.

The furry body of an Indian flying fox can be up to 16 in (40 cm) long.

Network of blood vessels

Small ears

Fox-like face with large eyes

DELECTABLE **DIETS**

Different bat species eat different foods, from fruit and nectar to blood, and other bats. Most bats, however, eat insects.

Fruit eaters
Flying foxes and fruit bats live mainly on fruit, such as bananas, guava, figs, or papaya.

Seychelles flying foxes feeding on breadfruit

Insectivores
Species such as this long-eared bat catch bugs, moths, and mosquitoes.

Bloodsuckers
Vampire bats get all their nutrients from blood, feeding on cows, pigs, horses, and birds.

Long finger bones form the wing's framework.

BAT **BONES**

A bat's arms, legs, and very long fingers provide the frame for their large wings. Bats flap their wings using powerful chest muscles, which are attached to a central raised bone (keel) on the breastbone.

Hooklike thumb is used for grooming.

A **FLYING FOX WINGSPAN** CAN REACH **5 FT (1.5 M)**— NEARLY THE **ARM SPAN** OF AN ADULT **HUMAN!**

Thumb

Keel

Ribs

Elbow

Fingers

Legs

Thumb is separate, not covered by skin.

Skin connects a bat's long fingers, all the way to their tips.

MIDNIGHT **MUNCHER**

Mostly asleep in trees during the day, koalas wake up to eat eucalyptus leaves at night. The leaves are tough and poisonous, but koalas' digestive organs allow them to break down the leaves and get rid of the toxins.

Marvelous marsupials

Most marsupials live in Australia and nearby islands, and around one third in South America. Their young are born in a very underdeveloped state, and then usually suckled in a pouch.

1. *The joey embryo spends only around 30 days in the womb.*

2. *The tiny, underdeveloped joey is born through an opening here.*

4. *The newborn immediately latches on to drink milk.*

3. *Following a scent path licked by its mother through her fur, the joey crawls toward and into the pouch.*

KANGAROO **BIRTH**

When born, a joey is not ready for the outside world. But although hairless and nearly blind, the tiny newborn has strong little arms, which it uses to climb up into its mother's pouch. Inside, feeding on milk, it continues to develop for around six to eight months.

DEMON DINER

Tasmanian devils are fierce carnivores with a strong bite (see page 221). Once they've caught prey or found carrion, they eat it all—meat, bones, and hair. If they can't finish their meal, they sleep inside the carcass so they can continue eating when they wake up. They are noisy, scaring rivals with coughs, growls, snorts, and screeches.

Carnivores
Quolls prey on insects, birds, and even rabbits and possums.

Omnivores
Bandicoots love insects, earthworms, berries, and fungi.

Herbivores
Wombats spend hours chewing wild grasses and plant roots.

WOMBAT **POOP** COMES OUT **CUBE-SHAPED!**

MARSUPIAL **MENUS**

Different species of marsupial enjoy different foods, and diets vary depending on where they live. Their teeth differ too: carnivores need sharp, tearing teeth; omnivores have an array of tooth shapes; and herbivores use large, square molars to grind vegetation.

KANGAROOS CAN TAKE **LEAPS** OF UP TO **30 FT (9 M)**!

AIRBORNE **POSSUM**

The sugar glider, a type of possum, has flaps connecting its forelegs to its hind legs. With flaps extended, it is able to glide between trees, away from predators or toward sources of its favorite foods: tree sap and nectar.

OPOSSUM RIDE

The only marsupial in North America, opossums give birth to babies the size of bees. Once old enough to leave the pouch, the babies hitch a ride on mom's back, learning to scavenge, climb, and evade predators.

The mother can use her strong arms to guide the joey in and out.

Jump-in joey
Older joeys still want to snuggle up in the pouch now and then. They enter head-first, and then twist around in the now-cramped space to peer out.

1. Jump in ...

2. Spin around

GROWING **JOEY**

For the first few months, a joey stays hidden in its mother's pouch. Then, it begins to peek out and, at around six months, takes short trips out, learning to hop for itself. It still jumps back in for milk and comfort, but when a new helpless sibling takes over the pouch, the older joey has to suckle from outside.

IF IN **DANGER**, **OPOSSUMS** RELEASE A STRONG **ODOR** AND **PLAY DEAD!**

PERPLEXING PARTS

The skeleton of a platypus is as puzzling as the animal's outside. It reveals unusual features for a mammal, such as splayed legs, more common in lizards.

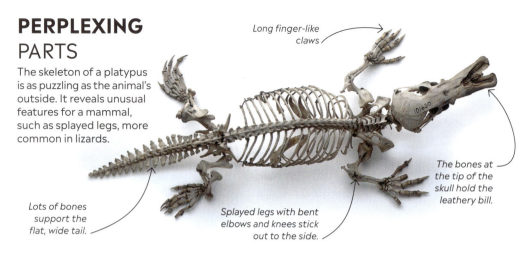

Long finger-like claws

The bones at the tip of the skull hold the leathery bill.

Lots of bones support the flat, wide tail.

Splayed legs with bent elbows and knees stick out to the side.

SPIKE ALERT!

Male platypuses have a venomous spur above the heel of each hind leg. Scientists think the males use it as a weapon to fight off rivals during breeding season.

Sensitive bill

More than 100,000 receptors on the platypus's bill help pick up the presence and location of prey. This is the same method sharks use to hunt.

Receptors detect electric fields and changes in pressure.

Prey send out faint electric currents when they move.

Eyes, just like ears, are closed during the dive.

Leathery bill sifts small invertebrates from the river bed.

PROPELLING PLATYPUS

During hunting dives, the platypus's webbed feet propel it through the water. With eyes closed, it uses its sensitive bill to locate prey in muddy river beds, including mollusks and crustaceans.

Thick fur keeps body temperature up in cold water.

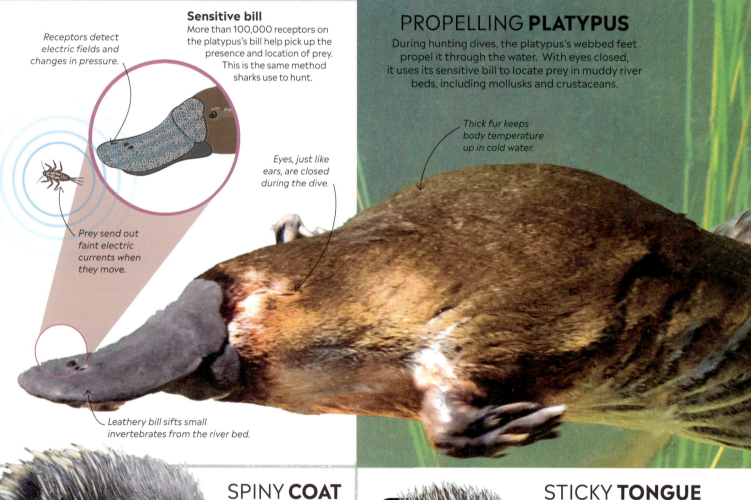

SPINY COAT

Echidnas have coarse hairs and spines that feel like fingernails but are large and hollow. When threatened, echidnas burrow into the ground with their spines sticking out to prevent attack.

Fur covers this short-beaked echidna, with spines poking through all over its back.

STICKY TONGUE

To catch all the food it needs, the echidna has a special tongue. Not only long, the tongue is also covered in gluey mucus, so termites and ants can't get away.

BABY ECHIDNAS ARE CALLED PUGGLES!

Egg-laying mammals

One group of mammals is very different from the rest—the egg-laying monotremes! Once hatched, their babies feed on milk, like other mammals.

Watertight nostrils

Web between claws helps swimming.

A GROUP OF ECHIDNAS IS CALLED A PARADE!

MONOTREME SPECIES

Of the five species of monotreme, four are different kinds of echidna. The fifth species is the platypus.

Platypus
The platypus lives in streams and rivers in eastern Australia and Tasmania.

Western long-beaked echidna
This echidna hunts for worms in the mountains of New Guinea.

Eastern long-beaked echidna
Also in New Guinea, the largest echidna has very thick fur, hiding most of its spines.

Sir David's long-beaked echidna
Smallest of the New Guinea echidnas, this rare species has a reddish-brown coat.

Short-beaked echidna
The only echidna found in Australia, it eats ants and termites.

HATCHING ECHIDNA

After she lays her egg, the female echidna scoops it up into her temporary pouch. Here the baby hatches and grows, lapping milk from glands hidden in its mother's fur.

1. Female lays soft egg and moves it into pouch.

2. Fetus emerges from the egg underdeveloped.

3. Embryo suckles on glands in the fur of the pouch.

4. Spines irritate the mother, who ejects the puggle from her pouch.

5. Juvenile leaves the burrow at six months.

UNIQUE ANATOMY

The sloth has a skeleton built for staying hooked onto branches, and muscles that pull and grip, rather than push. Its head can turn any direction to reach leaves and spot predators. Special membranes anchor its organs to a very large rib cage to stop them from pressing on the lungs while the sloth hangs upside down.

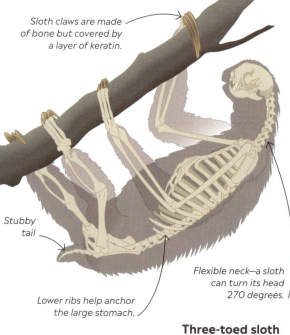

Sloth claws are made of bone but covered by a layer of keratin.

Stubby tail

Lower ribs help anchor the large stomach.

Flexible neck—a sloth can turn its head 270 degrees.

Three-toed sloth

HANGING OUT

Sloths can hang upside down for hours without moving, and when they move, they do so very slowly to save energy. Mothers give birth upside down too. The baby immediately finds a safe place on its mother's chest, where it spends the next six months, in a furry cradle. Soon, it will learn from her which leaves are tasty to chew, and which to avoid.

Two-toed sloth with her baby

ARMADILLOS CAN **SLEEP** UP TO 16 HOURS PER DAY!

Sloths
and relatives

Despite looking quite different, sloths, armadillos, and anteaters are related. They all live in the Americas and are adapted to carefully conserve and use energy.

SURPRISE SWIMMERS

Sloths rarely leave their trees, and can only crawl awkwardly on the ground. But they are strong swimmers! If they want to leave their territory, they take to nearby waterways, using their extended arms to move through the water.

ARMOR-DILLO!

For protection, armadillos have two large, hardened skin plates with smaller, movable "bands" around their middle. Head, legs, and tail are also covered. The three-banded armadillo, seen here in relaxed mode, can even roll up into a ball when threatened.

A giant anteater's tongue can be up to 23⅜ in (60 cm) long.

Tongue stretches down the long neck.

COOL CLAWS

Despite having different lifestyles, sloths, anteaters, and armadillos all have impressive claws. But they use them in different ways, whether for digging, for defense, or to hook onto branches.

TERRIFIC TONGUE

Anteaters have no teeth. Instead, they flick their long tongues in and out to lap up insects from mounds and nests, as fast as 160 times per minute. The tongue doesn't start at the back of the mouth, but all the way down at the animal's breastbone.

SLOW EATER

Sloths feed on leaves, which are not high in nutrients. But they take a long time to process food—a mouthful of leaves can take weeks to digest. Sloths don't need to poop very often but, around once a week, they climb sluggishly down a tree, using the ground at its base as a toilet.

Anteater claws
Anteaters break up termite mounds and fight off jaguars with their claws. They knuckle-walk to keep them sharp.

Armadillo claws
Armadillos use the long claws on their front feet to dig out insects and other food, and to make underground burrows.

Sloth claws
Sloths use their long, curved claws as hooks. Three-toed species have three on each hand, while two-toed sloths have two.

GIANT ANTEATERS CAN EAT UP TO 35,000 ANTS OR TERMITES EACH DAY!

THE APE **FAMILY**

Apes belong to the order of primates, which also contains monkeys. There are two main groups of apes—the lesser apes (20 species of long-armed gibbons) and the great apes.

Lesser apes
Gibbons are smaller than other apes, but have proportionally longer arms.

Orangutans
These gentle tree-dwellers share 96.4% of their genes with humans.

Gorillas
The largest great apes live in families led by a dominant male, called a silverback.

Chimpanzees
The closest relatives of humans can make tools and walk on their hind legs.

Humans
The world's 8 billion humans outnumber all other primates put together.

THE **BIGGEST** GORILLAS CAN WEIGH AS MUCH AS **4 ADULT MEN!**

Babies learn while clinging to mom.

All four limbs can hold on to branches.

Free arm can be used to snack, catch a falling baby, or reach for the next branch.

TREE **LIFE**

Orangutans spend most of their lives high in the trees, where they build a new nest every evening. Females even give birth in trees—babies are born with the instinct to hold on tight! They stay with their mothers for up to nine years.

Amazing **apes**

Apes are the largest, most intelligent, and longest-lived of the primate family. Unlike most monkeys, they can walk on their hind legs, build a nest to sleep in, and have no tail.

TOOL KIT!

Some chimpanzees hunt by sharpening sticks and using them to spear small primates! Others strip leaves from twigs and "fish" for ants in anthills.

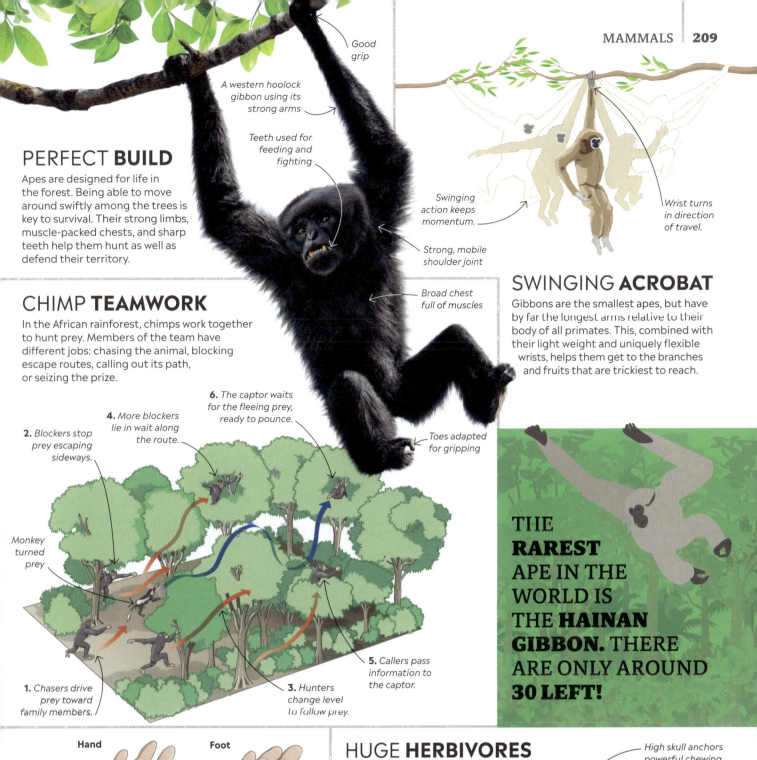

PERFECT **BUILD**

Apes are designed for life in the forest. Being able to move around swiftly among the trees is key to survival. Their strong limbs, muscle-packed chests, and sharp teeth help them hunt as well as defend their territory.

Good grip

A western hoolock gibbon using its strong arms

Teeth used for feeding and fighting

Swinging action keeps momentum.

Strong, mobile shoulder joint

Broad chest full of muscles

Toes adapted for gripping

Wrist turns in direction of travel.

SWINGING **ACROBAT**

Gibbons are the smallest apes, but have by far the longest arms relative to their body of all primates. This, combined with their light weight and uniquely flexible wrists, helps them get to the branches and fruits that are trickiest to reach.

CHIMP **TEAMWORK**

In the African rainforest, chimps work together to hunt prey. Members of the team have different jobs: chasing the animal, blocking escape routes, calling out its path, or seizing the prize.

6. *The captor waits for the fleeing prey, ready to pounce.*

4. *More blockers lie in wait along the route.*

2. *Blockers stop prey escaping sideways.*

Monkey turned prey

5. *Callers pass information to the captor.*

1. *Chasers drive prey toward family members.*

3. *Hunters change level to follow prey.*

THE **RAREST** APE IN THE WORLD IS THE **HAINAN GIBBON.** THERE ARE ONLY AROUND **30 LEFT!**

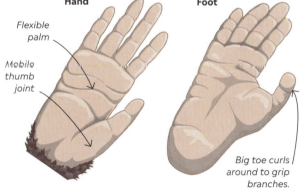

Hand | Foot

Flexible palm

Mobile thumb joint

Big toe curls around to grip branches.

HANDY **TOES**

Apes have opposable thumbs—they can move their thumbs to touch each individual finger. It means they can pick up and hold things, break open nuts, and even use tools. All apes except humans also have opposable big toes!

HUGE **HERBIVORES**

It takes a lot of leaves, stems, and berries to power a massive gorilla. They spend up to a quarter of their day eating the 55 lb (25 kg) of plant matter they need to survive.

High skull anchors powerful chewing muscles in the jaw.

Nimble fingers pluck food from nearby plants and trees.

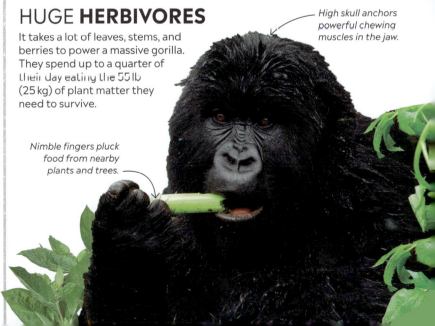

Mischievous monkeys

Like apes, monkeys are intelligent primates with grasping hands and forward-facing eyes. Most of them have a long tail and many are skillful climbers.

SPIDER MONKEYS USE THEIR **TAILS** LIKE AN **EXTRA LIMB!**

Black hair grows in spiky crests on top of the head.

MONKEY **WORLDS**

There are around 300 species of monkey, divided into two main groups. New World monkeys live in Mexico and Central and South America, while Old World monkeys (split into two types) are at home in Africa and Asia.

Old World monkeys

Mandrill, an omnivore

Omnivores
Species in this group eat anything from fruits and fungi to insects and reptiles.

Leaf-eating langur

Leaf eaters
Mostly long-tailed tree dwellers, these species like leaves and young shoots.

New World monkeys

Varied diets
Some are omnivores, others eat only fruit and leaves. Several have prehensile tails.

Howler monkey

NIGHT OWL

To see well enough to find food in low light, nocturnal owl monkeys have evolved huge eyeballs. Their lenses have a more spherical shape than those of monkeys that are active during the day. Their eyes also have more rod cells, which increase light sensitivity.

Smaller eyes for daytime life

Extra large eye sockets for holding large eyeballs

Owl monkey

Capuchin monkey

COLOBUS MONKEYS SHOW **FRIENDSHIP** THROUGH **BURPING!**

SOCIAL GROUPS

Monkeys are highly social animals. Many, such as these geladas, live in troops made up of many females and young, led by a dominant male. While the young play, adults spend time grooming each other.

CURIOUS COMRADES

These crested black macaques are nosy and eager to investigate new things. When monkeys live close to people, this curiosity can get them into trouble.

HOWLER MONKEYS CAN BE HEARD 3 MILES (5 KM) AWAY!

CHEEK POUCH

Old World monkeys, such as this baboon, have extended skin reaching down the side of their necks. These food storage pouches are very handy if a monkey is disturbed when foraging and needs to make a quick getaway without leaving its food behind.

BABY CARE

Infant monkeys are helpless, and cling on to their mothers. But marmosets and tamarins do things differently—the fathers have almost all the responsibility! As this golden lion tamarin dad shows, they carry their babies on their backs and take care of them, only giving them to the mother for nursing.

Long, golden guard hairs protect the underlying thick fur from snow and rain.

The flat shape of the nose, with flaps around its large nostrils, helps prevent frostbite.

Thick fur insulates from the cold.

IN SUMMER, FAMILY GROUPS GET TOGETHER IN GATHERINGS OF **UP TO 600 MONKEYS!**

CHILLING OUT

This snub-nosed monkey is taking a break from foraging. All adults have orange fur on their heads and a distinct bluish-white face, but the long golden guard hairs reveal that this one is an older male. His noisy family of several females and playful young ones is not far away.

YOUNG ARE **CREAMY BROWN** ALL OVER AND DON'T GROW **GOLDEN** HAIR UNTIL THE **AGE OF THREE!**

Golden snub-nosed **monkey**

These endangered monkeys live in remote mountainous forests in China. In temperatures that can fall to 14°F (−10°C), their thick coat is not just pretty, but essential.

CHILD **PROTECTION**

Like most primates, when there's a threat, snub-nosed monkeys form small huddles, keeping the youngsters in the middle for protection and comfort. The dominant male tries to stop the attacker, here a goshawk.

Baby surrounded by protective adults

Goshawk attacking

Male fights off goshawk.

TASTY **TREES**

On cold mountain slopes, being a plant-eater means a menu of pine needles, lichens, and bark. In summer, buds and fruit seeds offer some variety.

KEEPING **WARM**

Snub-nosed monkeys survive the longest winters and coldest temperatures of any nonhuman primate. Thick fur and group huddles keep them warm.

THESE **MOUNTAIN MONKEYS** LIVE AT HEIGHTS OF UP TO **13,000 FT (4,000 M)!**

MOVING AROUND

Long-limbed and agile, snub-nosed monkeys mostly travel by perching, climbing, and swinging in trees. But troops can move across land to look for food—and they sometimes hop across icy rivers too. Clinging on tight, young travel everywhere with their moms.

TOOTH **TALKING**

There's a lot of communication going on in a monkey family. Snub-nosed monkeys make many different sounds. But they also communicate by curling their lips, opening or closing their mouths, or showing their teeth.

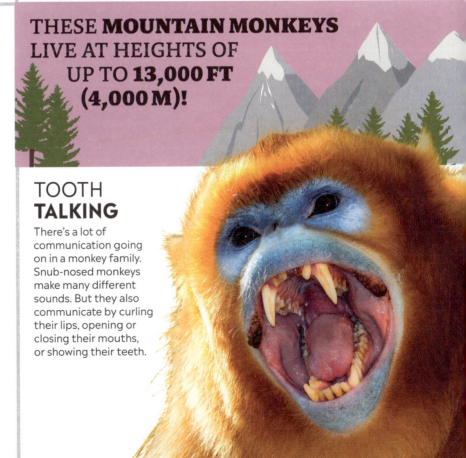

Primitive prosimians

Including lorises, tiny tarsiers, and long-tailed lemurs, prosimians are a group of primitive primates. Unlike monkeys, most have wet noses and many are active at night.

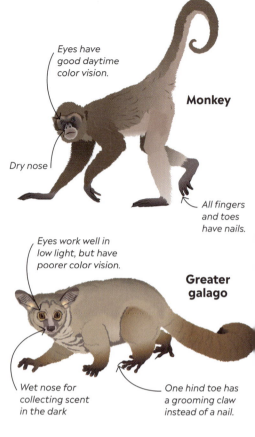

Eyes have good daytime color vision.

Monkey

Dry nose

All fingers and toes have nails.

Eyes work well in low light, but have poorer color vision.

Greater galago

Wet nose for collecting scent in the dark

One hind toe has a grooming claw instead of a nail.

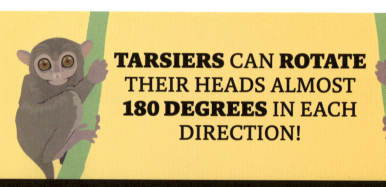

TARSIERS CAN **ROTATE** THEIR HEADS ALMOST **180 DEGREES** IN EACH DIRECTION!

MONKEY OR PROSIMIAN?

Monkeys are adapted to daytime activity, while smaller-brained, nocturnal prosimians have larger eyes and moist snouts for an advantage at night.

Dark, wiry fur is excellent camouflage in the nighttime forest.

Batlike ears hear even the faintest insect rustle.

Grooming claw is used to comb dirt off their bodies.

MISTAKEN IDENTITY

Measuring around 2 ft (60 cm) long, the spooky-looking aye-aye is the world's largest nocturnal primate. Like other members of the lemur family, it is only found in Madagascar. For centuries it was thought to be a type of rodent—like them, its sharp incisors never stop growing.

A reflective layer on the back of the eye gives excellent night vision.

Long finger is used to probe for grubs in tree bark and wood.

Ears can rotate like radar dishes.

Bush babies can't move their eyes, so they have to turn their whole head to look around.

SUPER SENSOR

Bush babies have big eyes and ears for detecting in the dark. The ears can rotate independently to sense prey from many directions, and fold back against the bush baby's head when not in use.

SLOW LORISES ARE THE ONLY KNOWN **VENOMOUS PRIMATE!**

ATTENTION **SEEKER**

When he is ready to breed, a ring-tailed lemur douses his tail in a fatty sweet-smelling musk secreted from his wrists. He then waves it toward potential female mates to encourage them to pick him over his rivals.

TO **COMMUNICATE** WITH EACH OTHER, RING-TAILED LEMURS USE UP TO **24** DIFFERENT CALLS!

The mouth contains a toothcomb, a row of tiny teeth used for grooming and peeling fruit.

Arms are used for balance when running.

Fur is long, fine, and silky.

DANCING QUEEN

Prosimians travel on all fours when not in the trees—except for sifakas. This Madagascan lemur skips and dances sideways across the ground at up to 12 mph (19 kph). Due to habitat loss it is now critically endangered.

Long tail helps the sifaka stay stable and upright.

Powerful legs allow them to jump 33 ft (10 m) from tree to tree.

Thumb-like big toe for gripping tree branches

TONGUE **TIED**

Sun bear tongues are up to 9¾ in (25 cm) long—perfect for getting termites, honey, and ants in hard-to-reach places such as insect nests and tree hollows. At just 5 ft (1.5 m) tall, this animal is the smallest of the bears.

SLEEP **TIGHT**

We used to think that bears hibernate through the winter in cold climates. Biologists now dispute this—though bears do sleep for extended periods, they can also wake up from time to time. Their body temperature and heart rate do not fall as low as those of "true" hibernators.

PANDAS SOMETIMES DO A HANDSTAND WHEN THEY PEE!

The fur of brown bears is long and thick. Its water-resistant properties mean it sheds moisture quickly, keeping the skin beneath dry.

This bear's claws are around 2 in (5 cm) long, but can grow to double that.

Black bear skull

ALL YOU **CAN EAT**

This American black bear skull has teeth for eating both plants and meat. Most bears are omnivorous, but some specialize—polar bears prefer meat and giant pandas eat bamboo.

Incisors cut and clip grass and plants.

Molars chew meat, nuts, fruit, and vegetables.

Canines (lower and upper) rip and tear at meat.

Long, curved claws give excellent grip.

UPWARD **MOBILITY**

Cubs and smaller bear species, such as black bears, easily scale trees when they feel threatened. Larger, heavier species, such as this brown bear, are less likely to climb trees unless they feel very unsafe or are gathering nuts or other food.

Brilliant bears

They vary in size and behavior, but all bears have short tails, small ears, are flat-footed, and have a keen sense of smell and relatively poor hearing and eyesight. Most bear species are omnivorous (they eat everything).

BROWN BEARS CAN RUN AT SPEEDS UP TO 40 MPH (64 KPH)!

TOP HUNTER

Bears' short, powerful limbs are ideally designed for foraging, digging, climbing, and swimming. Their sense of smell is better than a dog's, and their strong shoulders and flat feet mean they can run at great speeds on all fours over uneven terrain.

BLACK BEARS CAN EAT 30,000 BERRIES A DAY!

Standing on hind legs also allows the bear to better see and smell its opponent.

THREATENING POSE

Bears only fight as a last resort. Their main weapon, as this grizzly bear demonstrates, is intimidation. They show their teeth and claws to their opponent while bellowing at them in the hope they will back down. When a fight happens it is rarely lethal, usually ending when one bear has asserted its dominance over the other.

Polar bear

Polar bears live in the cold, harsh habitat of the Arctic, where they rely on snow and ice to hunt and to rear cubs safely. But warming oceans now mean these giants have to find new ways of living because their icy world is changing.

WAITING GAME

Patience is key on a polar bear hunt. Bears wait at holes in the ice to pounce on seals coming up for air. They also patrol the water's edge, ready to swim out and sneak up on seals resting on ice floes.

Seals are vulnerable when they come up to breathe.

One polar bear weighs roughly the same as two grand pianos

WEIGHING UP TO **1,765 LB (800 KG)**, MALE POLAR BEARS ARE THE **LARGEST LAND CARNIVORE!**

SUPERB **SWIMMER**

Polar bears are equally at home in the water as on ice or land. They can swim for hours between ice floes and icebergs. They paddle with their forepaws while their hind paws act as a rudder.

Ears are small and can flatten to stop water entering.

Nostrils can close to keep out water.

Oily coating on fur means it dries quickly, even when soaking wet.

A **GROLAR BEAR** IS A **HYBRID** OF A POLAR BEAR AND A **GRIZZLY!**

SNIFFING OUT **PREY**

With prey often hidden under ice, snow, or water, polar bears use their sense of smell to find food. They can detect scents from seal breathing holes in the ice or seals surfacing from underwater half a mile (1 km) away.

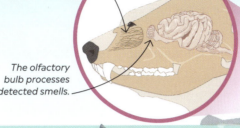

Curly bone plates increase the inside surface of the nose, which is full of smell receptors.

The olfactory bulb processes detected smells.

The seal's scent is picked up when the animal rises to the surface.

SAFE **DEN**

In late fall, a pregnant polar bear will dig a den in the snow and creep in. She'll stay there until spring, when her new cubs are ready to try life outside. During the whole time in the den, she doesn't eat anything but still produces fat-rich milk for the cubs so they can grow quickly.

DIET **CHANGE**

Polar bears prefer seals, though they also eat Arctic seabirds and their eggs. But with a changing, less icy habitat, they are increasingly forced to scavenge for any food, closer to sites of human habitation.

ONE TRACKED POLAR BEAR **SWAM NONSTOP** FOR MORE THAN **NINE DAYS!**

Cub on its way out for the first time

Small hole to let in air

The mother stays closest to the entrance.

Entrance tunnel

The den is warmer than the outside thanks to the insulating layers of snow.

One to three cubs are born tiny, blind, and helpless but grow fast.

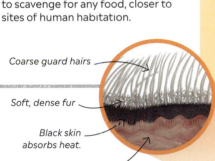

Coarse guard hairs

Soft, dense fur

Black skin absorbs heat.

Blubber

KEEPING **COZY**

In the Arctic, temperatures can go down to -50°F (-46°C). But polar bears stay warm with two layers of fur on top of their skin. The dense undercoat keeps the bear warm and is in turn shielded by thick guard hairs. A thick layer of blubber (fat) adds extra insulation.

PRACTICAL **PAWS**

Moving on ice is no easy feat, but polar bears' wide paws distribute their heavy weight perfectly and help them to grip the slippery surface.

Curved claws
Thick, curved, sharp, and strong claws give optimum grip on the ice.

Non-slip pads
The black footpads have small, soft bumps that prevent slipping.

PRESERVED
PREY

Some shrews inject their prey with venom, but to stun it rather than to kill it. This way, they can keep a supply of still-juicy worms.

**NORTHERN
SHORT-TAILED SHREW**

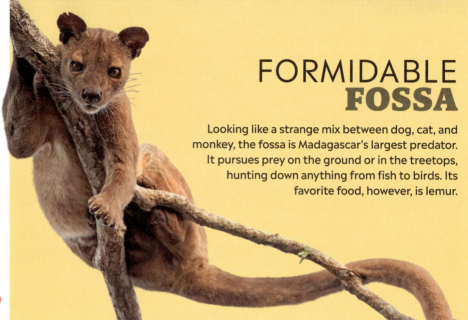

FORMIDABLE
FOSSA

Looking like a strange mix between dog, cat, and monkey, the fossa is Madagascar's largest predator. It pursues prey on the ground or in the treetops, hunting down anything from fish to birds. Its favorite food, however, is lemur.

FACT PACK!
PREDATORS

Many mammals are predators that actively hunt for prey to eat. On land and at sea, they need speed, strength, or clever methods to get the food they need for themselves and their young.

SMART STRATEGIES

Orcas have figured out how to use teamwork to get seals in their sights, even when the seal within range is out of the water.

1 SPY-HOP
Rising vertically out of the water, orcas peek for seals resting on ice floes.

2 MAKE WAVE
Together, orcas swim toward and under the floe to create a big wave.

3 ROCK THE FLOE
The wave rocks the floe, often breaking it into pieces in the process.

4 CATCH PREY
As the seal slips off the unstable floe, the orcas are ready to catch it.

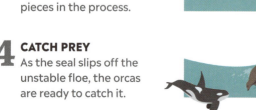

PACK HUNTERS

Hunting in packs isn't always successful, and predators often fail to catch their prey. This list shows how often different species succeed.

85% AFRICAN WILD DOGS

75% HYENAS

30% LIONS

20% GRAY WOLVES

TRIDENT **TEETH**

Leopard seals have super sharp teeth for grabbing and tearing flesh. But their scariest-looking teeth are for catching krill! These tiny prey are sifted through the seal's jagged, three-tipped molars.

SNEAKY STEALTH

A tiger's stripes help it blend in with its surroundings so it can sneak up on antelopes without being spotted. Most tigers have more than 100 stripes on their coat in patterns unique to each individual.

JAW POWER

A polar bear has a bite force of 5,000 newtons (N)—almost four times that of a human. But when measured in proportion to the animal's size, known as Bite Force Quotient (BFQ), smaller creatures, such as the Tasmanian devil, have a bigger bite.

When measured by BFQ, the Tasmanian devil has the strongest bite force.

Compared to its size, the polar bear has a relatively weak bite force.

BFQ 181
TASMANIAN DEVIL

BFQ 137
JAGUAR

BFQ 117
SPOTTED HYENA

BFQ 78
POLAR BEAR

SOLITARY HUNTERS

Some mammals go it alone, relying only on themselves to catch things to eat. These four creatures are all efficient hunters.

BLACK-FOOTED CAT
This African cat gets its prey 60 percent of the time.

INDIAN GRAY MONGOOSE
A king cobra is no match for this omnivore.

BOBCAT
First stalking its prey, this cat then ambushes by pouncing.

LEOPARD SEAL
Penguins are this sharp-toothed Antarctic seal's preferred prey.

SUPER TOOLS

Predators need good eyes, ears, and teeth. Some species have bigger ones than others compared to body size.

LARGEST EYES
The tiny, nocturnal tarsier has enormous eyes in comparison to its body size.

LARGEST EARS
With an ear length of nearly half its body, a fennec fox picks up the slightest sound.

LARGEST TEETH
Sperm whales have the largest teeth of mammal predators—up to 7¾ in (20 cm).

FISH LOVERS

These three fish-eating mammals have very different fishing styles.

GREATER BULLDOG BAT uses echolocation to catch fish in rivers.

WATER SHREWS jump into rivers to catch shrimp and small fish.

ELEPHANT SEALS chase squid and fish deep down in the ocean.

Greater bulldog bats can **catch** up to **40 fish** during a single nighttime **fishing trip!**

SNOWY LAIR

Ringed seals use their claws to make breathing holes in the Arctic ice. In winter, female seals create cave-like lairs in snowdrifts formed on top of the ice. Inside, they can nurse their pup in safety.

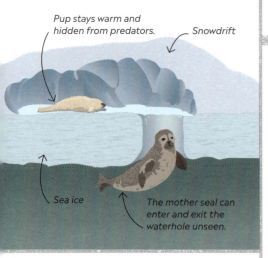

Pup stays warm and hidden from predators.

Snowdrift

Sea ice

The mother seal can enter and exit the waterhole unseen.

Seals, walruses, and sea lions

These marine mammals are known as pinnipeds (fin-footed). While true seals have small flippers and no visible ears, sea lions and fur seals have ear flaps and long, strong front flippers.

DEEP DIVERS

All pinnipeds dive to catch fish, but how deep and for how long varies between species. Elephant seals are champions: they can descend to depths of 5,570 ft (1,700 m) and stay under for two hours.

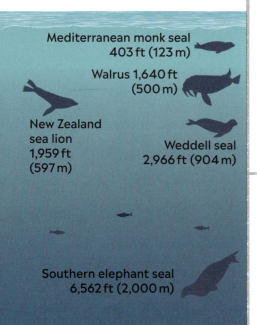

Mediterranean monk seal
403 ft (123 m)

Walrus 1,640 ft (500 m)

New Zealand sea lion 1,959 ft (597 m)

Weddell seal 2,966 ft (904 m)

Southern elephant seal 6,562 ft (2,000 m)

SWIMMING LESSONS

Most pups can swim soon after birth, but the fluffy pups of harp seals and some gray seals (above) usually stay on land for longer. The skills needed to elude predators and catch fish require a bit more practice.

WALRUS WHISKERS

The mustache of a walrus is composed of up to 700 sensitive whiskers called vibrissae. They can detect movement in water and changing currents, and let the walrus "feel" any tasty mollusks half-buried in the seabed.

EXTRA LAYER

Like other marine mammals, seals have a layer of blubber under the skin. Made up of fat and protein, it covers the whole body except the flippers. It keeps a seal's body warm in cold waters, stores energy, and boosts buoyancy (the ability to float).

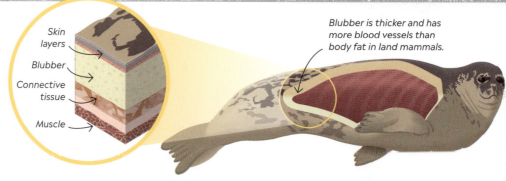

Skin layers

Blubber

Connective tissue

Muscle

Blubber is thicker and has more blood vessels than body fat in land mammals.

SEA LION PUPS CAN **WALK** AT 30 MINUTES OLD, LONG **BEFORE** THEY CAN **SWIM!**

Back flippers act as rudders, steering the animal through the water.

SEA LION STARS

Extremely flexible in water, sea lions twist their bodies for play or when winding through kelp forests in pursuit of prey. Their strong flipper muscles help them power through the water. On land, sea lions use their flippers to walk on all fours, unlike true seals, who use their front flippers to drag themselves forward on their bellies.

Bellybutton

Long, clawless front flipper covered in rubbery skin

Streamlined, torpedo-shaped body for easy gliding through the water

Short, thick fur turns darker when wet.

FURRY **MEET-UP!**

Adult fur seals spend more than 80 percent of the year in the sea. But when it's time to breed, they show up to their breeding shores in huge numbers. While on land, nursing mothers make quick fishing trips but males don't eat at all.

Eyes with small pupils adapt to the lower light levels in deep water.

Ear flaps

Dolphins and porpoises

Graceful, sleek swimmers, dolphins and porpoises are smaller, toothed relatives of whales. They exist in every ocean, and some rivers. From the giant orca to the small Māui, they vary in size but have many playful traits in common.

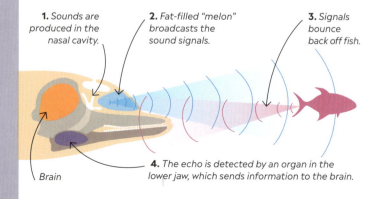

MEASURING UP TO **32 FT (10 M)** LONG, THE **ORCA** IS THE **LARGEST** OF THE **DOLPHINS!**

The tail flukes help create momentum to fly out of the water.

RIVER DOLPHINS

Some dolphin species are only found in freshwater. The largest is the Amazon river dolphin (left); others live in India and Southeast Asia. Rivers can be murky and lined with mangrove roots, making prey hard to see—meaning echolocation is even more vital there than in the ocean.

ECHO**LOCATION**

Dolphins send out high-frequency clicks, and listen for the bounce-back to navigate and to locate prey. When communicating with each other, they also produce various whistling sounds.

1. *Sounds are produced in the nasal cavity.*

2. *Fat-filled "melon" broadcasts the sound signals.*

3. *Signals bounce back off fish.*

Brain

4. *The echo is detected by an organ in the lower jaw, which sends information to the brain.*

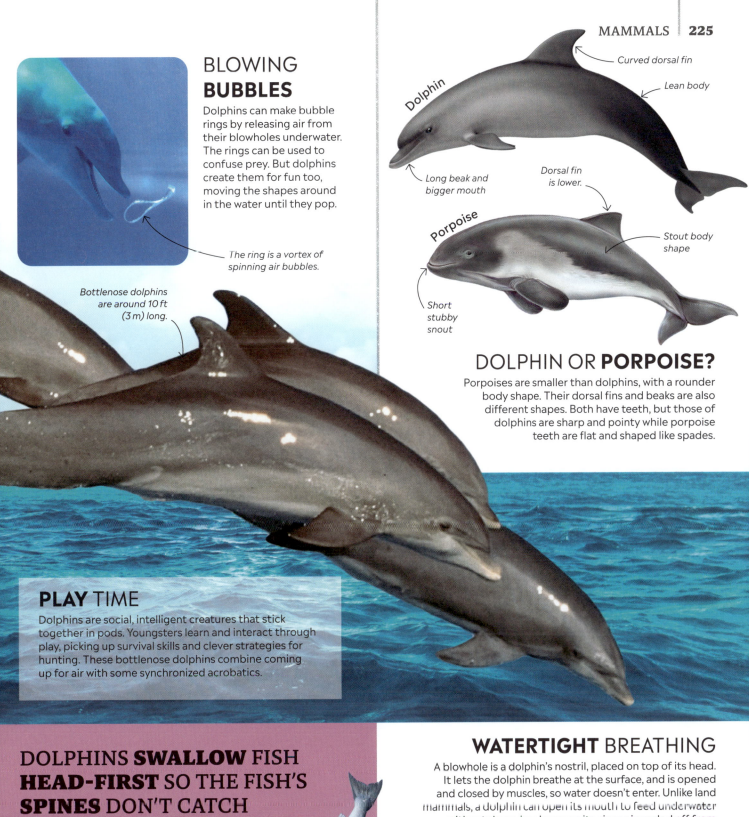

BLOWING BUBBLES

Dolphins can make bubble rings by releasing air from their blowholes underwater. The rings can be used to confuse prey. But dolphins create them for fun too, moving the shapes around in the water until they pop.

The ring is a vortex of spinning air bubbles.

Bottlenose dolphins are around 10 ft (3 m) long.

Curved dorsal fin

Dolphin

Lean body

Long beak and bigger mouth

Dorsal fin is lower.

Porpoise

Stout body shape

Short stubby snout

DOLPHIN OR PORPOISE?

Porpoises are smaller than dolphins, with a rounder body shape. Their dorsal fins and beaks are also different shapes. Both have teeth, but those of dolphins are sharp and pointy while porpoise teeth are flat and shaped like spades.

PLAY TIME

Dolphins are social, intelligent creatures that stick together in pods. Youngsters learn and interact through play, picking up survival skills and clever strategies for hunting. These bottlenose dolphins combine coming up for air with some synchronized acrobatics.

DOLPHINS SWALLOW FISH HEAD-FIRST SO THE FISH'S SPINES DON'T CATCH IN THEIR THROAT!

WATERTIGHT BREATHING

A blowhole is a dolphin's nostril, placed on top of its head. It lets the dolphin breathe at the surface, and is opened and closed by muscles, so water doesn't enter. Unlike land mammals, a dolphin can open its mouth to feed underwater without drowning, because its airway is sealed off from the back of its throat.

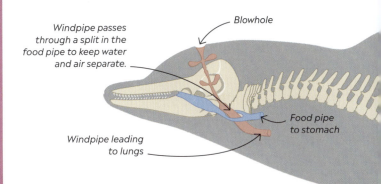

Windpipe passes through a split in the food pipe to keep water and air separate.

Blowhole

Food pipe to stomach

Windpipe leading to lungs

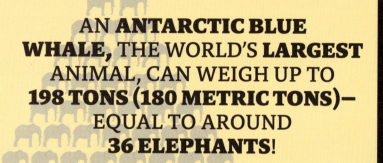

AN ANTARCTIC BLUE WHALE, THE WORLD'S **LARGEST** ANIMAL, CAN WEIGH UP TO **198 TONS (180 METRIC TONS)**— EQUAL TO AROUND **36 ELEPHANTS!**

Eyes sit on the sides of the head, so the whale cannot see straight ahead.

Long pectoral fins measure one third of the whale's body length.

Bumps on the face, called tubercles, each hold a strand of hair.

HUMPBACK WHALE

The humpback whale is present in every ocean of the world, traveling alone or in small pods. A baleen whale, it eats about 2.2 tons (2 metric tons) of krill a day and can grow up to 55 ft (17 m) long. It uses many varied noises to communicate, including the famous whale songs.

WHALE MIGRATION

Many whales migrate between feeding and breeding grounds. Some gray whales travel from the Arctic to warmer breeding grounds off Mexico. Then they swim back—a 12,000-mile (19,000-km) round trip!

ASIA

NORTH AMERICA

PACIFIC OCEAN

■ Gray whale habitat
--- Migration route, eastern Pacific

WHO'S WHO?

Whales, dolphins, and their relatives are aquatic mammals called cetaceans. They all have flippers for swimming and blowholes for breathing, and feed in two main ways. Baleen whales have sievelike plates in their huge mouths for straining krill and other plankton. Toothed whales and dolphins, including orcas, use their teeth to grab and tear at bigger prey.

Baleen whale

Two blowholes for breathing

Baleen plates

UP TO **1,100 LB** (500 KG) OF **BARNACLES** CAN **FREE-RIDE** ON A WHALE WITHOUT IT BEING BOTHERED!

Barnacles

One blowhole

Toothed whale

The orca, part of the dolphin family of cetaceans (see pages 224-225) has very sharp teeth.

The wide tail is made up of two boneless fins called flukes. It makes a big, loud splash when slapped through the ocean surface.

Long grooves running down from the whale's mouth allow the skin to expand when it gulps large quantities of water.

Narwhal tusks grow in a tight spiral around a core of nerves. The outer layer is not hard but porous, making them very sensitive!

Whale world

There are more than 43 different whale species. Some are majestic giants, gracefully gliding through the oceans, others playful predators. But all surface to breathe air through their blowholes.

MYSTERY **TUSK**

The narwhal tusk is an elongated tooth, but experts are not sure of its function. Since it's usually males that have them, they might be a signal of strength to display during breeding season.

SPERM WHALE

With a head taking up one third of its length, the sperm whale has the largest brain of any animal. Sperm whales can dive as deep as 3,300 ft (1,000 m), in search of prey such as giant squid and octopus.

The head contains an organ, used as a sonar.

Sperm whales only have teeth on the lower jaw.

Triangular tail flukes

TAIL PRINTS!

Just like human fingerprints, humpback tail flukes are unique: the markings are specific to each whale. Scientists can use them to identify and track individual whales and learn about their behaviors.

Unique markings on underside of tail

NAME THAT... WATER MAMMAL

Do you know a seal from a sea lion? What's an otter and what's not-a? Can you find the right whale, and is there a wrong one? Dive in with these water-loving mammals and name as many as you can.

1 Sperm whale
2 Sea otter
3 Humpback whale (mother and calf)
4 Ribbon seal
5 American mink
6 Hawaiian monk seal
7 Hippopotamus
8 Bowhead whale
9 Pygmy right whale
10 Capybara
11 Gray whale
12 Walrus
13 Shepherd's beaked whale
14 Gervais's beaked whale
15 Polar bear
16 Asian short-clawed otter
17 Long-finned pilot whale
18 Blue whale
19 Narwhal (sparring males)
20 European otter
21 Short-beaked common dolphin (mother and calf)
22 North American beaver
23 Whale shark
24 Franciscana
25 Orca
26 California sea lion
27 Vaquita
28 Harbor seal
29 North Atlantic right whale
30 Duck-billed platypus
31 West Indian manatee
32 Beluga whale
33 Pacific white-sided dolphin
34 Indus river dolphin
35 Water shrew

The odd one out is the whale shark (23). Whale sharks are fish, like all sharks—they have gills instead of lungs and don't feed milk to their young.

CAN YOU SPOT THE ODD ONE OUT?

Mighty **elephants**

The largest land mammals on Earth combine strength, incredible senses of smell and touch, and amazing memory to live together on savannas and in forests.

African savanna elephants

Trunk used in friendly greeting

Packed with muscles but no bones, the trunk can curl, bend, and twist.

The trunk can produce snorts, trumpets, and low-frequency rumbling.

TRUNK **TALK**

Elephants use their trunks to bond, with both adults and calves touching and stroking each other. They also use their excellent sense of smell to tell family and nonfamily members apart, and can hold smell memories for up to 12 years.

AN ELEPHANT CAN **STORE WATER** IN A **POUCH** INSIDE ITS MOUTH!

The African elephant has two "fingers" to manipulate objects.

Terrific tool

Trunks are strong but also useful for delicately investigating surroundings. The tip has prehensile "fingers," used to curl around objects and pick them up.

The Asian elephant only has one finger.

TREE TOPPLER

Elephants are fantastic ecosystem engineers. They change their habitats by pushing down trees, distributing seeds through their poop, and creating waterholes. The result is a healthy habitat that benefits other animals too.

CHARGING **BULL**

Most elephants will only charge when necessary, usually when they feel threatened. Male elephants charge as a display of strength too, with flapping ears and swinging trunk. Like this African savanna bull, they often mock-charge other males when wanting to show off.

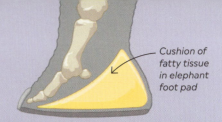

Cushion of fatty tissue in elephant foot pad

FOOT PADS ACT LIKE SHOCK **ABSORBERS** AND MUFFLE HEAVY **STOMPS**!

ELEPHANT **LINEUP**

There are three different species of elephant. All are of impressive weight and height, but they can be distinguished by some easily identifiable traits.

African savanna elephant
The largest species of elephant has huge, wide, flapping ears. Their color is lighter than forest elephants.

African forest elephant
Smaller than their savanna cousins, they have tusks that point downward.

Asian elephant
This species has smaller ears and a dome on the left and right sides of its head. Only the males have tusks.

DUST **BATH**

At the waterhole, elephants spray water on themselves to cool down. But taking a dust bath works just as well. This Asian elephant uses suction to gather dust in its trunk, and then blows it out over its back and ears. The dust cloud may also give relief from insect bites.

DISTANCE **CALL!**

Elephant trumpeting is loud. But very low-frequency rumbles, produced through the trunk and mouth, can reach twice as far. These vibrations travel through the ground and are detected by other elephants. Receivers can sense where the message came from and who was calling.

MEET THE **CAMELIDS**

There are seven species of camelid. The wild vicuña and guanaco and the domesticated alpaca and llama live in South America. Wild and domesticated Bactrian camels are at home in Mongolia and northwestern China. The domesticated dromedary is found in West Asia and North Africa.

A **CAMEL** CAN DRINK **32 GALLONS** (**145 LITERS**) OF **WATER** AT ONCE!

Vicuña
The smallest of the camelids lives highest up in the Andes mountains. Its shoulder height is just less than 3 ft (85 cm).

Alpaca
A domesticated species descended from vicuña, alpacas are bred across the world for their wool.

Guanaco
Wild herds roam the arid Atacama Desert and rugged plateaus in the Andes and Patagonia.

Llama
Descended from the guanaco, llamas were bred to carry cargo on narrow mountain roads.

Dromedary
These one-humped camels tolerate the heat of the Sahara and Arabian Deserts.

Bactrian camel
Shaggy coats keep these two-humped camels warm in cold Asian deserts.

The camel family

The camel family, a group known as camelids, takes extreme living to the next level. They thrive in tough, arid terrains and harsh climates. Some species survive breathing thin mountain air while others endure hot or cold deserts.

WOOLLY **ALPACAS**

Thick hair keeps alpacas warm in the cold, dry air of the Andes mountains. The people of the ancient civilizations of this region, including the Inca, bred alpacas to make warm clothing from their wool, and it is still highly prized. If sheared in summer, the fleece grows back in time for winter.

Hair fibers grow directly outward in small bundles with a tight crimp (wave).

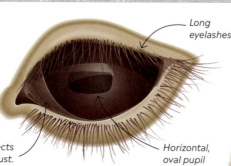

EYE OF A CAMEL

Camels live in sandy, dusty, and often windy places. To protect their eyes, they have a double row of super-long eyelashes and a thin membrane in each eye, like a see-through third eyelid.

Long eyelashes

Third eyelid protects eye from dust.

Horizontal, oval pupil

Fat held in humps, rather than spread out under the skin, stops the camel's body overheating.

TWO-TOED **WALKERS**

Camels walk long distances over sandy dunes. They have two toes on each foot, with a wide pad underneath. This helps spread their body weight and stops their feet sinking through the sand. The pads' leathery surface can withstand stepping on extremely hot desert sand.

Hard, naillike tip at the end of each toe

ENERGY **SUPPLY**

Almost all of a camel's body fat is stored in its humps. This rich fat supply helps camels go a long time without food and water. Eventually, the fat reserve is reduced and the humps slump over, until the camel can top it up by eating again.

CAMEL **LIPS**

Camels have cleverly shaped lips. The flexible upper lip is split in two, so the camel can easily nibble plants and grass very close to the ground. Since their lips are tough, thorny desert plants don't bother them, which is helpful in arid surroundings where vegetation is scarce.

Alpacas have shorter noses and are smaller than llamas.

WHEN **THREATENED,** LLAMAS **SPIT** OUT **SALIVA** MIXED WITH **VOMIT!**

Wild **pigs**

Found throughout Africa, Asia, and Europe, wild pigs are sociable, hoofed animals with bristly coats. Their broad, flattened snouts are perfect for sniffing out food as varied as fruit, leaves, fungi, and animal prey.

Size 7 basketball

THE **SMALLEST PIG** SPECIES IS THE **PYGMY HOG**. IT GROWS TO A **HEIGHT** OF ONLY **9¾ IN (25 CM)**!

RIVER PIG

The most colorful of all pig species, red river hogs live close to water in West and Central Africa. They wade in looking for water plants to eat, but also feast on fruit, roots, and worms on land.

White hair raised when pig is excited or threatened

Long tufts of hair on tips of the ears flick flies away.

White markings distort the pig's outline and confuse predators.

Nostrils stay above the waterline.

CLOSE **COMPANY**

Warthogs are often seen in the company of oxpeckers. These birds peck their way around the warthog's body, feasting on ticks (bloodsucking mites). Oxpeckers feed on their hosts' blood too, and their sharp beaks can cause sores, but the warthogs don't seem to mind.

Oxpecker cleaning the snout of a warthog kneeling down for a drink

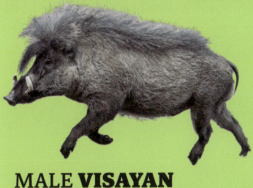

MALE **VISAYAN WARTY PIGS** GROW A LONG **MANE** FOR **MATING SEASON!**

ECOSYSTEM **ENGINEERS**

This wild boar sow and her boarlets are looking for food by snuffling and digging through woodland. Boars leave the soil in a bit of a mess, but they play a vital role in distributing seeds and creating space for plants to grow.

MUD **BATH**

Like all pigs, this warthog lacks sweat glands. To cool down in its warm Kenyan habitat, it wallows in mud to prevent its body from overheating. It might not look like it, but the mud helps cleanse the skin as well.

FAST **FORWARD!**

Quick on their feet, wild pigs can pick up some serious speed. This means they are able to sprint to evade predators, or charge at potential threats at pace.

Wild boar
25 mph (40 kph)

Warthog
30 mph (48 kph)

Face glands located around the eyes

Mouth glands around the tusks

Rear glands all around the bottom

Glands on front legs are scraped on the ground to leave scent marks.

SUPER **SCENTED**

Pigs aren't just great at picking up scents, they have nine different glands to produce unique odors too. These are used to communicate a wide variety of smelly messages from one pig to another.

This male babirusa's long upper tusks touch its forehead.

Lower tusk growing from lower jaw

TUSK **TROUBLE**

All pigs have long canine teeth that grow into tusks. Most upper tusks flare outward and curve upward from the side of the mouth. But those of the babirusa grow up through its skull and bend in toward its forehead.

Hairy skin, known as velvet, supplies nutrients to growing antlers.

MINI **GRAZER**

Chevrotains, or mouse deer, are tiny, with a shoulder height of only around 12 in (30 cm). Surprisingly for a grazer, they have long canine teeth—but they use these for fighting, not for eating.

Leaves are plucked off by incisors, then chewed by molars

Paired antlers get bigger every time they regrow, spanning up to 6 ft 6 in (2 m).

MIGHTY **MOOSE**

Largest of the deer family, moose roam northern forests in America and Eurasia. Standing up to 6 ft 6 in (2 m) tall, they can easily reach leaves and pine cones. They are good swimmers, and often feed on mineral-rich aquatic plants too.

BISON HAVE LIVED IN **YELLOWSTONE NATIONAL PARK** IN THE US SINCE **PREHISTORIC TIMES!**

Ruminant animals

These cloven-hoofed mammals are famous for chewing the cud (regurgitating food for a second chewing). At home in habitats that range from the African savanna to the Arctic tundra, they are a diverse group of animals, many crowned with striking horns or antlers.

1. Animal chews and swallows food for the first time.

5. The fourth chamber uses acidic digestive juices, like the human stomach.

6. Digestion and nutrient absorption are completed in the intestine.

2. The first and biggest chamber mixes food with microbes to start digestion. Nutrients are released—along with methane gas, which the cow burps out!

3. From the second chamber, balls of softened food, called cuds, return to the mouth for a second chewing.

4. Twice-chewed food returns to the third chamber to release more nutrients.

GREAT GUTS

Ruminants have a four-chambered stomach to help digest tough plants. The chambers contain microbes that break down plant fiber, and the animals regurgitate meals to give them a second chew.

MUSK OXEN CHARGE INTO HEADBUTTS AT 37 MPH (60 KPH)!

Giant eland horns

Hard outer sheath (cover) of dead keratin

Bone

Horn

Red deer antlers

Antler

Exposed, calcified bone

Velvetlike layer of living skin, rubbed off as antler grows

Pedicle, a growth connecting the antler to the skull

HORN OR ANTLER?

They might look similar, but there is a big difference between a horn and an antler. Horns grow continuously as extensions of the skull, whereas antlers are shed and regrown each year.

A COW PRODUCES 154–264 LB (70–120 KG) OF METHANE GAS PER YEAR!

A springbok arching its back as it pronks into the air.

HIGH JUMPER

Gazelles and springbok leap across the savanna to escape from predators. Many can spring vertically—or pronk—as high as 10 ft (3 m) up in the air. They do it as a warning sign and, sometimes, just to show off their strength.

MOUNTAIN CLIMBER

The mountain goat's cloven hooves have two padded toes that spread wide to provide grip on the steepest of cliffs. It scales rugged North American mountains in search of shrubs, moss, and even lichen.

Ask a …
FILMMAKER

Alex Walters is a producer and director with the BBC Natural History Unit, helping to make world-famous documentaries such as *Planet Earth III* with David Attenborough. Before that, she worked on conservation projects in Madagascar and a turtle sanctuary in Costa Rica.

Q Why did you become a wildlife TV producer?

A Growing up in the New Forest (southern England) I was completely obsessed with the natural world and loved taking photos of it, so this seemed a natural fit!

Q How did you become a TV producer?

A I studied Cinematography, then spent ten years working my way up, from runner to camera assistant and doing story research on British natural history shows shot in the UK and Alaska, then becoming Assistant Producer and directing on *Planet Earth III*. With perseverance and hard work, I am now living my dream.

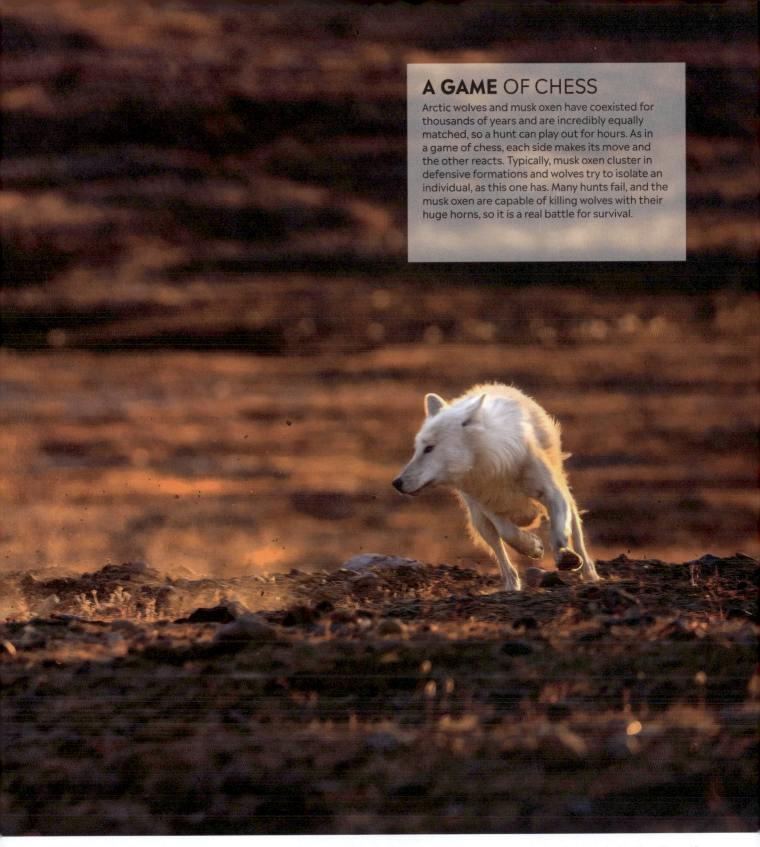

A GAME OF CHESS

Arctic wolves and musk oxen have coexisted for thousands of years and are incredibly equally matched, so a hunt can play out for hours. As in a game of chess, each side makes its move and the other reacts. Typically, musk oxen cluster in defensive formations and wolves try to isolate an individual, as this one has. Many hunts fail, and the musk oxen are capable of killing wolves with their huge horns, so it is a real battle for survival.

Q What does a wildlife TV producer do?
A Producers work as part of a big team on every stage of the film, from initial idea to planning, filming, and editing the show so the story makes sense to the viewer.

Q What is it like to film a wolf hunt?
A We camped in the Arctic for nearly three months. It really is an extreme world and after seeing the struggle for survival there, we left with a huge amount of respect for both the wolves and their musk oxen prey.

Q Is it hard to bathe in remote locations?
A In the Arctic it was below 5°F (–15°C), so having to undress to bathe with a bucket and washcloth was not very inviting! I definitely skipped bathing for several days.

Q Were you ever afraid of being eaten?
A There was one moment in the Arctic when I thought I might become lunch! The wolf pack came to visit and I didn't spot them until I was nearly surrounded. Luckily they were more interested in trying to steal our gear!

Q Do the animals mind being filmed?
A It varies—the Arctic wolves are fearless, but snow leopards and hornbills are so nervous that you have to hide away. On the African plains the animals gradually get used to you. For BBC's *Dynasties II*, the team followed a cheetah and her cub for two years!

Q What do you want viewers to feel?
A For me the most important feelings that viewers go away with are understanding, love, and compassion for the animals we film.

Giant giraffes

The tallest animal on Earth, giraffes are adapted for life on the savanna. They use their soaring height to reach succulent top leaves, and their strong legs to kick predators.

MALE GIRAFFES CAN GROW UP TO 19 FT (6 M) TALL!

A tufty mane runs the length of the neck.

Each giraffe has its own unique fur pattern.

Hard, bony, fur-covered ossicones, used for fighting by male giraffes

Large ears to listen for predators creeping up

Purple tongue

TWISTY **TONGUE**

Juicy acacia leaves make for a favorite meal, although they're not easy to get to. But giraffes have long, rough, flexible tongues, perfect for maneuvering around the spiky thorns that protect the leaves.

FAR **REACH**

A long neck is not always helpful. To drink, a giraffe has to splay its legs wide to reach the water, dipping its head. This position makes it vulnerable, so herd members take turns to watch for predators while at the waterhole.

Hard ossicones inflict damage.

NECK **FIGHT**

In breeding season, males engage in neck-to-neck combat. They swing their heads together, bony ossicones clashing, until the weakest give up. The winner gets to breed with the herd of females.

GIRAFFES HAVE **SEVEN BONES** IN THEIR NECKS, THE SAME NUMBER **AS HUMANS!**

Large vertebrae (neck bones)

BLOOD SUPPLY

A giraffe's heart is strong enough to pump blood up to its head. But when the animal bends down to drink, a special network of tiny vessels stops a sudden rush of blood to the brain. If it wasn't for this clever adaptation, the giraffe would get very dizzy.

Artery carries blood from the heart.

Vein carries blood back to the heart.

Valves in the vein stop blood from flowing back to the brain.

Brain shifts nearly 19 ft (6 m) between "head down" and "head up" positions.

Network of vessels under brain acts like a sponge, slowing down the blood flow.

WHO'S **WHO?**

There are several kinds of giraffes in different parts of Africa. You can tell them apart by the patterns on their fur, as shown by these examples.

Kordofan giraffe
Patches are pale tan and irregular, framed by thick, off-white borders.

Southern giraffe
Light brown patches sit close together on a pale cream base.

Reticulated giraffe
Orange-brown patches are set off by a network of thin white lines.

Masai giraffe
Very jagged, dark-brown patches contrast with the creamy-brown base color.

Baby emerging, ready to drop

SAVANNA **STRIDER**

Taking long strides, giraffes can cover quite a lot of ground. They don't run regularly, but when being chased—as this adult and juveniles are—they can briefly reach speeds of up to 37 mph (60 kph).

LONG **DROP**

Life starts with a fall for giraffe calves, who are born 6 ft (1.8 m) above the ground and land with a bump. But they are up on their feet within minutes, a key survival skill because predators are often close.

GIRAFFE FEET ARE AS WIDE AS A **DINNER PLATE:** 12 IN (30 CM)!

Hooves have two halves, or toes.

AFRICAN **WILD ASS**

Asses (also known as donkeys) are smaller, stockier equids, adapted to rocky, arid environments. The African wild ass is native to the dry climate of East Africa, where it can go without water for three days. Fewer than 600 wild asses survive today, due to habitat loss and hunting.

Striped, zebralike legs with small hooves

SUPER **STRIPES**

Zebras are the most striking members of the horse family. The three species—plains zebra, mountain zebra, and Grevy's zebra—live on grassy savanna in eastern and southern Africa. Each zebra's pattern of stripes is unique, like human fingerprints.

Horse family

Horses, zebras, and asses are all equids: long-limbed, single-toe-hoofed animals. They are sociable and are well adapted for running, especially in open spaces. Equids have a mainly grass-based diet, which their digestive system can process quickly.

Zebra stallions fight each other for dominance, usually by biting and butting heads.

Stripe pattern may deter disease-carrying tsetse flies.

Equids may have evolved a single-toed hoof to help them run more efficiently.

THE **OLDEST** DOMESTICATED **BREED OF HORSE** IS THE **ARAB**, BRED **4,500 YEARS AGO** BY THE BEDOUINS OF NORTH AFRICA!

HERD **MENTALITY**

Horses live in herds. This gives them protection against predators such as mountain lions and wolves. A herd is made up of many family groups, each protected by a male known as a lead stallion. Young horses, or foals, stay close to their mothers.

BORN TO **RUN**

Equids' main form of defense is their speed. The fastest equids can reach 43 mph (70 kph). When threatened, equid legs also become weapons: a zebra kick can kill a lion.

Big gluteal (bottom) muscles provide both power and speed.

Spine and rib cage supported by strong muscles.

Long limbs increase stride length.

Large foreleg joints bear 60 percent of the horse's weight.

Lower legs have less muscle, making them lighter and easier to move quickly.

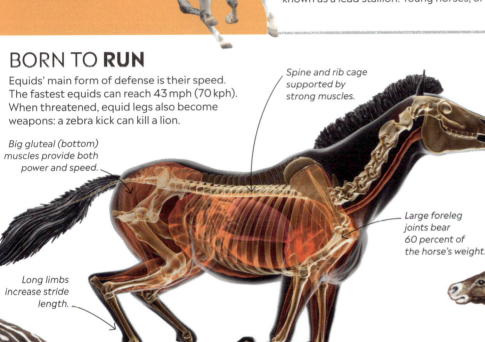

HORSES **SLEEP** STANDING UP AND **TAKE TURNS TO NAP** IN A HERD!

HORSE **VISION**

Located on the sides of their head, equids' eyeballs are the largest of any land mammals. This means that—like most prey species—they have a near 360-degree field of vision. But they are vulnerable at the rear, which is why their hind legs are capable of delivering potentially deadly kicks.

Both eyes 65°

Left eye vision 146°

Right eye vision 146°

Blind spot 3°

DISTANT **ANCESTOR**

The oldest known equid ancestor lived 55 million years ago. *Eohippus* was about the size of a fox and became extinct approximately 34 million years ago. Experts believe it had a spotted coat that may have provided camouflage in a jungle habitat.

PRZEWALSKI'S HORSE IS THE LAST SURVIVING **WILD HORSE SPECIES**. A BREEDING PROGRAM HAS **ENSURED ITS SURVIVAL!**

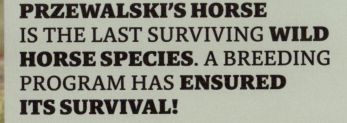

Rhinoceroses and tapirs

Although they look very different, the large, horned, and thick-skinned rhinoceros and the smaller, hairier tapir are closely related descendants of the horse family.

YOUNG CAMO

Tapir calves are born with stripes, which camouflage them in forests to keep them safe from predators. They stay with their mothers for 12–18 months.

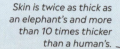

RARE ANIMAL

Southern white rhinos live in South Africa and northern white rhinos in Kenya. There are fewer than 16,000 southern white rhinos alive today but only two northern white rhinos, their species having been hunted almost to extinction by poachers.

Skin is twice as thick as an elephant's and more than 10 times thicker than a human's.

Each ear moves independently.

Horns made of keratin can grow 7 in (18 cm) a year.

Despite their short legs, rhinos can run at 31 mph (50 kph).

Three wide toes on each foot spread the rhino's weight evenly.

Wide, straight mouth is perfectly shaped for grazing on grass.

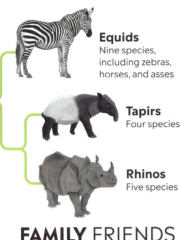

Equids
Nine species, including zebras, horses, and asses

Tapirs
Four species

Rhinos
Five species

FAMILY FRIENDS

Tapirs and rhinos branched off from equids 56 million years ago. Equids have one toe (or hoof) on each foot; tapirs and rhinos have shorter legs with multiple toes.

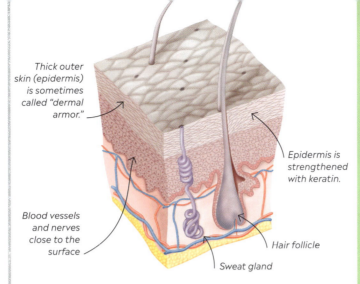

Thick outer skin (epidermis) is sometimes called "dermal armor."

Epidermis is strengthened with keratin.

Blood vessels and nerves close to the surface

Hair follicle

Sweat gland

UNDER THE SKIN

Rhino skin is up to 2 in (5 cm) thick, but is very sensitive to touch, sunlight, and vibration. It is arranged in layers, all of which contain the protein collagen, which gives it added strength.

TAPIRS KEEP **RAINFORESTS HEALTHY** BY DISPERSING UP TO 122 DIFFERENT **SEEDS IN EACH POOP!**

A **MALE WHITE RHINO** WEIGHS THE SAME AS A SMALL TRUCK: **3.4 TONS (3.5 METRIC TONS)!**

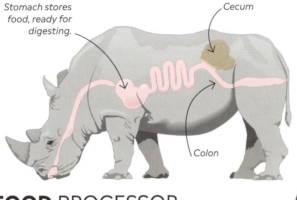

Stomach stores food, ready for digesting.

Cecum

Colon

FOOD PROCESSOR

Rhinos have an enlarged digestive system containing billions of "good" bacteria that extract nutrients from the tough, fibrous plants. This process, called hindgut fermentation, takes place in a large sac in the intestine called a cecum.

MUD BATHERS

Tapirs and rhinos both like to wallow in pools of mud. This keeps their sensitive bodies cool in hot weather. It's believed that tapirs also do it to remove ticks from their skin.

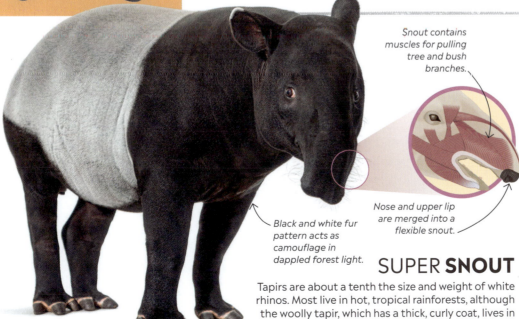

Snout contains muscles for pulling tree and bush branches.

Black and white fur pattern acts as camouflage in dappled forest light.

Nose and upper lip are merged into a flexible snout.

SUPER SNOUT

Tapirs are about a tenth the size and weight of white rhinos. Most live in hot, tropical rainforests, although the woolly tapir, which has a thick, curly coat, lives in the higher, cooler altitudes of the Andes Mountains.

TAPIRS ARE EXCELLENT **SWIMMERS** AND USE THEIR SNOUT AS A **SNORKEL!**

FACT PACK!
FAMILY LIFE

While many mammals live solitary lives, others spend more time together. From birth to death, how they live, and for how long, varies considerably from species to species.

TOGETHER FOREVER

In 3–5 percent of mammal species, males and females stay together for life. These are some of the happiest-ever-afters:

1 DIK-DIKS
Once these small antelopes (below) form a couple, they share a territory and graze close by each other in the area.

2 EURASIAN BEAVERS
Unusually for rodents, beavers mate with only one partner. The couple live together in carefully constructed lodges.

3 COYOTES
A coyote couple does everything together—hunting, building dens, and raising pups.

FAMILY BONDING

Many animals live in family groups. They hunt or forage for food together, but once those chores are done, it's time for other activities!

GROOMING
A family of vervet monkeys bonds by picking ticks off each other.

PLAY FIGHTING
Brown bear cubs learn to defend themselves by fighting for fun.

LANGUAGE LESSONS
Wolf cubs learn to howl from an adult pack member.

BOWHEAD WHALE 200 years

ELEPHANT 56 years

ORCA 50 years

BRANDT'S BAT 41 years

WESTERN GORILLA 35 years

LOWLAND TAPIR 30 years

LONGEST LIFE

Young animals become adults much earlier than humans, and most mammals live for many years. These species have some of the longest typical lifespans. The record is held by the bowhead whale—this marine mammal can live for more than 200 years!

LONG **WAIT**

All mammals except monotremes give birth to live babies, but the time spent developing in the womb varies between species. An African elephant is pregnant for almost 2 years, the longest pregnancy of all mammals.

In the womb, an **elephant** has time to **develop** an impressive **brain**—with **3 times** as many **neurons** as a human one!

HAMSTER 17 days
BROWN RAT 21 days
RABBIT 31 days
SQUIRREL 44 days
DOG 63 days
CAT 63 days
PIG 115 days
SHEEP 152 days
COW 280 days
HORSE 365 days
AFRICAN ELEPHANT 660 days

GESTATION PERIODS (LENGTH OF PREGNANCY)

MILK DRINKING

Mammal babies feed on milk produced by their mothers until they can hunt, forage, or graze. But not all milk is the same! Cow's milk contains 3–5% fat, 1% sugar, and 3.55% protein, but these animals have different mixes of milk.

 **60%**

MOST FAT
Hooded seal pups feed on rich, fatty milk for 6 weeks.

 **0.2%**

LEAST FAT
Rhino calves drink nearly fat-free milk for 18 months.

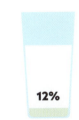 **12%**

MOST SUGAR
Tammar wallabies feed on very sweet milk.

 **15%**

MOST PROTEIN
The milk of the cottontail rabbit is packed with proteins.

WATER **BIRTH**

These mammals all give birth underwater. Their newborn babies need to get to the surface quickly to take their first breath of air.

💧 **WHALES** (one baby every 2–3 years)
💧 **DOLPHINS** (one baby every 1–6 years)
💧 **HIPPOS** (one baby every 2 years)
💧 **SEA OTTERS** (one baby every year)
💧 **MANATEES** (one baby every 2–5 years)

HARDWORKING MOMS

Lions are the only big cats that live together in large family groups. Grandmother, mother, sister, and daughter lions form the core of each pride, and do a lot of the work. They hunt, take care of each other's cubs, and protect them against outside threats.

LIFE **LESSONS**

Young meerkats learn how to eat deadly scorpions without being bitten. Taught by their parents, they practice first on a dead scorpion, then on an injured one, and then—only when they are ready—the real deal.

ANIMAL
LIFE

Partners and **parasites**

Most animals are in competition with each other for food and living space, but some join forces, becoming partners in the struggle for survival. Others are parasites that live in or on a host animal to survive.

PLANT **PARTNERS**

Many different plants recruit animals to help them reproduce—either by transporting their pollen from flower to flower, or by distributing their seeds far and wide. The plants attract their helpers by offering them a tasty treat, such as sugary nectar or juicy fruits.

European robins eat a variety of fruits, such as red berries, grapes, and cherries.

Fruit and seeds
Red berries are a favorite among birds. The soft flesh is easily digested, but the berry seeds pass through the birds' digestive system and are dropped far away from the parent plant.

Nectar and pollen
The Australian honey possum is one of many animals that visit flowers to sip nectar. As the possum feeds it is dusted with pollen, which it transfers to other flowers.

MUTUAL **BENEFITS**

On coral reefs, big fish line up for a visit from "cleaners" who pick off parasites and eat them as a free meal. This cleaner shrimp is working fearlessly inside the mouth of a predatory moray eel.

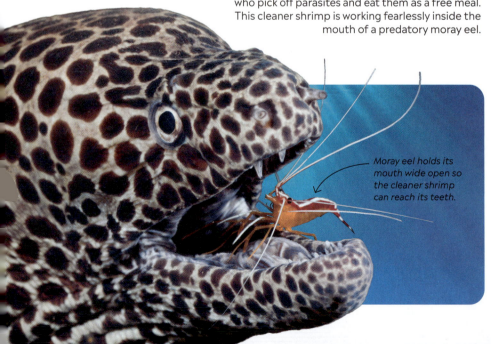

Moray eel holds its mouth wide open so the cleaner shrimp can reach its teeth.

The skua's luckless target is an Arctic tern.

Arctic skua can fly at speeds of up to 31 mph (50 kph).

INSIDE JOB

Many kinds of parasites live inside other animals. They include thousands of species of worms that settle in the intestines of their hosts, such as this pork tapeworm. It feeds by absorbing the host's food through its skin.

SOME TAPEWORMS CAN GROW TO MORE THAN 12 FT (3.5 M) LONG INSIDE A HUMAN GUT!

DAYLIGHT ROBBERY

Some animals specialize in stealing food or prey from other animals instead of finding their own, saving themselves time and energy. Known as kleptoparasites, this group includes seabirds such as this skua, which forces other birds to give up their food by chasing and harassing them until they drop it.

GETTING ATTACHED

Some parasites kill other animals while feeding on them. This sea lamprey attaches itself to a fish and uses its teeth to rasp through its skin and feed on its blood. A single lamprey kills around 40 lb (18 kg) of fish every year.

Mouth works like a large suction cup.

Small teeth are sharp and pointy.

FLEETING FEEDERS

Mosquitoes, leeches, and vampire bats are among the many parasites that drink blood. Another is this Galápagos vampire finch, which uses its sharp beak to peck into the skin and feathers of large seabirds to drink their nutritious blood.

CON TRICK

Brood parasites fool other animals into raising their young. Most notorious are the cuckoos and cowbirds that lay their eggs in the nests of host birds. When the cuckoo chick hatches first, it pushes other eggs out of the nest, so it has no competition for food.

Well-fed cuckoo chick grows larger than its host parent.

TAGGING ALONG

Sometimes one animal benefits from another without affecting it at all. This cattle egret follows—or even rides on—zebras and other grazing animals to snap up the invertebrates they disturb with their hooves. The zebra is neither helped nor harmed.

Cattle egrets look for insects such as grasshoppers and crickets.

SHARP **TEETH**

Typical predators, such as this Nile crocodile, are armed with sharp teeth and claws, which they use to seize prey and then eat it. They tear big animals apart and eat them bit by bit, but meat and fish are so easy to digest that many hunters swallow their smaller prey whole.

Powerful jaws give prey little chance of escape.

Sharp senses are vital to hunting success.

Crocodile teeth are simple sharp spikes.

Top predators such as wolves are naturally rare.

Mid-level predators are rarer than their prey.

Plant-eaters are relatively common.

Energy transfer

Ultimately all land animals rely on plants.

TOP **DOG**

When animals eat plants, only a proportion of the food is turned into animal flesh and bone. The rest is lost as waste or released as energy. So a bigger mass of plants is needed to support a much smaller mass of plant-eaters. The same is true when predators eat prey, so there are far fewer predators than plant-eaters. A top predator needs a large territory to catch its food.

AN ASIAN PYTHON CAN EAT ENOUGH AT **ONE MEAL** TO FEED IT FOR **MANY MONTHS!**

Hunters and hunted

Meat is easier to digest than plant material—but getting it can be difficult or even risky. Prey may have fast escape tactics and use defenses such as horns or poisons. But predators have weapons that kill, and the high food value of meat makes hunting worthwhile.

Armor plates protect the crocodile's back.

STAYING **ALIVE**

Most prey animals have ways to avoid being eaten. They can hide, escape, or fight back. Some are even poisonous, and they advertise this with warning colors.

Poison!
As caterpillars, cinnabar moths eat poisonous ragwort and they keep the foul-tasting toxins as adults.

Caterpillar stands on back legs.

Twig mimic
This brimstone moth caterpillar looks like a twig, so it is ignored by hungry predators.

Faking it
The stripes of harmless hoverflies make birds think they are wasps with dangerous stingers.

Blending in
Excellent camouflage enables this frog to hide in plain sight—so long as it stays still!

DRAGONFLIES ARE EXPERT HUNTERS, WITH A 95% SUCCESS RATE WHEN CATCHING PREY!

FEARSOME **ADAPTATIONS**

Some predators are equipped with extreme adaptations for finding, catching, and eating their prey. They include such terrifying weapons as the deadly venoms used by some snakes, spiders, and scorpions.

This snake will swallow the frog whole!

Open wide!
A snake has specialized jaws that allow it to swallow prey bigger than its own head.

Fiendish fangs
Spiders inject venom into their prey using a pair of very sharp, hollow fangs.

Toxic terror
This assassin bug stabs insect prey and injects toxic saliva that liquefies their flesh.

THE TROPICAL STONEFISH IS PROTECTED BY FIN SPINES WITH VENOM THAT CAN KILL AN ADULT HUMAN!

A **SLOTH CARRIES** ITS OWN ECOSYSTEM OF **ALGAE, BEETLES,** AND **COCKROACHES** IN ITS **FUR!**

Biomes and habitats

A biome is a place with a specific climate and distinct forms of life. Biomes cover many habitat types—including deserts, grasslands, and forests on land, and fresh and salty water.

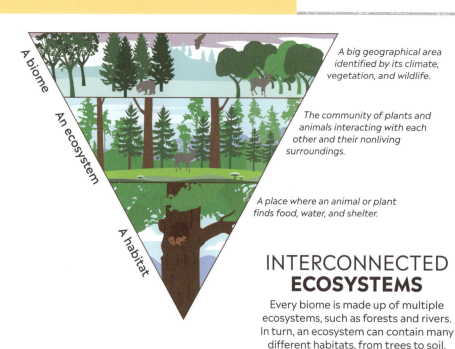

A biome
An ecosystem
A habitat

A big geographical area identified by its climate, vegetation, and wildlife.

The community of plants and animals interacting with each other and their nonliving surroundings.

A place where an animal or plant finds food, water, and shelter.

INTERCONNECTED ECOSYSTEMS

Every biome is made up of multiple ecosystems, such as forests and rivers. In turn, an ecosystem can contain many different habitats, from trees to soil.

EPIC JOURNEYS

Many animals make long migrations from one habitat to another. Sockeye salmon hatch in freshwater and then swim to the sea where they spend several years. They return to freshwater spawning grounds to reproduce.

FRESHWATER HABITATS

Only about 2.5 percent of Earth's water is freshwater. However, rivers, ponds, and lakes—including the areas on and around the water—are crucial habitats for animals such as insects, frogs, turtles, beavers, and freshwater fish.

Nearly half of all fish species live in freshwater.

MARINE HABITATS

Making up three-quarters of the Earth's surface, oceans, estuaries, and coral reefs such as this one are home to all kinds of diverse marine life, from sharks to butterfly fish. The deep sea is the largest habitat on Earth.

LAND HABITATS

Terrestrial habitats are typically categorized by their plant life as well as by their temperature and the amount of rainfall they experience. Here are a few examples of some of the many land habitats around the world.

Forests

Forests contain many habitats, from the floor to the roof of the forest, called the canopy, where marmosets such as this spend most of their time.

Grasslands

Grasslands are typically open, flat habitats. They are covered in grasses that provide food for herbivores such as these prairie dogs.

Deserts

In hot areas with less than 10 in (25 cm) of rain per year, finding water is hard. To stay hydrated, this fog-basking beetle collects fog droplets.

Tundra

In these cold, treeless arctic and subarctic areas with permanently frozen soil, animals including this snowy owl have thick plumage to stay warm.

GEOGRAPHIC ZONES

Earth can be divided into three different zones: polar regions at the top and bottom of the globe, tropical regions in the middle, and temperate regions in between. Each zone has a very different climate with well-adapted animals.

- ■ Tropical zone
- ■ Temperate zone
- ■ Polar zone

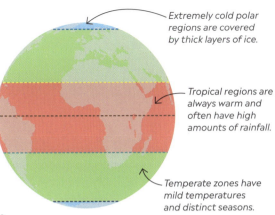

Extremely cold polar regions are covered by thick layers of ice.

Tropical regions are always warm and often have high amounts of rainfall.

Temperate zones have mild temperatures and distinct seasons.

ROADRUNNERS DON'T NEED TO DRINK TO SURVIVE IN DRY CONDITIONS—THEY ABSORB ALL THE MOISTURE THEY NEED FROM FOOD!

POLAR LIFE

Animals living in polar regions are well adapted for the cold weather. These gentoo penguins have plenty of body fat and layers of feathers to keep them warm in cold weather. They can dive to depths of 721 ft (220 m) to find food.

TEMPERATE LIFE

Earth's temperate zones have four seasons (spring, summer, fall, and winter), and animals need to adapt throughout the year to survive. For example, deer shed their heavy antlers in the winter to save energy, and then regrow them in the spring.

TROPICAL LIFE

Bulging red eyes to startle predators so the frog can escape.

In tropical regions the climate is warm and humid. Tropical rainforests have rainfall all year round, while places with wet and dry seasons have monsoon forests or open savanna with scattered trees. Many tropical animals, such as red-eyed tree frogs, breed during the wettest seasons.

Toes have sticky pads for grip while climbing.

SALMON TRAVEL HUNDREDS OF MILES FROM FRESHWATER TO THE SEA!

Colin Beale is Professor of Ecology at the University of York and has been exploring the natural world since he was a child. His research includes the effect of fire on the African savanna (grassy plains).

Ask an ...
ECOLOGIST

Q Why did you become an ecologist?
A I've loved animals since I was small, but I wanted to know more: why can I only find one type of bird in a few places, but another nearly everywhere I go? And how can we protect this amazing nature for the future?

Q What does an ecologist do?
A We study how animals, plants, and the environment interact. From watching nature in amazing places, to testing samples in the lab, to running analysis on supercomputers, ecology has something for everyone!

Q Were you nervous about starting fires?
A We're always very careful: if the day is too hot, dry, or windy, we don't light fires. We also leave safe gaps where there is nothing that can burn, so it can't spread to forests or homes. Then we light the fire and set it free!

Q How can fire be good for nature?
A Fires in the wrong place are very bad, but savannas have always had them, and all the plants and animals that live there not only survive, but may even need fires to thrive!

Q Don't animals get hurt by fires?
A Almost all the animals will walk, run, or fly away, or hide in a hole when they smell smoke. A few don't escape, but then baboons or storks come to feast on the toasted locusts.

Q How long does it take the savanna to recover after a fire?
A Antelopes often come back the very next day to lick the nutrient-rich ash. A few days later the grasses start to regrow, and animals gather to eat these tasty new shoots. As soon as the rains arrive, life returns in all its glory.

Q What can I do to help nature near me?
A Connect with others! Wherever you are, there will be local groups of volunteers who monitor nature to help us see changes in real time. Together we can make a much bigger impact than individually.

TOASTED SNACKS

Fire sweeps slowly across the savanna, giving most animals plenty of time to escape. Some birds, like these white storks, even flock to the flames to pick off fleeing insects or snack on barbecued grasshoppers. One small bird called the Temminck's courser only nests on recently burned ground, so cannot reproduce without regular fires. Around half of the grassland in the Serengeti Reserve of Tanzania burns each year and these fires help sustain a wide range of bird and mammal species.

GREENHOUSE EFFECT

A layer of gases in the atmosphere, including carbon dioxide (CO_2), traps heat energy from the Sun, keeping Earth at a warmer temperature—a bit like the glass of a greenhouse. When humans burn fossil fuels such as gasoline, they release extra CO_2, which traps more heat, increasing the temperature. As a result, Earth is now heating up faster than ever before. This is called global warming and it is threatening animal life around the globe.

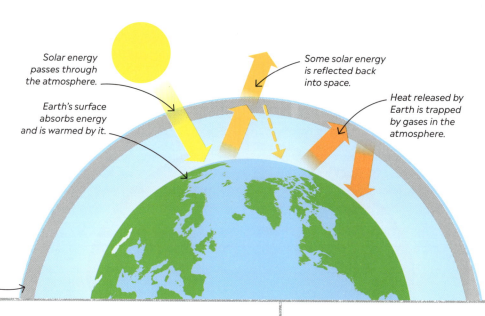

Solar energy passes through the atmosphere.

Earth's surface absorbs energy and is warmed by it.

Some solar energy is reflected back into space.

Heat released by Earth is trapped by gases in the atmosphere.

Atmosphere contains gases that trap infrared radiation.

Human impact

Humans have a huge impact on Earth, and this affects the other animals that share our planet. When habitats are polluted, destroyed, or rapidly altered, it can cause drastic changes in animal populations. Species may relocate, die out, or overwhelm their environments.

RISING TEMPERATURES

Average temperatures around Earth are now about 2°F (1.1°C) higher than in the 1800s. This may seem like a small change, but it is affecting animals' access to food and water and making it harder for them to survive.

Melting sea ice
Higher global temperatures are melting the Arctic sea ice, shrinking the polar bear habitat. Some polar bears are coming into settlements to find food, causing conflict with humans.

Wildfires
Higher temperatures mean bigger and more frequent wildfires. Animals may be trapped, or have their homes and food sources destroyed by the fire, while the smoke carries harmful toxins.

ANIMALS OFTEN MOVE INTO **URBAN AREAS** FOR **FOOD**. THERE ARE ABOUT **10,000 FOXES** LIVING IN **LONDON**, UK!

LITTER

CLEAR **OUT**

Deforestation means that trees and other plants are cleared, as here in the Amazon. This is usually to make space for buildings and roads, or to create grazing land for farm animals. This destroys the habitats of birds, mammals, insects, and reptiles who make their homes in and around trees.

Animals sometimes eat plastic, thinking it's food.

PLASTIC **WASTE**

Plastic is a useful material, but it's a big problem when it escapes into the environment. Animals can get trapped in plastic packaging, unable to escape, or they may eat it, where it can choke or poison them, or fill up their stomachs so they can't eat.

OIL **SPILLS**

Oil tankers sometimes spill their cargo at sea, or illegally release oily water when cleaning their tanks, and the oil spreads for miles. The chemicals inside it poison animal life, and oil on birds' feathers or sea mammals' fur prevents them from swimming efficiently, flying, or just keeping warm.

Oil-soaked birds are weighed down and struggle to stay afloat.

OVER**FISHING**

As human populations increase, so does the demand for food, leading to ever larger catches of fish. This reduces the food available for other marine animals. In time fish stocks could collapse completely.

FEWER **INSECTS**

One-third of all insect species may currently be at risk of extinction due to factors such as deforestation, pesticide use, light pollution, and climate change. This matters because insects are a key food source for other animals, and vital pollinators for more than three-quarters of all plant species.

Leg hairs can pick up pesticide particles, which are taken back to the hive and stored with pollen.

Tiny pollen grains stuck on the bee are carried to other plants.

INVASIVE **SPECIES**

When humans introduce new species into a habitat, it can have disastrous effects on the animals living there. In the 1700s, European settlers brought rabbits to Australia. With no natural predators, the rabbits bred rapidly and wiped out plants, causing other animals to run out of food.

EXTINCTION

The dodo—a large, flightless bird that lived on the island of Mauritius in the Indian Ocean—is a famous example of a species that went extinct. When explorers arrived in the 1500s, they killed dodos for food and damaged the bird's natural habitat, causing it to die out completely in 1681.

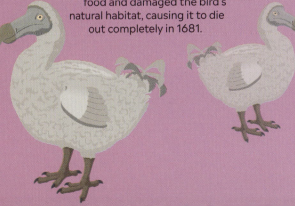

Madame Berthe's mouse lemur is categorized as "Critically Endangered" by the IUCN.

RED LIST

In 1964, the International Union for Conservation of Nature set up the Red List of Threatened Species. To identify which species are in need of protection, animals are placed into groups such as "Vulnerable" and "Critically Endangered."

THANKS TO A GLOBAL INITIATIVE, THE NUMBER OF WILD TIGERS HAS INCREASED BY 74% SINCE 2010!

Saving animals

In the last two hundred years or so, people have begun to understand the importance of protecting animals. This work includes fighting against poaching and illegal animal trades, monitoring endangered animals, and building nature reserves.

HELPFUL HUMANS

Conservationists work to protect animals and their environment. Dian Fossey, a well-known US conservationist, lived with mountain gorillas in Rwanda for more than 20 years and fought against illegal hunting.

Fossey built a strong bond with the gorillas she studied.

SUCCESS STORY

The Lord Howe Island stick insect was thought to be extinct in 1920, until a tiny population was found on the islet of Ball's Pyramid, Australia, in 2001. Although still critically endangered, there is a breeding program to grow their numbers.

MOUNTAIN GORILLAS WERE EXPECTED TO BECOME EXTINCT IN 2000, BUT THEIR NUMBERS ARE NOW INCREASING DUE TO CONSERVATION EFFORTS!

NATURE **RESERVES**

A nature reserve, or wildlife sanctuary, is a protected area of land that is home to certain species of plant, animal, or even fungi. The goal is to preserve and protect the living things there as well as prevent uncontrolled hunting. They can be on land or at sea.

Gorongosa National Park, Mozambique

At 1,544 sq miles (4,000 sq km), this national park is a section of the Great African Rift Valley system in Mozambique. It is home to ground pangolins such as this one, which was rescued from poachers.

Palau National Marine Sanctuary

This sanctuary in Oceania was the first marine protected area of its kind, placing 80 percent of Palau's national waters and 800 marine vertebrate species in a no-fishing zone.

AFTER A BAN ON **COMMERCIAL WHALING** IN THE 1970s, THE NUMBER OF **FIN WHALES HAS DOUBLED!**

RECOVERY PLAN

The South Island takahē, a flightless bird from New Zealand, was thought to be extinct until birds were found in 1948. Since then, the Department of Conservation has set up a recovery program that involves breeding and monitoring takahēs. Work is ongoing, but there are now around 500 birds.

Brightly colored wings are used for defense and courtship displays.

HEDGEHOG **HIGHWAYS**

Hedgehog Street is a conservation project in the UK. It works by asking people to create "hedgehog highways": holes in their fences that allow hedgehogs to move freely while searching for food and nesting sites.

CORAL **CARE**

Rising ocean temperatures due to climate change cause "coral bleaching," where coral is damaged and turns white. To restore reefs, organizations grow coral in nurseries, plant them onto damaged reefs, and monitor their health, as here in Mayotte's lagoon, off Africa's east coast.

ELEPHANT **UNDERPASS**

In 2010, a 15-ft- (4.5-m-) high tunnel was built in northern Kenya to connect two wilderness areas and two isolated elephant populations that had become divided. The underpass allows the elephants to travel safely through the region to find food and mates without being separated by highways and fences.

Glossary

abdomen
In vertebrates, such as mammals, the part of the body containing the digestive and reproductive organs; in arthropods, the rear part of the body.

adaptation
A special feature of an organism that makes it better suited to its way of life.

algae
Plantlike organisms that usually live in water and use energy from sunlight to make their own food. The largest are seaweeds and the smallest are a type of plankton.

ampullae of Lorenzini
Sensory organs in the snouts of cartilaginous fish that detect the electric fields of other animals. Sharks use them to precisely locate prey during an attack.

Andes
Mountain range running the length of South America, from north to south.

antennae
A pair of sense organs on stalks that detect movement and chemicals in the air.

apex predator
An animal that is at the top of a food chain and has no natural predators.

aquatic
Living in water all or most of the time.

arthropod
An invertebrate with an external skeleton and jointed legs.

biodiversity
The variety of all living things, on Earth or in a particular area.

bioluminescence
Light emitted by living things, such as animals that live in the deep, dark zones of the ocean where sunlight cannot reach.

bivalve
A mollusk such as a clam with two half-shells that can open and close, joined by a hinge.

brood
A set of young animals produced at one time by the same mother.

buoyancy
The ability to keep afloat.

burrow
A hole or tunnel dug into the ground by a small animal, which is then used as a place to live.

camouflage
Animal colors, patterns, or shapes that match surroundings to avoid being seen by others.

carapace
The hard protective shell on the back of some animals.

carbon dioxide
A gas found in air, produced as a waste product of organisms and burning fuels, and used by plants and algae to make food.

carcass
The body of a dead animal.

carnivore
An animal that feeds on meat.

carrion
The rotting flesh of a dead animal, eaten as food by scavengers.

cartilage
A tough, flexible type of connective tissue that helps support the body and covers the ends of bones and joints. Human ears are made from cartilage.

cartilaginous fish
Fish with skeletons made not of bone, but of cartilage.

cephalopod
One of a group of mollusks that includes octopuses and squid.

chrysalis
The hard protective case that a butterfly caterpillar forms when it turns into a pupa.

climate change
Long-term shifts in the usual weather patterns of the Earth or a particular area. Often refers to the severe effects caused by human actions.

cocoon
The silk case that some moth caterpillars spin around their body before turning into a pupa.

cold-blooded
Describes animals whose body temperature is the same as that of the environment. They cannot self-regulate their temperature.

colony
A group of animals or other organisms that live together.

compound eyes
In insects and crustaceans, eyes made up of hundreds of elements, each with its own tiny lens.

conservation
The work of protecting plants, animals, and their natural habitats.

copepod
A type of small crustacean, many of which are part of the ocean plankton.

coral
A small marine animal made up of numerous tiny polyps. Coral reefs form from the hard skeletons of coral that live in large colonies.

courtship
Behavior that forms a bond between a male and female before mating.

crustacean
An animal with a hard external skeleton and paired, jointed legs, such as a crab or shrimp.

depth perception
The ability to tell how close or far away an object is. This is particularly useful when hunting.

detritivore
An organism that feeds on dead and decaying organic material.

DNA
The common abbreviation for deoxyribonucleic acid, a material found in the cells of all living things that carries instructions for how a living thing will look and function.

domesticated species
Wild animals that have been tamed to make them useful to humans.

dormant
In a state of inactivity.

dorsal fin
A fin on the back or top of a fish or aquatic mammal, which acts as a stabilizer.

drag
The resistance formed when an object pushes through a gas or liquid, such as air or water. Drag slows an object down.

echinoderm
One of a group that includes spiny-skinned marine animals such as starfish and sea urchins.

echolocation
A way of locating prey or objects in air or water by transmitting sound pulses and detecting the echoes.

embryo
An unborn animal or plant in the very early stages of development.

endangered
At risk of going extinct in the near future. Animals become endangered due to habitat loss, poaching, or invasive species.

evolution
The process of gradual change in living things over many generations.

exoskeleton
A hard outer layer that supports and protects soft-bodied animals without an internal skeleton. Many invertebrates have these.

extinction
The disappearance from Earth of all living members of a species.

eye of a storm
The center of a big storm, which is relatively quiet and still.

face disk
A concave area of flattened feathers on the face of some birds, especially owls. It is surrounded by a ring of stiff feathers.

fang
A pointed tooth or other type of mouthpart, typically used to inject venom.

feline
Members of species that are part of the cat family, and the larger group of catlike animals called Feliformia.

fertilization
The joining together of male and female sex cells, when sperm fertilizes an egg.

fossil
The remains or traces of an animal or plant from long ago, preserved in rock.

fossil fuel
Fuel burned for energy such as oil, gas, or gasoline. It is formed from long-dead plants or animals compressed underground over millions of years and cannot be replaced once used.

fungi
A group of organisms that reproduce by releasing spores, feed on organic matter, and typically help decompose dead and waste material.

genes
Units of DNA that control how cells behave and bodies grow and look. They are passed on from parents to children.

gills
Organs in aquatic animals, such as fish, that help them extract oxygen from water.

grooming
Describes an animal's behavior when it cleans itself or another animal.

hatchling
A young animal that has recently broken out of its egg.

herbivore
An animal that feeds on plants.

herd
A large group of animals that feed and travel together.

hibernate
A resting state like very deep sleep that occurs in some animals during winter.

hoof
The hard-capped foot of an animal such as a horse or a pig, or the hard cap itself. Hooves help animals to run quickly.

ice floe
A slab of floating ice.

insectivore
An animal that mainly eats insects or other invertebrates.

insulation
Reduction of heat loss by a body layer such as fur, blubber, or feathers.

iridescent
Showing colors that seem to change when seen from different angles.

keel
An enlarged part of the breastbone of a bird. The large flight muscles of birds are anchored to the keel.

keratin
A tough, waterproof protein found in hair, feathers, scales, and claws.

krill
Small, shrimplike crustaceans that drift in huge numbers in the ocean and provide vital food for many marine animals.

larva
The immature stage of animals that hatch from eggs and undergo metamorphosis to become adults.

leaf litter
Rotting leaves on the ground.

ligament
A tough band of tissue that holds bones together where they meet at joints.

mandible
The paired jaws of an arthropod, used to bite, cut, and hold food.

metamorphosis
A dramatic change in the body of an animal as it develops. Caterpillars turn into butterflies by metamorphosis.

microscopic
Something that is so small that it is only visible under a microscope.

migration
A long journey regularly undertaken by an animal to reach a new habitat. Many birds migrate every year between their summer and winter homes.

mollusk
One of a group of invertebrates that includes snails, clams, and squid.

molt
In arthropods, the shedding of the exoskeleton to allow growth. In vertebrates, shedding skin, hair, or plumage, so it can regrow. Mammals and birds molt to keep in good condition, to adjust to the weather, or to get ready to breed.

mucus
A thick, slippery liquid produced by animals for various reasons. Clown fish are coated in mucus to avoid being stung by sea anemones.

mutation
A permanent change in the DNA of an organism.

nectar
A sugar solution produced by flowers to attract pollinating animals.

newton
A unit used to measure the strength of a force.

nocturnal
Active at night but inactive during the day.

nursing
Referring to a female mammal feeding her young on her milk.

nutrients
The useful parts of food, such as sugars, proteins, fats, oils, vitamins, and minerals. An animal's digestive system extracts these from food.

omnivore
An animal that eats both plants and meat.

ossicone
A small horn covered with skin that is found in giraffes.

ovipositor
In female insects, an organ at the end of the abdomen, used for laying eggs. The ovipositor often has a tubular or bladelike shape, so it can insert eggs in the ground, in plants, or in other animals.

oxygen
A gas that makes up 21 percent of Earth's atmosphere. Most living things take in oxygen from the air and use it to release energy from food in a process called respiration.

papillae
Small rounded structures on the tongue, which can serve many purposes, including tasting and gripping.

parasite
An organism that lives in or on another (its host), and has a negative effect on it.

pectoral fins
Paired fins located on both sides of a fish or marine mammal. In most fish these help it steer up, down, or sideways. In rays, the flexible pectoral fins are used for movement and feeding.

photophore
A light-emitting organ, especially one of the luminous spots on some deep-sea fish.

pigment
Chemicals that give color to an organism.

plankton
Organisms that drift in the ocean, rather than swimming against the current. Most plankton are tiny but they exist in large numbers. They are an important source of food for bigger animals, such as whales.

plumage
The layer of feathers that covers a bird to provide protection and insulation, and streamlines them.

pollen
Tiny grains produced by flowers or cones of seed-producing plants, which contain male sex cells that fertilize eggs so the plant can produce seeds.

pollinator
Anything that carries pollen from the male anther to the female stigma of the same or another flower, helping to fertilize it. Examples include bees, bats, and wind.

polyp
A form taken by some marine animals, such as jellyfish, sea anemones, and corals. Polyps have a mouth at one end, and are attached firmly at the base to a rock or the seabed.

powder down
Special soft feathers that break up at the end to form a powder that cleans and waterproofs the other feathers. They grow continuously to replace the lost ends.

predator
An animal that kills other animals for food.

preening
When a bird cleans and smooths its feathers with its beak.

prehensile tail
A tail that can curl around branches or stems, acting like an extra limb to grip and swing.

prey
An animal that is eaten by another animal.

pupa
The resting stage in the life cycle of an insect that undergoes metamorphosis.

raptor
A bird of prey, such as an eagle, hawk, or owl.

regenerate
Regrow a part of the body.

regurgitate
Bring swallowed food back up into the mouth. Many birds regurgitate food to feed their young.

retract
Draw something back in, such as a cat's claws.

savanna
Open grassland in tropical or subtropical areas, especially Africa; flat, grassy plains with some wooded areas.

school
A large number of fish that swim in a coordinated way.

scute
A bony external plate with a layer of horn over the top. Found on the shell of a turtle and the skin of a crocodile.

seabed
The solid ground that lies under the ocean or sea. It is also called the sea floor.

sensory pit
Tiny hole or dip full of nerve endings, used to sense changes in pressure.

serrated
Having a jagged edge.

spawning grounds
Areas of water where aquatic animals lay their eggs.

species
A group of similar organisms that can interbreed and produce fertile offspring like themselves.

streamlined
Smoothly shaped to move easily through air or water. Penguins are streamlined to help them swim faster.

swarm
A large group of flying insects.

talons
Sharp, hooked claws that curve downward. They are found on birds, reptiles, many mammals, and some amphibians. They are used for digging, climbing, or clutching.

tendon
A tough, fibrous band of tissue that anchors a muscle to a bone. When the muscle contracts, the tendon pulls the bone, making the animal's body move.

tentacle
Seen mainly in invertebrates, a mobile extension of an animal's body, sometimes armed with stinging cells.

terrestrial
Living on land.

tetrapod
A vertebrate with four limbs, or descended from four-limbed ancestors.

thorax
The middle part of an insect's body or the part of a mammal between the neck and abdomen.

tube feet
Water-filled mobile projections in echinoderms, used for movement, feeding, and respiration.

umbilical cord
A cord-like structure that carries food, oxygen, and other vital substances between an unborn baby mammal and its mother's body.

upwash
Rising air behind the wingtips of a flying bird, caused by air traveling past the wings.

variation
The differences between living things.

venom
Poison that a biting or stinging animal injects into another animal for hunting or defense.

warm-blooded
Warm-blooded animals can regulate their internal body temperature to maintain a stable level, even when the local environment is colder or hotter.

Index

Page numbers in **bold** show the pages with the main information. Quiz pages are shown in italics.

Acknowledgements

DK would like to thank:
Kathakali Banerjee, Michelle Crane, Ian Fitzgerald, Vicky Richards, and Rona Skene, for additional editorial help; Kelly Adams, Vikas Chauhan, and Prateek Maurya for additional design help; Manpreet Kaur, Vagisha Pushp, and Samrajkumar S for picture research assistance; Hazel Beynon for proofreading; Elizabeth Wise for the index; and all of the experts who agreed to be interviewed for the Q&As.

The publisher would like to thank the following for their kind permission to reproduce their photographs:

(Key: a-above; b-below/bottom; c-centre; f-far; l-left; r-right; t-top)

1 123RF.com: Serg_v (sky). **Alamy Stock Photo:** Michel Poinsignon / Nature Picture Library. **2 Dreamstime.com:** Rinus Baak (cla); Isselee (ca); Yothin Piyatrakul (cl); David Dennis (r); Feathercollector (clb); Nynke Van Holten (bl). **Getty Images:** Life On White (br). **3 Alamy Stock Photo:** Tim Plowden (tc). **Dreamstime.com:** Ziga Camernik (cra). **5 123RF.com:** Thawat Tanhai (tc). **Alamy Stock Photo:** Buiten-Beeld / Jelger Herder (br). **Dreamstime.com:** Steve Byland (crb); Natakuzmina (cra); Parfentevamaya (ca). **Getty Images / iStock:** GlobalP (tl). **Shutterstock.com:** Independent birds (tr). **6 Dreamstime.com:** Vitalii Bondarenko (cla/glow); Panupong Ponchai (tl); Graphics.vp (cla); Robisklp (cb); Mark Turner (crb). **Shutterstock.com:** Liliya Butenko (clb); Zero Smany (cb/shark). **7 Alamy Stock Photo:** Arterra Picture Library / Clement Philippe (cl); Michele Falzone (clb); Rick & Nora Bowers (clb/Squirrel). **Dreamstime.com:** Musat Christian (c). **naturepl.com:** Tui De Roy (tc, tr). **8 123RF.com:** Marek Poplawski / mark52 (tr/crab); Pavlo Vakhrushev / Vapi (bc); Thawat Tanhai (tr). **Alamy Stock Photo:** Alfred Pasieka / Science Photo Library (br). **Dreamstime.com:** Feathercollector (clb); Aldona Griskeviciene (cl); Siedykholena (c). **Getty Images / iStock:** RomoloTavani (bc/sea). **Shutterstock.com:** Simon Shim (cla). **9 123RF.com:** Andrzej Tokarski / ajt (snail); Michael Zysman / deserttrends (snake); Pavlo Vakhrushev / Vapi (jellyfish); Visarute Angkatavanich / Bluehand (fish). **Alamy Stock Photo:** Nature Picture Library / SCOTLAND: The Big Picture (crb). **Dorling Kindersley:** Gary Ombler / Cotswold Wildlife Park (panda). **Dreamstime.com:** Amwu (Kingsnake); Vladimir Melnik / Zanskar (Walrus); Isselee (Mouse, macaw); Daniel Thornberg (trout); Abeselom Zerit (Leopard); Kazoka (Frog); Xunbin Pan / Defun (worm); Matthijs Kuijpers / Mgkuijpers (dart frog); Viacheslav Dubrovin (turtle); Mirecca (Angel fish); Ziga Camernik (Caterpillar). **Fotolia:** Shchipkova Elena (jaguar). **Getty Images / iStock:** Antagain (Budgerigar); Enrique Ramos Lopez (Toucan). **Getty Images:** Life On White (Giraffe). **10 Alamy Stock Photo:** Rob Crandall (cra). **Dreamstime.com:** Marielemerle157 (cb); Stephen Noakes (ca). **Getty Images / iStock:** LIgorko (br). **Shutterstock.com:** Independent birds (bl). **11 Alamy Stock Photo:** robertharding / Louise Murray (tc). **Dreamstime.com:** Wirestock (bl); Yakub88 (tr). **Getty Images / iStock:** GlobalP (bc); rancho_runner (tc/butterfly). **12 Dorling Kindersley:** Frank Greenaway / Natural History Museum, London (cb). **Dreamstime.com:** Johnbell (bl); Max5128 (bc). **naturepl.com:** Eric Medard (crb). **Shutterstock.com:** AngelaLouwe (tl). **13 123RF.com:** Surya Zaidan / dagadu (clb). **Alamy Stock Photo:** Imagebroker / Arco / TUNS (bl). **Depositphotos Inc:** ftlaudgirl (tr). **Shutterstock.com:** Daniel Danckwerts (tl). **14 Alamy Stock Photo:** Papilio / Robert Pickett (crb). **naturepl.com:** Tui De Roy (c, bl). **15 Dreamstime.com:** Joergspannhoff (tl); Timothy Stone (bl). **naturepl.com:** Phil Savoie (br). **Shutterstock.com:** Danny Ye (tr). **16 Dorling Kindersley:** Thomas Marent (cb, clb, cr). **Dreamstime.com:** Frenta (cl); Stevehullphotography (br). **17 Alamy Stock Photo:** Darren5907 (tl). **Dreamstime.com:** Slowmotiongli (tr); Laurie L. Snidow (br). **naturepl.com:** Dr. Axel Gebauer (cb). **18 Dreamstime.com:** Alslutsky (c); Surabhi25 (tl). **Shutterstock.com:** Zaferkizilkaya (cr). **19 123RF.com:** Pavlo Vakhrushev / Vapi (tl). **Dorling Kindersley:** Thomas Marent (br). **Dreamstime.com:** Blackslide (tr); Vasyl Helevachuk (tc); Henrikhl (cb). **20 123RF.com:** Pavlo Vakhrushev / Vapi (ca/jellyfish). **Dreamstime.com:** Blackslide (crb); Zestmarina (cla); Seadam (cra). **Getty Images / iStock:** RomoloTavani (ca/bc). **21 Dreamstime.com:** Hot99 (cla); Teh Soon Huat (ca/Spider); Tetiana Kozachok (br). **Fotolia:** CPJ Photography (clb). **Getty Images / iStock:** Chushkin (ca). **Shutterstock.com:** tienduc1103 (crb). **22 Alamy Stock Photo:** Minden Pictures / Thomas Marent (cl, cr). **Dreamstime.com:** Az Septian (bl/Insect). **Getty Images / iStock:** Ani_Ka (bl). **23 Alamy Stock Photo:** Avalon.red / Stephen Dalton (bl); imageBROKER.com GmbH & Co. KG / Ulrich Reichel (tr); Minden Pictures / Thomas Marent (cl, cr). **Dreamstime.com:** Stanislav Judas (br); Andy Nowack (crb). **24 Dreamstime.com:** Amplion (cla/cockroach); Hhurzhi (cla); Razvan Cornel Constantin (r); Alexander Kovalenko (br). **Fotolia:** Eric Isselee (cl). **Science Photo Library:** Thierry Berrod, Mona Lisa Production (bl). **25 Alamy Stock Photo:** Jan-Luc van Eijk / Buiten-beeld / Minden Pictures (br). **Getty Images:** Yasuyoshi CHIBA / AFP (cl); Moment / Shawn E Thomas (tr). **26 Alamy Stock Photo:** Scenics & Science (tc). **Dreamstime.com:** Artushfoto (cl); Seamartini (tr, br); Linas Toleikis (bl). **naturepl.com:** Ingo Arndt (cla). **26-27 Getty Images:** renekoo1978 / 500px (c). **27 Alamy Stock Photo:** MYN / Gil Wizen / Nature Picture Library (cr). **Dreamstime.com:** Alain Lacroix / Icefields (bl/background); Leo Malsam (clb). **Getty Images / iStock:** R-DESIGN (bl). **naturepl.com:** Piotr Naskrecki (br). **28 Dreamstime.com:** Godruma (crb); Jason Ondreicka (cl). **naturepl.com:** Pete Oxford (tl); Robert Thompson (cla); Michel Poinsignon (cr). **29 Alamy Stock Photo:** Avalon.red / Anthony Bannister (cra/termites); blickwinkel / Hartl (crb). **naturepl.com:** John Cancalosi (cr); Nature Production (cra). **30 Dreamstime.com:** Vasyl Helevachuk (cla); Hilary Rivers / Hilarywren (cla/Hand); Yodke67 (crb). **30-31 Dreamstime.com:** Jmrocek. **31 Alamy Stock Photo:** Thomas Marent / Minden Pictures (br). **Dreamstime.com:** Anita Patterson Peppers (tr). **naturepl.com:** Jane Burton (cr). **32 Dreamstime.com:** Nicolas Fernandez (cl). **Getty Images / iStock:** engabito (r). **33 Alamy Stock Photo:** Mark Moffett / Minden Pictures (tr). **Dreamstime.com:** Anjazz Anjazz Doz Santoz (cla); Alexander Zhiltsov / Whizzard (bc). **Getty Images / iStock:** Igor Krasilov (fbl); panom (cr). **Science Photo Library:** THOMAS SHAHAN (bl). **Shutterstock.com:** SIRITAT TECHAPHALOKUL (c). **34 Dreamstime.com:** Alslutsky (c); Eivaisla (br). **Science Photo Library:** Karl Gaff (crb). **35 123RF.com:** Richard E Leighton Jr (bl). **Dorling Kindersley:** Thomas Marent (cl, crb). **Dreamstime.com:** Nicolas Fernandez (tc); Vlasto Opatovsky (cra); Palex66 (bc). **Shutterstock.com:** Cocos. Bounty (tr). **36 123RF.com:** Richard E Leighton Jr (fcra). **Dorling Kindersley:** Frank Greenaway / Natural History Museum, London (tl, tc, c, fcrb, bc); Tim Parmenter / Natural History Museum, London (cla). **Dreamstime.com:** Feathercollector (tr); Stephanie Frey (cra); Nexus7 (cr); Weerapat Kiatdumrong (crb); Matee Nuserm (bl). **Fotolia:** Tan Kian Khoon (br). **Getty Images / iStock:** Antagain (ca). **Shutterstock.com:** Simon Berenyi (cl). **37 Alamy Stock Photo:** PhotoSpin,Inc (tc). **Dorling Kindersley:** Thomas Marent (ca); Colin Keates / Natural History Museum, London (ftl, tl); Frank Greenaway / Natural History Museum, London (fcla, c, cl, clb). **Dreamstime.com:** Melinda Fawver (fbl); Acharaporn Kamornboonyarush (bc); Sutisa Kangvansap / Mathisa (br). **Getty Images / iStock:** epantha (bl). **38 Alamy Stock Photo:** Mircea Costina (tl). **38-39 naturepl.com:** Nick Garbutt (c). **39 Getty Images / iStock:** ConstantinCornel (crb). **40 Alamy Stock Photo:** Papilio / Robert Pickett (crb). **Dreamstime.com:** Meisterphotos (tl). **41 123RF.com:** Daniel Prudek (tr/Bees). **Dreamstime.com:** Le Thuy Do (br); Maksym Fesenko (tr); Kkovaleva (clb); Serg_velusceac (bc). **naturepl.com:** Palo Alto JR Museum / MD Kern (crb). **42 Minden Pictures:** Stephen Dalton (b). **43 Alamy Stock Photo:** Blickwinkel / H. Bellmann / F. Hecker (bc). **Science Photo Library:** Claude Nuridsany & Marie Perennou (cra). **Shutterstock.com:** Cathy Keifer (t, cla). **44 Alamy Stock Photo:** Jürgen Kottmann (tl). **Dreamstime.com:** Stefan Rotter (ca); I Wayan Sumatika (tr). **Science Photo Library:** Power And Syred (bl). **44-45 Shutterstock.com:** I Wayan Sumatika (b). **45 Dreamstime.com:** Cosmin Manci (tc); Larry Rains (cla). **46 Alamy Stock Photo:** Adisha Pramod (tl); Science History Images / Photo Researchers (c). **Shutterstock.com:** Pee Paew (ca); Sinhyu Photographer (cra). **47 Alamy Stock Photo:** Blue Planet Archive BPA (br); Nature Picture Library / Andy Jackson / 2020VISION (tl); imageBROKER.com GmbH & Co. KG / Norbert Probst (tc); Science Photo Library / Juan Gaertner (clb); Nature Picture Library / Sue Daly (bl); Science History Images / Photo Researchers (fbl). **Dreamstime.com:** John Anderson (tr); Bernhard Richter (cl). **naturepl.com:** Nature Production (ftr); Nick Upton (fclb). **48 Alamy Stock Photo:** Bazzano Photography (tr). **Dreamstime.com:** Corey A Ford (cla). **48-49 Dreamstime.com:** Yothin Piyatrakul (c). **49 Dreamstime.com:** Danolsen (br); Rueangsin Phuthawil (bl). **Shutterstock.com:** BlueRingMedia (tc). **50 Dreamstime.com:** Salvatore Ianniello (cl); Johninpix (bl). **50-51 Alamy Stock Photo:** Terence Dormer (b). **51 Alamy Stock Photo:** Natural Visions / Heather Angel (crb). **52-53 Alamy Stock Photo:** blickwinkel / F. Teigler (b). **52 Alamy Stock Photo:** blickwinkel / Hecker (bc). **53 Alamy Stock Photo:** dpa picture alliance (cla). **Dreamstime.com:** Irina Andreeva (crb); Andrii Bezvershenko (cra); Aldona Griskeviciene (cb); Fredweiss (fcrb); Yisi Li (br). **naturepl.com:** Doug Perrine (tr). **54 123RF.com:** Marek Poplawski / mark52 (tr). **Alamy Stock Photo:** Connect Images / Albert Lleal Moya (cl); Alan Gregg (fbr). **Dorling Kindersley:** Linda Pitkin (crb). **Dreamstime.com:** Serge Bertasius (cla); Natakuzmina (tl); Eyeblink (cra); Bluehand (ca); Isselee (clb); Henrikhl (cb); Digitalimagined (bc); Shaffandi (br). **55 Dreamstime.com:** Bluehand (bl); Puntasit Choksawatdikorn (clb). **56 Dreamstime.com:** Vladwitty (c). **Science Photo Library:** ANDREW J. MARTINEZ (tr). **56-57 Dreamstime.com:** Carol Buchanan (br). **57 Depositphotos Inc:** cheattha (tr). **58 Alamy Stock Photo:** Chris Newbert / Minden Pictures (tc). **Dreamstime.com:** Blueringmedia (cla); Bokasana (cl); Ekaterina Mikhailova (tr); Surabhi25 (clb); Dmitry Rogatnev (bl). **Shutterstock.com:** Zaferkizilkaya (cb). **58-59 Alamy Stock Photo:** Gabriel Barathieu / Biosphoto (c). **59 BluePlanetArchive.com:** Steven Kovacs (crb). **Dreamstime.com:** Seamartini (cra). **60 naturepl.com:** Gary Bell / Oceanwide (tl). **60-61 Shutterstock.com:** Thierry Eidenweil (b). **61 Alamy Stock Photo:** Reinhard Dirscherl (bc); James Peake (tl, tr); WaterFrame_fur (cb/Octopus). **Getty Images / iStock:** blueringmedia (cra); Luca Gialdini (cb). **62-63 naturepl.com:** SCOTLAND: The Big Picture. **62 Alamy Stock Photo:** Album (br); WaterFrame_fba (cla). **63 Dorling Kindersley:** Frank Greenaway / Natural History Museum, London (cra). **Dreamstime.com:** 3drenderings (tl); Alexander Ogurtsov (cb); Lgor Dolgov / Id1974 (crb). **Science Photo Library:** Kjell B. Sandved (fcrb). **Shutterstock.com:** Laura Dts (br). **64 Laurie Raymundo:** (bl). **64-65 Alamy Stock Photo:** James T Carnehan / Stephen Frink Collection. **66 123RF.com:** Visarute Angkatavanich / Bluehand (cra). **Dorling Kindersley:** Frank Greenaway (tr). **Dreamstime.com:** Isselee (tl, ca); Vladvitek (tc); Igor Zubkov (cr); Surachet Khamsuk (bc). **67 123RF.com:** Bonzami Emmanuelle / Cynoclub (tl). **Alamy Stock Photo:** Andrey Nekrasov (br). **68 Dreamstime.com:** Arsty (ca). **Getty Images / iStock:** RomoloTavani (cra/background). **Getty Images:** Westend61 (cla). **68-69 Dreamstime.com:** Seadam. **69 123RF.com:** Visarute Angkatavanich / Bluehand (crb). **Dreamstime.com:** Iadamson (tl); Vladvitek (cl); Isselee (ca); Mgkuijpers (tr); Vitas (br). **Getty Images / iStock:** marrio31 (cb); RomoloTavani (c/Underwater x3). **70 Dreamstime.com:** Tazdevilgreg (bc). **Shutterstock.com:** Tetsuo Arada (bl); Sebastian Kaulitzki (c). **70-71 Shutterstock.com:** Lindsey Lu (t). **71 Dreamstime.com:** Snehitdesign (br/truck); Torsten Velden / Tvelden (br). **Getty Images / iStock:** RomoloTavani (bc/water). **naturepl.com:** Doug Perrine (clb). **72 Alamy Stock Photo:** Media Drum World (bl). **Getty Images / iStock:** RomoloTavani (bl/water). **72-73 Dreamstime.com:** Steven Melanson (b). **73 Dreamstime.com:** Seadam (tl). **74-75 Alamy Stock Photo:** blickwinkel / A. Hartl (c). **Dreamstime.com:** Krzysztof Odziomek (c/water). **74 Alamy Stock Photo:** www.pqpictures.co.uk (br). **Dreamstime.com:** Slowmotiongli (clb). **75 Alamy Stock Photo:** Wolfgang Pölzer (tr). **naturepl.com:** Piotr Naskrecki (bl). **Shutterstock.com:** Arip Apandi (cr); BOONCHUAY PROMJIAM (br). **76 Dreamstime.com:** Stevehullphotography (Background). **naturepl.com:** Tony Wu. **Science Photo Library:** Dante Fenolio (tr). **77 Alamy Stock Photo:** Andrew Walmsley (c); Poelzer Wolfgang (tr, cl).

Dreamstime.com: Md Annur Ahamed (crb); Isselee (cra/Eel). **Getty Images / iStock:** Stevehullphotography (cra). **Shutterstock.com:** Takamaru (tl, tl/2, tl/3). **78 Alamy Stock Photo:** imageBROKER / Mathieu Foulquie (bl). **Dreamstime.com:** Slowmotiongli (cl). **78-79 Getty Images / iStock:** bbevren. **79 Alamy Stock Photo:** Jorge García / VWPics (br). **Getty Images / iStock:** llazarus (tr). **Shutterstock.com:** Martin Pelanek (cr); Tristan Tan (tl). **80 naturepl.com:** David Shale. **81 Alamy Stock Photo:** blickwinkel / Schmidbauer (c). **Science Photo Library:** Solvin Zankl / Nature Picture Library (br). **UWA Deep Sea Research Centre:** Alan Jamieson (cr). **82-83 ORCA:** Edith Widder. **82 Ocean Research & Conservation Association (ORCA):** (bl). **84 123RF.com:** macrovector (crb); Micha Klootwijk / michaklootwijk (cla). **Dreamstime.com:** Duncan Noakes (cb). **Getty Images / iStock:** Andykrakovski (cl); LUNAMARINA (b). **naturepl.com:** Norbert Wu (tc). **Shutterstock.com:** Michael Bogner (tl). **85 Alamy Stock Photo:** Blue Planet Archive MVA (bl); Nature Picture Library / Alex Mustard. **Getty Images / iStock:** RainervonBrandis (tr). **86 Alamy Stock Photo:** Tosh Brown (tl); Minden Pictures / Pete Oxford (c). **Dreamstime.com:** Hery Siswanto (crb). **OceanwideImages.com:** Chris & Monique Fallows (ca). **86-87 naturepl.com:** Henley Spiers (c). **87 naturepl.com:** Ralph Pace (b). **88 Shutterstock.com:** Elonsy (tl). **89 Alamy Stock Photo:** Minden Pictures / Fred Bavendam (clb/Handfish, br); James Peake (c). **naturepl.com:** David Fleetham (cb); Birgitte Wilms (clb); Shane Gross (tc); Alex Mustard (ca/frogfish); Linda Pitkin (ca); Andy Murch (c/skate). **NOAA Office of Ocean Exploration and Research, 2019 Southeastern U.S. Deep-sea Exploration:** (bl). **90 BluePlanetArchive.com:** Steven Kovacs (Seahorse). **Getty Images / iStock:** Stevehullphotography. **91 Alamy Stock Photo:** Andrey Nekrasov (br); Todd Winner (clb). **BluePlanetArchive.com:** Rudie Kuiter (c). **Dreamstime.com:** Patrimonio Designs Limited (crb/x17). **92 Alamy Stock Photo:** Colin Marshall (ca); Stocktrek Images, Inc. / Brook Peterson (tr). **92-93 naturepl.com:** Franco Banfi. **93 Alamy Stock Photo:** FB-StockPhoto-1 (tr); David Fleetham (cr). **Dreamstime.com:** Orpoliii (br). **Shutterstock.com:** Heiko Jetzkowitz (crb). **94 Alamy Stock Photo:** Marli Wakeling (c). **Dorling Kindersley:** Frank Greenaway (cb). **Dreamstime.com:** Daniel Thornberg (tr). **Getty Images / iStock:** Addillum (bl); Pe-Art (clb). **Shutterstock.com:** Hennadii H (clb/Puffer fish). **95 Dreamstime.com:** John Anderson (c/Background). **Getty Images:** Universal Images Group / Wild Horizon (tr). **96 123RF.com:** Bonzami Emmanuelle / Cynoclub (tc); livingpitty (bc). **Adobe Stock:** Tomas Drahos (cla). **Dreamstime.com:** Arsty (tr); Peter Leahy / Pipehorse (tl); Sneekerp (ca); Isselee (cra, crb/18, bl); Planetfelicity (crb); Parfentevamaya (br); Surachet Khamsuk (fbr). **naturepl.com:** David Shale (ca/9). **96-97 Dreamstime.com:** Fenkie Sumolang / Fenkieandreas (c). **97 123RF.com:** Visarute Angkatavanich (tl). **Alamy Stock Photo:** David Cook / blueshiftstudios (cb). **Dorling Kindersley:** Jerry Young (cl). **Dreamstime.com:** Bluehand (clb); Mirkorosenau (tc, cla, bl); Isselee (ca). **98 Dreamstime.com:** Dirk Ercken / Kikkerdirk (ca). **Getty Images / iStock:** GlobalP. **99 Alamy Stock Photo:** Daniel Borzynski (br); Gillian Pullinger (tr). **Dorling Kindersley:** Twan Leenders (bl). **Dreamstime.com:** Am Wu / Amwu (ca). **Shutterstock.com:** Bildagentur Zoonar GmbH (tl). **100 Alamy Stock Photo:** David Chapman (clb). **Dorling Kindersley:** Twan Leenders (cr). **Dreamstime.com:** Dirk Ercken / Kikkerdirk (tr); Slowmotiongli (c/newts). **Getty Images / iStock:** Azureus70 (c). **101 Alamy Stock Photo:** Reinhard Dirscherl (tr). **Dreamstime.com:** Bobhilscher (cr); Alain Lacroix / Icefields (beamsx2); Anusorn Thongpasan (c); Shane Myers (c/Turtle); Isselee (crb). **Getty Images / iStock:** Mark Kostich (c/Viper). **102 Alamy Stock Photo:** Buiten-Beeld / Jelger Herder (c). **Dreamstime.com:** Liliya Butenko (bl); Kamensky (tl); Patrick Guenette (tl/small liz). **102-103 Shutterstock.com:** Bildagentur Zoonar GmbH (ca). **103 Alamy Stock Photo:** Cris Ritchie Photo (crb). **Dreamstime.com:** Nynke Van Holten (br); Javier Alonso Huerta (cra). **Science Photo Library:** Roger Hall (tc); Luis Montanya / Marta Montanya (tc/newt); Carlyn Iverson (tc/red-black, tr); Roger Hall / Science Source (ftr). **104-105 Alamy Stock Photo:** Minden Pictures / Buiten-beeld / Ernst Dirksen (ca). **104 Alamy Stock Photo:** Alistair and Jan Campbell UKCI (cb). **Dreamstime.com:** Dirk Ercken / Kikkerdirk (cl). **Getty Images:** Rosemary Calvert / Photographer's Choice (br). **naturepl.com:** Michael & Patricia Fogden (bl). **105 Alamy Stock Photo:** Daniel Borzynski (br). **Getty Images / iStock:** Rob Jansen (tr). **naturepl.com:** Stephen Dalton (tl); Andrew Murray (cr). **106 Dreamstime.com:** Kerstiny (cla, clb). **naturepl.com:** Kim Taylor (cra). **106-107 Alamy Stock Photo:** Ivan Kuzmin (b). **107 Alamy Stock Photo:** Natural History Archive (br). **Getty Images / iStock:** Wirestock (c). **naturepl.com:** Melvin Grey (cr). **108-109 Jaime Culebras. 108 Jaime Culebras:** (tl). **110 123RF.com:** Artem Mykhaylichenko / artcasta (sky). **naturepl.com:** Tui De Roy. **Shutterstock.com:** chrisbrignell (bl). **111 Alamy Stock Photo:** Gregory Johnston (tc). **Dorling Kindersley:** Colin Keates / Natural History Museum (cra). **Dreamstime.com:** Kim Deadman / Kimdeadman (br). **naturepl.com:** Jordi Chias (cb). **112 Dorling Kindersley:** Eleanor Bates (tl). **naturepl.com:** Tui De Roy (tr); Solvin Zankl (br). **112-113 123RF.com:** Chonlasub Woravichan (c). **Dreamstime.com:** Almir1968 (Underwater). **113 Alamy Stock Photo:** Laura Romin & Larry Dalton (clb); Jan Wlodarczyk (br). **Dreamstime.com:** Annstasag91 (bl). **Shutterstock.com:** 4LUCK (tr). **114 Alamy Stock Photo:** Danita Delimont (tc). **Dreamstime.com:** Valentyna Chukhlyebova / Vac (cl); Sergey Uryadnikov (clb); Pindiyath100 (bc). **114-115 naturepl.com:** Anup Shah (b). **115 Dreamstime.com:** Stu Porter (tr). **naturepl.com:** Alex Mustard (tl). **116-117 Getty Images:** McDonald Wildlife Photography Inc. (tl). **116 Shutterstock.com:** Scott Delony (crb); bluedog studio (cr); Reynaldo Graca Lopes (br). **117 123RF.com:** radiantreptilia (c). **Alamy Stock Photo:** Media Drum World (cla). **118 Getty Images:** Photodisc / Ascent Xmedia / Adam Goessaert (tc). **119 Alamy Stock Photo:** Giovanni Giuseppe Bellani (tc); John Sullivan (cl). **Getty Images / iStock:** Uwe-Bergwitz (c). **naturepl.com:** Paul Bertner (cla); Richard Herrmann (tl); Pete Oxford (cla/gecko). **120-121 Shutterstock.com:** Kurit Afshen. **120 Dreamstime.com:** Amwu (bc, br); Seamartini (tc); Arifkdh (tc/Monitors); Ekaterina Muzyka (tr); Godruma (crb). **121 Alamy Stock Photo:** Blickwinkel / Fotototo (clb); Nature Picture Library / Bence Mate (tl); Imagebroker / Arco / TUNS (bc). **Dreamstime.com:** Ken Griffiths (br); Mollynz (tr); Rudmer Zwerver (cb). **122-123 Shutterstock.com:** I Wayan Sumatika. **122 Alamy Stock Photo:** Ivan Kuzmin (bl). **Shutterstock.com:** Neos1am (tl). **123 Alamy Stock Photo:** Gillian Pullinger (tc). **Science Photo Library:** Power and Syred (clb). **124 123RF.com:** Teerayut Yukuntapornpong / Joesayhello (crb). **Dreamstime.com:** Amwu (br); Isselee (tl). **Getty Images / iStock:** GlobalP (tc, crb/Gila monster). **125 Dorling Kindersley:** Twan Leenders (c). **Dreamstime.com:** Am Wu / Amwu (c/Turtle); Rinus Baak (br); Mgkuijpers / Matthijs Kuijpers (bc). **Getty Images / iStock:** Cellistka (cl). **126 Getty Images / iStock:** Freder (bl). **Getty Images:** Image by David G Hemmings (c). **naturepl.com:** Christian Ziegler (tl). **126-127 Dreamstime.com:** Isselee (tc). **127 123RF.com:** Sergei Uriadnikov (cb/African penguin). **Alamy Stock Photo:** MichaelGrantBirds (cb); Michel Poinsignon / Nature Picture Library (tr). **Dorling Kindersley:** Frank Greenaway / National Birds of Prey Centre, Gloucestershire (bl). **Dreamstime.com:** Charles Brutlag (cra). **Getty Images / iStock:** Enrique Ramos Lopez (clb). **Shutterstock.com:** muhammadadeel007 (br). **128 Alamy Stock Photo:** Science Photo Library / Steve Gschmeissner (cl). **129 Alamy Stock Photo:** Biosphoto / Daniel Heuclin (cr). **Dreamstime.com:** Yuriy Balagula (ca); Slowmotiongli (tr); Natalia Golovina (cl); Flowersofsunny (Background); Anna Lopatina (crb); David Herraez (bc). **Shutterstock.com:** Oded Ben-Menachem (clb). **130 123RF.com:** santonius (br). **Dreamstime.com:** Tadeasvonh (tr). **naturepl.com:** Christian Ziegler (b). **131 Alamy Stock Photo:** Nicolas Fernandez (b); Octavio Campos Salles (cr). **Dreamstime.com:** Hel080808 (clb). **Shutterstock.com:** Tara N Salgado (tr). **132-133 Alamy Stock Photo:** Praxis Creative (c). **132 123RF.com:** Artem Mykhaylichenko / artcasta (tc/sky). **Alamy Stock Photo:** Dave Collins (tc/osprey). **Getty Images / iStock:** Freder (bl). **133 Alamy Stock Photo:** ZUMA Press, Inc. (br). **Shutterstock.com:** Rudy Umans (bl). **134 Dreamstime.com:** Harry Collins (tl); Dennis Jacobsen (tc); Mikelane45 (tc/Buzzard). **naturepl.com:** Ian McCarthy (ca). **Shutterstock.com:** Rob Palmer Photography (b, crb). **135 Getty Images / iStock:** David Johnson (bc). **Shutterstock.com:** Mualvi. **136 Alamy Stock Photo:** Media Drum World (tl). **Dreamstime.com:** Pavel Naumov (cl/clb); Ondrej Prosicky (t/Background). **Getty Images / iStock:** evilknevil (b/Background). **naturepl.com:** Lynn M. Stone (bl). **Shutterstock.com:** Spirit Mouse (clb). **136-137 Alamy Stock Photo:** Media Drum World (c). **Shutterstock.com:** Josef Pittner (ca). **137 Alamy Stock Photo:** BSIP SA / Jacopin (tr); FLPA (crb). **Dreamstime.com:** Spineback (cla). **naturepl.com:** Michael Quinton (cra). **138 Dorling Kindersley:** Frank Greenaway / National Birds of Prey Centre, Gloucestershire (bc, bl, c); Frank Greenaway / The National Birds of Prey Centre (ca); Liberty's Owl, Raptor and Reptile Centre, Hampshire, UK (br, crb). **Dreamstime.com:** Dennis Jacobsen (cr/13); Yaroslava Polosina (cl). **Getty Images:** Daniel Parent (cr). **naturepl.com:** Joel Sartore / Photo Ark (crb/falconet). **139 Dorling Kindersley:** Gary Hanna / Mattscott (tl). **Dreamstime.com:** Isselee (cb); Jmrocek (c); Martin Mecnarowski (ca). **Getty Images / iStock:** JBLumix (cl). **140 Getty Images / iStock:** BrianEKushner (tr). **naturepl.com:** Anup Shah (c). **141 Dreamstime.com:** Abxyz (cla); Meunierd (tr); Stepanjezek (tl); Lukas Blazek (clb). **naturepl.com:** Jen Guyton (cb). **142-143 naturepl.com:** Luke Massey. **144 123RF.com:** Serg_v (t/sky). **naturepl.com:** Ben Cranke (crb). **144-145 naturepl.com:** Bruce Thomson (cb). **145 123RF.com:** Serg_v (b/sky). **Alamy Stock Photo:** Steve Bloom Images (b/bird). **Dreamstime.com:** Agami Photo Agency (cr). **naturepl.com:** David Tipling (tl). **Shutterstock.com:** Maquiladora (tr). **146-147 Getty Images / iStock:** David Keep (c). **147 Alamy Stock Photo:** Danita Delimont / Martin Zwick (cra); Alain Poirot (tc); Michel Poinsignon / Nature Picture Library (tl); FLPA / Mike Jones (bl); Ivan Kuzmin (bc). **Dreamstime.com:** Séligour Christophe (br). **Fotolia:** Impala (tr). **148 Alamy Stock Photo:** Brown Pelican bird (cla). **naturepl.com:** Alan Murphy / BIA (tr). **148-149 Alamy Stock Photo:** Malcolm Schuyl. **149 Dreamstime.com:** Mogens Trolle (tr). **Shutterstock.com:** Martin Blazicek (bc). **151 Alamy Stock Photo:** Chris Robbins (cb). **naturepl.com:** Robin Chittenden (tl); Bruce Thomson (br). **152 Dorling Kindersley:** Eleanor Bates (bl). **Dreamstime.com:** Kjersti Joergensen (clb); Jan Martin Will (crb/Emperor Penguin). **153 123RF.com:** ambeon (cl); Sergei Uriadnikov (bc/group). **Alamy Stock Photo:** James Caldwell (tl); MichaelGrantBirds (bl). **Depositphotos Inc:** NedoB (bc/rockhopper penguin). **Dreamstime.com:** David Dennis (br). **naturepl.com:** Klein & Hubert (tr). **154-155 Dyan deNapoli. 154 Dyan deNapoli:** (tl). **156 Alamy Stock Photo:** Gary and Donna Brewer (tr). **Shutterstock.com:** Independent birds (bc); muhammadadeel007 (l). **157 Alamy Stock Photo:** Allen Creative / Steve Allen (crb). **Dreamstime.com:** Kenneth Keifer (bc); Sdbower (tr). **Shutterstock.com:** Nadine Wagner (cl). **158 Dreamstime.com:** Holainsemar (tl). **naturepl.com:** Nick Upton (tc). **158-159 Shutterstock.com:** Wang LiQiang (c). **159 Alamy Stock Photo:** jack perks (cla). **Shutterstock.com:** Agnieszka Bacal (tr). **160 Getty Images:** Image by David G Hemmings (c). **160-161 123RF.com:** serezniy (bc). **161 123RF.com:** Artem Mykhaylichenko / artcasta (b). **Alamy Stock Photo:** Robin Chittenden (cl); imageBROKER / S & D & K Maslowski (cra). **Dreamstime.com:** Gallinagomedia (br). **Shutterstock.com:** Amadeu Blasco (bc). **162 Alamy Stock Photo:** Natalia Kuzmina (tc); Rolf Nussbaumer Photography / Bill Draker / Rolfnp (ftr). **Dreamstime.com:** Slowmotiongli (clb). **Getty Images:** Moment / Marcia Straub (tl). **naturepl.com:** David Kjaer (tr). **163 Alamy Stock Photo:** Science History Images (br). **Dreamstime.com:** GCapture (cb); Smitty411 (crb). **164-165 Alamy Stock Photo:** alantookthis. **164 Dreamstime.com:** Panuruangjan (br). **165 Dreamstime.com:** Stu Porter (cla). **Getty Images / iStock:** Ian Fox (crb). **naturepl.com:** Angelo Gandolfi (tr); Dave Watts (cb). **Shutterstock.com:** Stock for you (cra). **166-167 Dreamstime.com:** Christoph Lischetzki (c). **167 Alamy Stock Photo:** Duncan Usher / Minden Pictures (ca); Octavio Campos Salles (tr). **Dreamstime.com:** Viktoria Protsak (cr). **naturepl.com:** Douglas Herr / BIA (br). **168 Dreamstime.com:** Mark Aplet (c); Gilles Malo (bl). **Shutterstock.com:** George J Alukkal (ca). **168-169 Dreamstime.com:** Isselee (c). **169 Dreamstime.com:** Isselee (c). **naturepl.com:** Mark Carwardine (tr). **Shutterstock.com:** Daiquiri (crb). **170 Dorling Kindersley:** Andrew Beckett (Illustration Ltd) (bl). **170-171 naturepl.com:** Guy Edwardes (c). **171 Alamy Stock Photo:** blickwinkel / B. Zoller (tl). **Dreamstime.com:** Linncurrie (bl). **Shutterstock.com:** Reimar (tr). **172-173 naturepl.com:** Markus Varesvuo. **172 Alamy Stock Photo:** Duncan Usher (br). **Dreamstime.com:** Zagrosti (cla). **173 Alamy Stock Photo:** imageBROKER / Paul Sawer (cr). **Dreamstime.com:** Edwin Butter (br). **174 Alamy Stock Photo:** Tim Plowden (tr). **Dorling Kindersley:** Geoff Dann / Barleylands Farm Museum and Animal Centre, Billericay (crb). **Dreamstime.com:** Charles Brutlag (cb/13); Steve Byland (fcla); Michael Truchon (cla); Phichak Limprasutr (ca); Vasyl Helevachuk (cb); Isselee (clb); Narupon Nimpaiboon (cb/16). **Getty Images / iStock:** drakuliren (cra); Leopardinatree (tc). **175 Depositphotos Inc:** steve_byland (c). **Dreamstime.com:** Charles Brutlag (cb/32); Isselee (cla); Vasyl Helevachuk (ca, cl); Wildlife World (cb, cb/34); Svetlana Foote (clb). **176 Alamy Stock Photo:** Auscape International Pty Ltd (cl). **Dreamstime.com:** Rudmer Zwerver (tr/x13). **naturepl.com:** Suzi Eszterhas (tl). **Science Photo Library:** Peter Chadwick. **177 Alamy Stock Photo:** Asbjorn M.

Olsen (tr); Westend61 GmbH / Gemma Ferrando (bl). **Depositphotos Inc:** lifeonwhite (bc). **naturepl.com:** Pete Oxford (tl). **178-179 Dreamstime.com:** Cornelius20 (bc). **Getty Images / iStock:** Preto_perola (cb). **178 Dreamstime.com:** Andegraund548 (bl); Abeselom Zerit (ca); Lucielang (bc); Pokec / Jan Pokornì (cb); Stu Porter (cb/ cheetah); Neelsky / Nilanjan Bhattacharya (c). **Science Photo Library:** Gustoimages (cra). **179 Alamy Stock Photo:** Auscape International Pty Ltd (clb/squirrel); John Porter LRPS (ca). **Dreamstime. com:** Mealmeaw (cl); Emmanuel Nalli (fcla); Slowmotiongli (bl); Rudmer Zwerver (clb). **Getty Images:** Ariel Skelley (tr). **naturepl.com:** Vincent Grafhorst (cla). **Shutterstock.com:** Gallinago_ media (br). **180 Dreamstime.com:** Marina Pissarova / Byheaven87 (t/grey clouds); Photomo (t). **Getty Images:** Ibrahim Suha Derbent. **181 Alamy Stock Photo:** André Gilden (ca); Stu Porter (crb). **Dreamstime.com:** Dima1970 (cb); Ana Vasileva (br); SaveJungle (bl, clb/x2); Fredweiss (tr/ x11); Hhurzhi (cla). **182 Alamy Stock Photo:** Pardofelis Photography. **Dreamstime.com:** Mariia Klymenko (tr); Zafi123 (clb). **183 123RF.com:** Serg_v (ca). **Alamy Stock Photo:** Biosphoto / Sylvain Cordier (cra); Imagebroker / Arco / G. Lacz (bl); Survivalphotos (br). **Dreamstime.com:** Elena Abramovich (tc); Geoffrey Kuchera (c). **184 Dreamstime.com:** Borja Xanela (bc). **naturepl. com:** Peter Blackwell (tl). **184-185 Shutterstock. com:** Elana Erasmus (c). **185 Dreamstime.com:** Appfind (tr); Denisa Prouzová (tc); Keith Wheatley (bl); Stu Porter (br); Ndp (cla). **186-187 Alamy Stock Photo:** Nature Picture Library / Nick Garbutt (b/red fox). **Getty Images / iStock:** evilknevil (b). **186 Dreamstime.com:** Volodymyr Byrdyak (tl); Mythja (cl). **naturepl.com:** Luiz Claudio Marigo (br). **187 Alamy Stock Photo:** imageBROKER.com GmbH & Co. KG / Ronald Wittek (cr). **Dreamstime.com:** Pavel Naumov (ca). **naturepl.com:** Will Burrard-Lucas (tl). **188 Dorling Kindersley:** Tracy Morgan / Berry (c). **Dreamstime.com:** Chris Brignell (bl); Isselee (cra, crb, cb/12); Eriklam (c/9); Willeecole (cb/14); Cynoclub (cla, br); Gurinaleksandr (cla/6); Viorel Sima (clb); Jagodka (ca). **Shutterstock.com:** Ivanova N (tl); Rita_Kochmarjova (tr). **189 Alamy Stock Photo:** Grossemy Vanessa (ca/23). **Dreamstime.com:** Adogslifephoto (ca, c); Jagodka (bl, clb); Volodymyr Melnyk (cb); Judith Kiener (cla); Aleksandr Tarlokov (cr); Isselee (bc, cl, tc); Eastmanphoto (ca/25); Mila Atkovska (tl). **190 Dreamstime.com:** Holly Kuchera (clb). **190-191 Dreamstime.com:** Andrey Gudkov (t). **191 Alamy Stock Photo:** Arterra Picture Library / Arndt Sven-Erik (tr); Jason Hornblow (bc). **192-193 Getty Images:** The Washington Post. **192 Monterey Bay Aquarium:** (tl). **194 Getty Images:** Moment / Stan Tekiela Author / Naturalist / Wildlife Photographer (tl). **194-195 Alamy Stock Photo:** imageBROKER. com GmbH & Co. KG / Dieter Mahlke (b). **195 Dreamstime.com:** Isselee (cr). **naturepl.com:** Klein & Hubert (cla); Photo Ark / Joel Sartore (cra); Andy Sands (c). **196 Dreamstime.com:** Edurivero (cra); Grafxart (cr). **naturepl.com:** Jeff Foott (l). **197 Alamy Stock Photo:** David Sewell (bl). **Dreamstime.com:** Sarah2 (clb). **Getty Images:** Gamma-Rapho / Xavier Rossi (cra). **198 Alamy Stock Photo:** Auscape International Pty Ltd (tl). **Dorling Kindersley:** Exmoor Zoo, Devon / Gary Ombler (bc); Marwell Zoological Park, Winchester / Frank Greenaway (ca). **Dreamstime.com:** Farinoza (cra); Isselee (cla, c); Oleg Kozlov (cb); Irina Kozhemyakina / Ir717 (crb); Eduard Kyslynskyy (fcrb). **199 Dreamstime.com:** Musat Christian (cb); Isselee (tc); Poeticpenguin (clb). **Getty Images / iStock:** GlobalP (tl). **200 123RF.com:** yotrak (ftl). **Alamy Stock Photo:** Stephanie Jackson - Australian wildlife collection (cla); Ivan Kuzmin (bl). **Depositphotos Inc:** Myimagine (tl). **Dreamstime. com:** Rudmer Zwerver (tr/x13). **Science Photo Library:** merlintuttle.org (br). **201 Alamy Stock Photo:** blickwinkel / M. Woike (cra/flying fox). **Dreamstime.com:** Michael Lynch (cr); Roman Nazarov (br). **naturepl.com:** Kim Taylor (cra). **202 Alamy Stock Photo:** Imagebroker / Arco Images / Mosebach, K. (cb/Bandicoot); imageBROKER.com GmbH & Co. KG / Gerry Pearce (cl). **Dreamstime. com:** Isselee (cb); Slowmotiongli (tl); Marco Tomasini (crb). **203 Alamy Stock Photo:** Album (t); Auscape International Pty Ltd (tr); Westend61 GmbH / Gemma Ferrando. **Shutterstock.com:** Evelyn D. Harrison (crb). **204-205 Alamy Stock Photo:** Minden Pictures / D. Parer & E. Parer-Cook (c). **204 Alamy Stock Photo:** Ben Nottidge (br). **Ardea:** (cb). **naturepl.com:** Roland Seitre (tr); Bruce Thomson (bl). **206 Dreamstime.com:** Micha Klootwijk (br). **naturepl.com:** Suzi Eszterhas (l). **207 Alamy Stock Photo:** adrian hepworth (clb); Minden Pictures / Suzi Eszterhas (tr). **Depositphotos Inc:** lifeonwhite (c). **Shutterstock.com:** Ekaterina Gerasimchuk (crb); GR92100 (cr). **208 Getty Images:** Stone / Anup Shah (br). **naturepl.com:** Suzi Eszterhas. **209 Alamy Stock Photo:** Minden Pictures / Thomas Marent (br). **Dorling Kindersley:** Andrew Beckett (Illustration Ltd) (tl). **210 Dreamstime.com:** Ksenyalim (br); Jenny Mendoza (clb); Anna Kucherova (tr). **210-211 Alamy Stock Photo:** Nature Picture Library / Anup Shah (c). **211 Alamy Stock Photo:** blickwinkel / Layer (br); Buiten-Beeld / Ronald Messemaker (bl); imageBROKER.com GmbH & Co. KG / GTW (tr). **212 Alamy Stock Photo:** Hemis.fr / Sylvain Cordier (cra); Minden Pictures / Cyril Ruoso; Nature Picture Library / Wild Wonders of China / Staffan Widstrand (tc). **naturepl.com:** Cyril Ruoso (br). **213 Alamy Stock Photo:** Asbjorn M. Olsen (br). **Dreamstime.com:** Rawin Thienwichitr (tr/ background). **naturepl.com:** Cyril Ruoso (tl, clb); Xi Zhinong (c). **214 Alamy Stock Photo:** imageBROKER.com GmbH & Co. KG / Thorsten Negro (b). **215 Alamy Stock Photo:** Danita Delimont / Pete Oxford (bl); Mediadrumimages / AndreCloete (r). **Dreamstime.com:** Nynke Van Holten (tl). **naturepl.com:** Anup Shah (clb). **Shutterstock.com:** PurpleShine (cla). **216-217 Barrett Hedges. 216 Dreamstime.com:** Volodymyr Byrdyak (tc); Johnbell (bl). **Getty Images / iStock:** wrangel (tl). **naturepl.com:** Willi Rolfes / BIA (bc); Will Burrard-Lucas (cl). **217 Science Photo Library:** WILLIAM ERVIN (br). **218 Getty Images:** Stone / Paul Souders (b). **219 Alamy Stock Photo:** Arterra Picture Library / Clement Philippe (tl); Matthias Breiter / Minden Pictures (cr). **Dreamstime.com:** Mirage3 (ca); Sergey Uryadnikov / Surz01 (bc). **Getty Images:** Moment / MB Photography (cl). **Science Photo Library:** Claus Lunau (clb). **220 naturepl.com:** Bernard Castelein (tr); Jabruson (crb). **221 Alamy Stock Photo:** Avalon.red / Anthony Bannister (clb); Tarun Chopra (tr); Alf Jacob Nilsen (bl). **Ardea:** Pascal Goetgheluck (clb/mongoose). **naturepl.com:** Michael Quinton (clb/,obcat); Christian Ziegler (br). **222 Depositphotos Inc:** aleksei.ee (crb). **Shutterstock.com:** Colin Seddon (cr). **223 naturepl.com:** Tui De Roy. **Shutterstock.com:** LouieLea (bl). **224-225 123RF.com:** Iakov Kalinin (c). **Alamy Stock Photo:** imageBROKER / P. Wegner (c/ dolphins). **224 naturepl.com:** Kevin Schafer (bl). **225 Alamy Stock Photo:** David Jefferson (bl); Karina Tkach (tl). **Shutterstock.com:** Anna L. e Marina Durante (cra); Triduza Studio (tr). **226-227 Shutterstock.com:** Craig Lambert Photography (t). **226 Dreamstime.com:** Evgenia Kotozhekova (clb). **naturepl.com:** Flip Nicklin (bl). **NOAA:** (clb/ map). **227 Alamy Stock Photo:** Blue Planet Archive FBA (bl). **Dreamstime.com:** John Abramo (br); Chase Dekker (fbr). **naturepl.com:** Eric Baccega (cr). **228 123RF.com:** Eric Isselee / isselee (br). **Dorling Kindersley:** Gary Ombler / Cotswold Wildlife Park (cl). **Fotolia:** Eric Isselee (ca). **Shutterstock.com:** Aleksei Verhovski (bl). **228-229 Dreamstime.com:** Torsten Velden / Tvelden (c). **229 Dorling Kindersley:** Harry Taylor (clb). **Dreamstime.com:** Jnjhuz (ca); Rudmer Zwerver (bc). **230-231 Dreamstime.com:** Johannes Gerhardus Swanepoel (c). **230 Alamy Stock Photo:** AfriPics.com (crb). **Dreamstime.com:** Sharon Day / Shaday365 (bl). **231 Alamy Stock Photo:** Christine Johnson (tc). **naturepl.com:** Yashpal Rathore (bc). **232 Dreamstime.com:** Dima1970 (l/x6); Peer Marlow (tc). **232-233 naturepl.com:** Pete Oxford (br). **233 Getty Images:** Tuul & Bruno Morandi / The Image Bank (tl). **Shutterstock.com:** SeraphP (ca). **234 Dreamstime.com:** Rudolf Ernst (b). **235 Alamy Stock Photo:** Steve Taylor ARPS (cr); Roger de La Harpe / Biosphoto (tc). **Depositphotos Inc:** NataliiaMelnyc (cla). **Getty Images:** Riza Marlon (br); Mark Newman / The Image Bank (tr). **236 Alamy Stock Photo:** John Bennet (tr). **Dreamstime.com:** SaveJungle (bl/x2). **236-237 Alamy Stock Photo:** Steve Boice (c). **237 Alamy Stock Photo:** Andrey Podkorytov (bc). **Dreamstime.com:** Insima (tr/x2); Lequint (ca). **Shutterstock.com:** Amadeu Blasco (tl). **238-239 Ronan Donovan. 238 Alex Walters:** (bl). **240-241 Getty Images:** Sølve Fredheim / 500px (c). **240 Alamy Stock Photo:** J-FRANCOIS DUCASSE (clb). **Dreamstime.com:** Isselee (c). **241 Alamy Stock Photo:** Roger de La Harpe / Biosphoto (cb); Kevin Schafer (crb). **Shutterstock.com:** GUDKOV ANDREY (tl). **242 Science Photo Library:** Peter Chadwick. **243 Alamy Stock Photo:** inga spence (tr). **Dreamstime.com:** Olga Itina / Olikit (tl). **244 Dreamstime.com:** Isselee (cra); Sandra Van Der Steen (c/background). **Shutterstock.com:** Krakenimages.com (c). **245 Alamy Stock Photo:** JACOPIN / BSIP (tc). **Dreamstime.com:** Zzizar (tl). **Getty Images:** Ger Bosma (cr). **Shutterstock.com:** Eric Isselee (bl); MyImages - Micha (br). **246 Alamy Stock Photo:** David Cantrille (clb); GPNaturePhotos (cra); Arco / TUNS / Imagebroker (crb); J & C Sohns / imageBROKER.com GmbH & Co. KG (cr). **247 Alamy Stock Photo:** Robin Hoskyns / BIOSPHOTO (br); Diana Rebman (bl). **Dreamstime. com:** Anankkml (cra). **248 Alamy Stock Photo:** J-FRANCOIS DUCASSE (bl). **Getty Images / iStock:** Yann-HUBERT (c). **naturepl.com:** Andrew Parkinson (tr). **Shutterstock.com:** Milan Zygmunt (tl). **249 Alamy Stock Photo:** Buiten-Beeld / Jelger Herder (bl); Reinhard Dirscherl (tr). **Getty Images / iStock:** Luis Espin (tl). **Shutterstock.com:** Cavan-Images (br). **250 Alamy Stock Photo:** Helmut Corneli (br); Reinhard Dirscherl (bl). **Dreamstime. com:** Addict (bc). **Getty Images / iStock:** Gordon Magee (c). **naturepl.com:** Jiri Lochman (cr). **251 123RF.com:** Artem Mykhaylichenko / artcasta (tl/ sky). **Alamy Stock Photo:** Buiten-Beeld / Jelger Herder (cr); Runk / Schoenberger / Grant Heilman Photography (tc); Tui De Roy / Nature Picture Library (cb). **Getty Images / iStock:** nomis_g (bl). **naturepl.com:** Oliver Richter / BIA (br); Andrew Parkinson (tl). **252-253 Alamy Stock Photo:** J-FRANCOIS DUCASSE (c). **252 Dreamstime.com:** Supertrooper / alex (cl). **253 Alamy Stock Photo:** Michel Rauch / Biosphoto (bc). **Dreamstime.com:** lancphotography (bl). **Getty Images / iStock:** Luis Espin (fbl); KeithSzafranski (cr); Yann-HUBERT (crb). **Shutterstock.com:** BenOBrienPhotography (c); Hugh Lansdown (tr); Marek R. Swadzba (tc). **254 Dreamstime.com:** Seadam (br); Sekarb (cr). **Getty Images / iStock:** Rike_ (bc). **Shutterstock.com:** Milan Zygmunt (tl). **255 Alamy Stock Photo:** Jim Cumming (bl); Ann and Steve Toon (clb); turventur. com (cb). **Dreamstime.com:** Rinus Baak (cla); Heiti Paves / Heitipaves (tl); Hotshotsworldwide (crb). **Getty Images / iStock:** Bkamprath (bc). **256-257 Elza Friedlaender. 256 Victoria Beale:** (tl). **258 Alamy Stock Photo:** Morley Read (cb). **Dreamstime.com:** Volodymyr Byrdyak (br). **Getty Images / iStock:** NiseriN (cr). **259 Depositphotos Inc:** titoslack (crb). **Getty Images / iStock:** DamianKuzdak (bl); sezer66 (cla). **naturepl.com:** Gerrit Vyn (tr). **Shutterstock.com:** Cavan-Images (tl). **260 Alamy Stock Photo:** Liam White (clb). **naturepl.com:** Emanuele Biggi (br); Nick Garbutt (tl). **261 Alamy Stock Photo:** AP Photo / Jason Straziuso (br); Gabriel Barathieu / Biosphoto (cr); Jen Guyton / Nature Picture Library (cla). **Dreamstime.com:** Izanbar (cl). **Getty Images / iStock:** Robert CHG (cra). **262 Dreamstime.com:** Geoffrey Kuchera (bl). **263 Dreamstime.com:** Le Thuy Do (br); Serg_velusceac (bc). **264 123RF.com:** Sergei Uriadnikov (bc). **Alamy Stock Photo:** MichaelGrantBirds (bl). **Depositphotos Inc:** NedoB (br). **Dreamstime.com:** David Dennis (fbr); Jan Martin Will (fbl)

Cover images: *Front:* **Alamy Stock Photo:** Gabriel Barathieu / Biosphoto ftl; **Dreamstime.com:** Atalvi clb, Sean Beckett fbl, Dashark c, Kristof Degreef bl, Jakub Krechowicz br, Dmitry Petlin fcrb, Channarong Pherngjanda cra, Elena Sanchez crb, Tiberiu Sahlean / Tiberiusahlean tc; **Fotolia:** Eric Isselee ftr; **Getty Images / iStock:** cyoginan cra/ (flamingo), Mingfei Hou tl, JuliGin crb/ (starfish), kerkla cl, MicrovOne bl/ (insect), NatuskaDPI (algae), OGphoto fcl, Ekaterina Sheshina cla/ (snail); **Shutterstock.com:** HelloRF Zcool fcr; *Back:* **123RF. com:** Bonzami Emmanuelle / Cynoclub clb; **Alamy Stock Photo:** Urs Hauenstein c, blickwinkel / F. Teigler cra, Poelzer Wolfgang bc; **Depositphotos Inc:** Krakenimages.com bl, lifeonwhite fclb; **Dreamstime.com:** 2day929 ftr, Edi Hidayat fcr, Derek Holzapfel tr, Tae208 cb; **Getty Images / iStock:** Craig Lambert crb, MicrovOne (insect), MorePics fcla, NatuskaDPI (algae); *Spine:* **Dreamstime.com:** Isselee ca